Praise for *Exploring the Gaps*

"In the past several years I have been observing from the other side of the Ocean how Professor Lee's academic program has developed. Now, with this new and readable book, James Lee is directing both scholars and students to the right and balanced direction of conjunction."

Makitaro Hotta
Dean of International Affairs, College of Asia Pacific Studies
Ritsumeikan Asia Pacific University, Japan

"In Exploring the Gaps, *Professor James Lee brings cultural and historical understanding to the clash between trade liberalization and environmental protection and to the challenge of sustaining environmental goals in the face of globalization. His perspective is fresh, his insights sharp, and his conclusions worrisome in light of the struggles that lie ahead in a world of economic integration."*

Daniel C. Esty
Professor, School of Forestry and Environmental Studies
Yale University

"As we enter the new millennium, we face profound challenges to our ability to live ecologically sensitive and culturally fulfilling lives. James Lee's wide-ranging book moves us closer to surmounting some of those challenges by explaining the difficult task of linking trade, environmental wellbeing and cultural sustainability. Lee's book is expansive and insightful."

Paul Kevin Wapner
Director and Associate Professor, Environmental Policy Program
American University

EXPLORING THE GAPS

EXPLORING THE GAPS

VITAL LINKS BETWEEN TRADE, ENVIRONMENT AND CULTURE

JAMES R. LEE

KUMARIAN
PRESS

Dedicated to James P. and Dorothy M. Lee

Exploring the Gaps: Vital Links Between Trade, Environment and Culture

Published 2000 in the United States of America by Kumarian Press, Inc.,
14 Oakwood Avenue, West Hartford, Connecticut 06119-2127 USA.

Photo of author courtesy of American University by Chris Zimmer.

Production and design by The Sarov Press.
The text of this book is set in Sabon 10.5/13.5.
Index by Robert Swanson.
Proofread by Beth Richards.

Printed in USA on acid-free paper by
Thomson-Shore, Inc.
Text printed with vegetable oil-based ink.

∞ The paper used in this publication meets the minimum requirements
of the American National Standard for Information Sciences—Permanence of
Paper for Printed Library Materials, ANSI Z39.48–1984.

Library of Congress Cataloging-in-Publication Data

James R. Lee, 1951–
Exploring the gaps : vital links between trade, environment, and culture /
James R. Lee
p. cm.
Includes bibliographical references and index.
ISBN 1–56549–115–7 (cloth) — ISBN 1–56549–114–9 (pbk.)
1. International trade—Environmental aspects—Case studies. 2. International trade—Social aspects—Case studies. 3. International trade—Cross-cultural studies. 4. International trade—Effect of technological innovations on—Case studies. 5. Globalization—Cross-cultural studies. I. Title.
HF1379 .L44 2000
382—dc21 00–032133

09 08 07 06 05 04 03 02 01 00 10 9 8 7 6 5 4 3 2 1

First Printing 2000

CONTENTS

LIST OF FIGURES

LIST OF TABLES

PREFACE

THERE IS EXHILARATION about the wondrous pace of change in the world today and a serious unease about the globalization that results from it. In 1992, I was attracted and distracted by the real and intellectual aspects of this contradiction and set out to write a short concept paper. The paper sought to describe how globalization, spread through trade, was increasingly coming into conflict with local environment and culture issues. In the course of writing the paper, it became evident that this phenomenon had occurred before and the current trends are part of a long-standing dissonance. This intellectual understanding also coincided with a growing public recognition and concern over globalization. For personal and universal reasons, the book thus addresses this historic era and proposes how policy can meet the challenges that globalization poses.

This research was not only long, but also deep. More than twenty separate case studies were undertaken to support this effort. The book therefore only reveals one layer of a larger and richer research base. Beyond these twenty cases, the book draws from the six hundred case studies generated by the Trade Environment Database (TED) projects. The *TED Case Studies* provide comparative information on trade and environment (and more) issues that cross several disciplines to provide insight into globalization's impact on people and places. TED case studies are available at the following World Wide Web address (hereafter, the "Web").

<http://www.american.edu/TED/ted.htm>

A virtual venue was built to enhance the book beyond the printed pages. The Web site provides hyperlinks to the TED case studies, a search engine for them, sets of discussion questions, linkages with other classes that use the book, and other relevant virtual and real activities. It is available at the following Web address.

<http://www.american.edu/TED/culture/index.htm>

ACKNOWLEDGMENTS

I HAVE SPENT TEN YEARS writing this book about the pace of historical change and its meaning for today. I also had tremendous help from students, research assistants, and experts in the academic and policy worlds.

The book uses background case studies provided by more than twenty of my students and I note them at the appropriate points in the text. These case studies are in many ways the backbone of the book. Several of my graduate assistants played key roles in formulating, researching, and producing the book. Kathryn Bunting helped me write a concept paper and build up the idea of a relation between trade, environment, and culture. Later, Maren Brooks suffered with me through countless drafts and was critical in plotting out and filling in the essence of the idea. Barbara Pando worked on Web support and research and Jaya Mathur toiled to refine and sharpen the document. Liz Hipple, Margo Thorsen, Zoe Trohanis, and Jeremey Schanck helped make the document whole.

Many professionals have added their advice and commentary on the book, especially Nicholas Onuf. Nick, my teacher, would never turn down an opportunity to view another draft of the manuscript. On several occasions, he properly chastised me to go further and to seek out new ideas in this book. Other research and policy experts who provided valuable comments and feedback include Steve Charnovitz, David Walters, and Ismail Serageldin (as well as several anonymous reviewers). Lastly, Richard Rowson made this book happen in a number of ways and I thank him for it.

CHAPTER 1

THE CONJUNCTION: A THEORY ACROSS IDEAS, PLACES, AND TIMES

TODAY'S INSTITUTIONS are not effectively meeting the challenges of globalization. Globalization is undeniably making people's lives better in many ways. Globalization also redefines the human experience (the "social context") and this process of change extracts a cost to people and the world around them. As the carefully plotted relationships in the social context begin to unravel in the wake of breathtaking technological advances, people become uncertain about their place in society and in the world and more likely to feel anomie and alienation.

Because of the accumulating costs of change during periods of globalization, there occurs a disconnect in the social context. People rely on social institutions for stability and for preventing the fragmentation that change brings. The problem is that bureaucratic inertia constrains the role of institutions during these periods. This tension leads to an inability to effectively articulate a coherent institutional agenda for approaching the problem of globalization. This book provides one blueprint for people and institutions.

This book examines the disconnect resulting from globalization by comparing the social context over time in a historical and conceptual framework. The social context comprises elements of trade, environment, and culture. How these elements have become more disparate and increasingly disconnected from each other at the global and local levels was an idea described by Robert Merton over one-half century ago.[1] Then, the distinction was a theory; now it is a reality.

The book has four chapters. *Chapter 1* offers an approach for exploring the social context and the implicit disconnect in it. *Chapter 2* explores that context through three historical periods. *Chapter 3* applies that framework to the present social context, and *Chapter 4* looks in depth at today's trends and from them to future trends.

In this first chapter, it is necessary to begin by placing the story of the disconnect in human and theoretical terms. Thus, it defines key terms, describes the relationship between trade, culture, and environment, and discusses the idea of unique periods in human history.

ONE PLACE AND MANY PLACES

The specific and general conditions of disconnect have local and far-reaching impacts both across time and within the elements of the social context. The fact is that while this new period in history is emerging in many places, at other places on the planet people essentially exist in earlier historical periods, at least as measured by technological advancement. In one sense, it is as if traveling from one part of the world to another today is part ordinary transportation and part time travel. In the end, the distance in time for places and peoples will gradually but inexorably diminish in the new globalization.

ONE PLACE

In July 1999, I taught a course on trade and environment in Kuala Lumpur to American, Japanese, and Malaysian students. We took a trip to the Taman Negara National Park—a rainforest in northeast peninsular Malaysia—to look at the impact of tourism on it. Besides the prospect of experiencing the world's oldest rainforest, I also hoped to meet the Orang Asli, a people almost Neolithic in terms of their lifestyle and an ancient inhabitant of Southeast Asia. The Orang Asli preceded the modern Malaysians as inhabitants (the people who live there today are called Deutero-Malays or "second" people) and relatives of them live in the Philippines, Indonesia, Papua New Guinea, and Australia (in the latter they are known as the aborigines).

Early in the morning, we left Kuala Lumpur and took a four-hour bus ride on a road through the Malaysian highlands where the lanes went from four to two to one and our speed proportionately reduced. The bus stopped near the fork of two large rivers at a place called Jerantut. After lunch, we took a motorboat ride up the Tembeling River and passed wild water buffalo grazing along the banks and monkeys brachiating among the huge dipterocarp trees. The early morning departure, the lunch, the warm sun and the rhythmic purring of the motorboat engines combined to act like a sleeping pill and we all fell asleep (except the boatsmen). After three hours, we awoke to noise and our arrival at Kuala Tahan and the Taman Negara resort.

On one side of the river, there was a hotel resort, owned by a government-affiliated business, which took credit cards, served German beer, and offered hot showers, cabins, and buffet breakfasts. On the other side was a poor, rural town with dirt streets filled with children and chickens. The two sides met in the middle where there were four floating restaurants on the river. Most visitors to the park were young travelers from developed countries, whose budgets found the prices at these floating restaurants, run by the locals, more favorable to their wallets. Besides, the floating restaurants had a certain charm and life that the business side, with their Bavarian-style cabins, did not. The last restaurant, on the downstream side of the river, was "Won's." This place became our favorite for the food and atmosphere. Won, the father, sat in his chair, smoked cigarettes, drank tea or coffee all day, and when he laughed you saw only a few, long teeth in his mouth.

His son, also known as Won, was in charge of the restaurant and he really did all the work. Won wore his hair in a black ponytail and he never wore shoes. At first, he was large and imposing, but we found he had a gentle laugh and a big heart. He took us rafting on the river one day and worried like my own mother out of fear we would not survive. He also was a sort of tour guide, a fact made clear by Won's tiny, faded, hand-lettered sign that announced trips to meet the Orang Asli.

Like his father, Won the son traded with the Orang Asli on a regular basis, selling them both food (rice especially) and cooking utensils (knives and pans). As a result, he had built up a personal relationship with the tribe and the people in it. Won ran his unsanctioned tours even though he was in competition with legal tour guides. The "legal" tour guides, usually government employees (from the other side of the river) with official identification cards who rotated in and out every two years, were politely tolerated by the Orang Asli but were thought of as outsiders in a way Won was not. Won had lived alongside them all his life.

Won took us upstream in a motorboat with a refreshing spray of water on a hot, summer day in the tropics. Where a small creek emptied into the river, we saw some children and women swimming. You knew these people were different from the modern Malay by looking at them. Won was typical Malay with light brown skin color, straight, black hair, and a stocky build. These people had black skin and a brownish colored hair that was curly—but not in tight knots like the hair of Africans—and thin bodies. We hiked a short distance inland up a hill. You could smell a fire burning. Won walked towards the outskirts of a village and spoke to a woman. She went off and brought back the chief of the tribe.

Bi-yoong was less than five feet tall, gaunt in stature, and graying in the hair. He went barefoot but wore an old pair of slacks and a tee shirt; his head was topped off with a baseball cap that said "England." He was an old but still physically active man and sported only a few unevenly spaced teeth.

The name of the people is the Orang Asli or "original people" from the Malay language of Bihasa, but in their own language they call themselves the *Batek*. The word *orang* means "people" in Bihasa, suggesting that the early Deutero-Malays thought of orangutans in human terms.

Bi-yoong talked to us and smoked the cigarettes that Won had advised me to bring. Bi-yoong was part of a dynastic chain of chiefs that stretched back beyond his memory. To escape the encroaching Deutero-Malays, the Batek migrated to their current homes long ago from the Malaysian states of Pahang and Kelantan in the west. The Batek history was brief, their knowledge of the world limited, and Bi-yoong was one of the few people in the tribe who had even a narrow glimpse beyond a world that for all practical purposes was using Stone Age technologies.

Bi-yoong's worldliness derives from the fact that each year the chief of each of the several Batek tribes travels by bus to Kuala Lumpur to meet with government officials. The meetings are allegedly one-sided affairs and essentially the tribes learn the amount of government assistance they will receive in the upcoming year. Bi-yoong liked the trips on the bus because he was especially fond of air conditioning.

For the Batek, the position of chief in the tribe is like the king in a kind of liberal monarchy. The chief inherits his position, but the people can vote him out of office for some grave offense or malfeasance, but this is quite rare, akin to impeachment. Bi-yoong has ten children and wants another, but his wife refuses to bear him another child and tells him to find another wife.

All the while Bi-yoong is talking he is taking more cigarettes and stashing some away under his cap. Soon, some young men arrive and sit with us and start taking cigarettes, too. I, of course, mention the dangers of smoking, but Won says that they all smoke. Won points to a young girl who had wandered over and says, "You can give her one, too. She smokes already." As much as I wanted to have cross-cultural experiences, I could not bear giving a cigarette to this child. It seems most all in the village smoked a dried leaf commonly found in the forest, but universally would rather have a Marlboro.

Bi-yoong invited us to walk through the village, which was laid out in a spiral ring, starting with some key structures and homes in the center. Most homes were largely pole structures with palm leaf roofs, but some had plastic coverings. The tribe stayed in one place until one of three things occurred: a death, an attack by wild animals, or a lack of resources.

In the camp were a few metal knives and axes, along with an occasional pan and kettle. Lines of clothes hung drying and included pants, shirts, and an occasional dress. Only a few women owned or wore bras and these women usually held the higher positions of stature in the tribe. Won said that, in general, there was little resentment to the visitors touring the village, but if there was, it was more with the women. The men saw the tours as a way of making money but the women only saw them as an unnecessary disturbance.

The Batek are an environmentally conservative people. They do not fell trees or kill animals except for direct consumption. Their subsistence strategy relies almost solely on hunting and gathering. By Malaysian law, they can kill anything in the area, including elephant, although monkey is probably the most consumed meat, along with various birds, tapirs, and other sources. They do catch some fish but have no advanced fishing techniques (even though a river is nearby), catching fish by hand in the roots of enormous trees. Surely, they filled out their diet with an occasional reptile. The gathering part of Batek subsistence, as opposed to hunting, is limited and consists mostly of roots and a few seasonal fruits.

With Won interpreting, I asked almost everyone I encountered in the tribe if they had heard of or seen a computer. None had heard of it and even found it difficult to fathom what I was asking. In fact, Won had to invent a way to describe a computer, calling it a combination of a television and typewriter. Of course, none in the tribe had ever seen either a television or typewriter, so they all just shrugged their shoulders: all but Bi-yoong. He had seen a television (on the bus) and a typewriter (in the government office in Kuala Lumpur) but even he had never heard of a computer.

Poor Bi-yoong, I thought to myself. Here was this leader of a people possessing Stone Age technologies in the midst of the Computer Revolution. His people, who remember little, will eventually come to live in a world that remembers all and forgets nothing. These people had never gone through the Agricultural Revolution, much less the Industrial Revolution, but probably within a short period the Batek will have to come to terms with life in a world of computers and globalization. Yet Bi-yoong seemed remarkably unperturbed by this prospect. He believed that the Batek had benefited from the changes that had already come. After all, they had rice, pots, pans, and even cigarettes. They were also a very resilient people, Bi-yoong added, but he would look into this computer thing.

MANY PLACES

No people can escape the inevitable intrusion of today's globalization and the Batek too will discover the costs and benefits of progress. The gap between their social context and that of the globalized world is immense, but they will soon find the same sense of being out of time and out of place that more advanced societies are already experiencing. Today, a culture that is forty thousand years behind in technological progress may be able to close that gap over the course of a single generation. But while this would certainly be an amazing feat, the intense pace of change may be simply too much for a culture to bear, perhaps inducing a form of historical insanity.

For the Batek, and many other developing and developed peoples, the pace of technological and economic change in the world—the result of globalization—is on a collision course with their human and natural ability to absorb it. This book examines that process of globalization and change in a long-term perspective focusing on its contemporary meaning. The lens for this analysis is change in the human social context over time because of globalization. A prime force behind such change are multilateral trade negotiations and, in particular, events occurring in the World Trade Organization (WTO). The importance of the WTO to the globalization process and its ability to control local laws and usurp national sovereignty is surely overstated. Nonetheless, the WTO has become a focal point and key symbol for globalization and the unease that many people feel about it.

The book's focus is on the social context and the relationship between economic (trade), ecologic (environment), and social (culture) factors over time. The approach is to use case studies from periods of unique technological breakthrough (what I call a "conjunction") to illustrate the manifold but related influences of globalization. As a point of reference, the book examines the Tool, Agricultural, Industrial, and Electronic Conjunctions.

The conjunction reflects the view that these unique eras represent the coming together of many forces that produce change and the four periods provide a historical construct in which to describe these changes in the social context. From this construct and context, it is then possible to suggest cases for today's and tomorrow's conjunction issues. The story shows how cumulative conjunctions have upset the natural order of the social context.

The perspectives of culture, environment, and trade provide keen viewpoints from which to chart the course of conjunctions since they bring together a vital kaleidoscope of behavior, which of course is so critical to telling the disconnect story. The onset of a conjunction begins with the introduction of new technologies that spark new economic structures, which spread through trade to impact cultures and environments in other places. This book argues that there is an inherent tension between the spread of globalization through trade and the sustainability of culture and environment.

Conjunctions are extraordinary periods of technological, social, and environmental change that define new contexts of human behavior. Conjunctions locate the standard social context for many years to follow and set into place structures and patterns of behavior that echo through many generations. The social context changes only when the next unique technological period redefines the context and results in a new conjunction. This book examines each historical period to discover how, during these technological times of breakthrough, the three factors in the social context changed over time. The examination shows that there has been a slow but accelerating disconnect over time in the coherence of the social context.

Constant over these four periods is the natural interrelation between human culture, the economy of cultural survival and subsistence, and how that culture and economy interacts with and affects the environment. What has changed in today's period (at the global level) is the way that multilateral institutions have grown in power and how they have been singular and thus unidimensional in treating the three factors. Overall, the institutional approach has been to focus on one factor, but relatively ignore the other important factors in the social context. This singularity tends to weaken or sever the traditional well-integrated relationship between culture, trade, and environment and produce distorting policies and practices. The result is today's growing sense of disconnect between the goals of trade and those of environment and culture at the global level.

The disconnect is also a local problem. The local disposition of people tends to resist the conjunction, and the globalization that accompanies it, but the continuing forces of non-local change often win out. The human being is historically a local animal and its survival linked to the resources available in the immediate environment. This local lifestyle inherently reenforces the relation between trade, environment, and culture. As international trade has grown, the natural link between an economic subsistence strategy, the culture, and the local environment weakens and often breaks. By definition, international trade creates a new relation to the environment, since the resources come from far away and these culture and economic systems can be very different from ones nearby.

The disconnect at both global and local levels is significant for the future of the human condition and for conjunctions. The greater the disconnect, the more the discord. Over time, the discord will bear its own costs. The more disconnect, the less public and intellectual support for more trade liberalization and by implication for more globalization. Due to the accumulation of disconnects over time, today's disconnect is at a peak level. Thus, it is necessary to restore the natural relation between trade, environment, and culture or at least, in the short term, prevent further deterioration. Reconnecting means to reintegrate the three factors in an institutional fashion but also with respect to their role in civil society.

The reconnecting process will require more than one trade negotiation round, but in many real and symbolic ways the near-term efforts at trade liberalization will point the future down a path that will bear impacts deep into the twenty-first century. This direction may well point to more disconnects in future conjunctions. Now is a point in time to change the direction of these trends towards reconnecting the parts of the human social context.

There is no alternative to reconnecting. The failure to reconnect will result in meaningless wealth, consumer cultures, and degraded environments. The book suggests how to fairly treat environment, culture, and trade through some common civil and international principles. It also provides some hypothetical future cases of trade, environment, and culture, and some insights into new conjunctions just on the horizon.

TODAY'S TOWER OF BABEL

The launch of the WTO's December 1999 "Millennium Round" of trade negotiations in Seattle—surely as symbolic of timing as possible—produced riots, hundreds of arrests, and perhaps $10 million in business losses. What happened outside the convention hall was in stark contrast to what happened inside: nothing. The Seattle meeting fell apart within days. The disconnect was clear and the result of differing histories, worldviews, and expectations among the 134 government participants and the thousands of nongovernment organizations (NGOs). Some of these divisions were expressions of developing country fears of globalization. The Seattle riots, one of the largest in the United States since the Vietnam War, demonstrated that even people from developed countries have serious concerns about the direction of trade liberalization and with the WTO as the chief agent in the process of globalization.

Taken as a whole, the vocal positions on trade liberalization espoused by these many groups turned into a cacophony of differing tones and decibels. Pro-business groups touted the benefits of trade, countering anti-trade protests by labor and environmental groups. Pro-labor and pro-environment groups, on the other hand, have been bitter rivals for many years in the northwest United States, over controversial issues such as protecting the spotted owl versus cutting timber from old growth forests.

The environmental groups often espoused positions that intended to protect environments in developing countries (such as the Amazon rainforest) from exploitation. Governments such as Brazil and many private groups in developing countries, however, rejected their positions as eco-imperialistic. The disconnect spread to traditional trade allies: even within developed country governments there were serious disagreements over farming and services issues.

The deep problem of the disconnect is that the many viewpoints expressed in Seattle, and hence about the meaning and pace of globalization through trade liberalization, represent not just differing perceived worldviews based on logical determinations and deductions where some sort of coherent state of discussion and discourse can take place. Rather, the fragmented worldviews of the many groups underlie a social context that is clearly in a state of disconnect on a number of dimensions. The arguments are so discordant that there seems to be no common plane for discourse. It is as if the many groups in Seattle were speaking differing languages, almost like a modern day Tower of Babel. Perhaps relating the story of the Tower can provide an analogy for the state of today's discussion on globalization.

Described in the Bible at Genesis 11:1–9, the Tower of Babel was built of brick and mortar at a place called Shinar (modern day Iraq) and was the outstanding technological achievement of the time. Perhaps, in our time, it is the equivalent of going to the moon. Not only was the tower, probably a huge ziggurat, meant to reach the sky to make it easier for people to talk to God, it was thought to be insurance against God in case of another flood (as noted in the ancient Epic of Gilgamesh). The Tower also gave the people a sense of personal empowerment because it showed that with technology they could solve any problem. There was thus less of a need for them to rely on God.

The tower was a monumental construction effort, bringing together many differing people from many differing places. In the process of its planning and eventual construction, the tower became a sort of world federalist movement that attracted many differing peoples not just to build a tower but to "make ourselves a name, so that we will not be scattered all over the face of the earth" (Genesis 11:4). The many peoples of the world would unite, intermarry, and speak the same language and be one people.

In the Bible, it is clear that God did not like the idea of a tower, nor approve of a world populated by one people speaking one language. To show disdain for the tower and the one-world idea it symbolized, as the project neared its completion God made it so that the people working on the Tower of Babel could no longer understand one another. They spontaneously began speaking in differing languages. (Some believe this is where the term "babbling" comes from.) In confusion, the people of Shinar scattered to different parts of the earth and that was the end of the Tower of Babel.

The comparisons to today are compelling but interpretations are of course quite varied. Did it suggest rebelling against the idea of globalization and the idea of a single world language, culture, and economy? Was the Bible saying that "babbling," or the need for people to possess worldviews (languages) that were very different (what we think of as diversity), was a virtue? I think this answer is yes, but this inclination may only reflect a modern interpretation.

The story of the Tower of Babel gives the strong impression that the issues of technological progress and by inference globalization are not new in history. It also suggests a quite complicated story. This book attempts to translate these many worldviews on globalization, spoken in many languages, into a coherent story told over time and across ideas. It examines prior globalizations from the perspective of the social context to give some meaning and interpretability to the events of today. We are now living in one of these unique periods in human history known as a conjunction: a time when a coalition of special agents of change emerge and create substantial and widespread technological and social changes in the human condition. The conjunction is a time when globalization, the ongoing spread of economic and cultural ideas, travels from one group to another. Given sufficient time, the new technologies spread throughout the world. It is critical for people to understand the role that trade, environment, and culture will play in this conjunction—and its globalizing tendencies—so that they can have a hand in creating their own destiny and the destinies of their children.

The book employs a historic perspective by comparing the events and trends of today with those of the past. History offers both positive and negative examples in the instance of conjunctions and notions of progress. The Electronic Conjunction, the most recent conjunction in human history, is now emerging as a twenty-first-century lifestyle. Because of the historical human urge to institutionalize new ideas and behaviors, it is during a conjunction that stress in the social context is at its peak due to the collision of new technologies with the rigidities of ancient and cumulative human institutions. This conflict characterizes the disconnect.

Globalization through trade has brought environments and cultures into contact in a manner never before experienced or imagined. Consequently, cultures and environments are more at risk than ever before. Formulating a system that treats trade, environment, and culture fairly in this process is a formidable obstacle and requires new ways of thinking. In the past, dealing with the social changes brought about by technology largely fell outside most institutional realms. However, this will not be the case in the future, as institutions, especially the WTO, begin addressing a wide variety of issues that involve trade. Integrating institutional rulings with trade, environment, and culture norms will be an essential and difficult task.

Trade policy effectively acts as a social gatekeeper; in essence, it sets, and therefore controls, the rate of social change by allowing an influx of technology and economy, and from them a constellation of social changes. The greater the degree of trade liberalization, the greater the likelihood a society will adopt new technologies. Therefore, more trade openness increases the rate of social and economic change. If trade policy does act as a gatekeeper, how far should these trade policy negotiations proceed and at what pace in order to assure continued economic and social stability in the human social context? Furthermore, what is the role of trade and economy with respect to non-economic issues generated by trade liberalization, especially in the case of culture and the environment? This book suggests that the unique technological periods of history can produce considerable social and environmental instability that need addressing along with trade liberalization progress.

Negotiations carried out under the auspices of the WTO will result in important decisions about globalization and its impact on society. These negotiations on trade liberalization may take the form of complicated and long-term "rounds," more limited and short-term sector agreements, or other arrangements. Whichever the mechanism, the WTO will continue to act as a force for globalization and trade liberalization.

While it is appropriate to examine the WTO as the nexus of globalization, or at least to assume this viewpoint, it is also important to remember that the pace of globalization is proceeding ahead through many governmental and nongovernmental fora. Nearly 150 countries are either now in the WTO or trying to get in and almost every one of these countries is also involved in regional, bilateral, or customs agreements such as the European Union (EU), the North American Free Trade Agreement (NAFTA), or the Association of Southeast Asian Nations (ASEAN). At another level, a group of the most industrialized countries belongs to a sort of "Super-WTO" in the form of the Organization for Economic Cooperation and Development (OECD).

This book has a broad scope and its areas of intellectual interest cover several disciplines and historical periods. Therefore, the discussion must start with some basic definitions, concepts, and ideas that follow in three parts. The second section defines the three primary factors of interest in the social context (culture, environment, and trade). The third section describes the beliefs of some scholars on the relationship between culture and the environment and the role of trade. The final section lays out a timeline for the historical conjunctions of interest here.

DEFINING TERMS

This section defines the three critical parts of the social context (culture, environment, and trade) necessary to understanding that context and the historic conjunction. Given the right social context and a new technology, these combinations can lead to unique periods of change.

The definitions of these three terms cannot be divorced from their historical use. For each term, in the interests of consensus, the definitions are general and philosophical in orientation rather than specific and technical. Given the prior discussion on the differing languages spoken by the many viewpoints on globalization, it is essential to begin with a broad and comprehensive understanding and definition of the terms. One aspect of today's disconnect is the differing claims on the costs and benefits of globalization. These differing claims also reveal the fragmentation and narrowness of terms and ideas. "One consequence of this dispute has been the insufficient exchange of ideas between environmentalists and trade policy experts on how to make trade regulations better reflect the environmentalists' growing and legitimate concerns."[2] Add an anthropologist to the mix to reflect ideas on culture, and discussion about globalization and the disconnect becomes much more complicated. For many, agreeing on what even constitutes culture is itself a struggle.

WHAT IS CULTURE?

Defining culture is difficult because it is so ubiquitous and so ever-present in the human experience: almost every person has his or her particular definition and socialized idea of culture. This definitional problem is not limited to civil society. Even among anthropologists there is no consensus on an all-encompassing, single definition of culture. Lacking this common base for discourse naturally makes the task of discussing and examining culture difficult. "It is as though mammologists were not agreed upon the definition of 'mammal,'" or mathematicians in dispute about what is "zero."[3] The problem is not that there are too few definitions of culture but rather there are too many: "there are almost as many definitions of culture as there are anthropologists."[4] There is, however, good reason for a lack of consensus on the word.

Many scholars and language specialists believe that culture is one of the two or three most complicated words in the English language. This is partly due to its intricate historical development, in several European languages, but mainly because the word culture now represents important concepts in several distinct intellectual disciplines, where the meaning in one context is incompatible with another.[5]

Culture is probably the broadest concept of all those used in the historical social sciences. It embraces a very large range of connotations, and thereby it is the cause perhaps of the most difficulty.[6]

It is perhaps fitting that the definition of the word culture is rooted in ecology. Culture is a French word (and before that Latin) that migrated to the English language in the fifteenth century. In French, culture implies agricultural practices because "the primary meaning [of culture] was in its role in husbandry, the tending of natural growth."[7] The early French meaning focused on the cultivation of plants and animals, and the process of domesticating and cultivating them. In fact, the English word for "culture" does not translate into "culture" in French, but rather "civilization."

In the sixteenth century, the English borrowed the French word "culture." Over time, the English not only adopted but also extended the meaning to include the "process of human development." The English definition of culture focused on manners and breeding in the process of becoming civilized as humans, especially according to the European view of progress. The change in the definition of culture coincided with the Industrial Conjunction and the rise of urbanization and mass civil society. The shift in word meaning also reflected the need to "educate" and "socialize" a rapidly expanding middle class who had decent incomes but often lacked formal or social education.

Having or possessing culture is often a symbol and manifestation of power. Culture, like income, reflects the power and wealth of a country. Europeans believed that some societies "had done a better job than others" and, therefore, had "a higher level of culture."[8] Thus, a higher self-perceived culture not only indicated advancement, it gave license to spread that culture to others. Early on, culture was a rationale for colonialism built on a perceived social superiority. During this time culture, defined in terms of civil manners and used as a verb, was the subject of such diverse writers as Thomas Moore, Francis Bacon, Thomas Hobbes, and Samuel Johnson.

It was not until the mid-eighteenth century that culture became commonly used as a noun and denoted a particular belief and custom of a group, ranging from tribes to religions. As a noun, culture acquired a contextual definition that became more pluralist. The change in word use also reflected a changing social construct that "was especially important with the nineteenth-century development of comparative anthropology, where it has continued to designate a whole and distinctive way of life."[9]

Franz Boas and others challenged the Eurocentric definition of culture, asserting that intellect "constitutes" culture but does not measure it.[10] In the early twentieth century, a less absolute definition of culture emerged. The belief in cultural relativism "understood that people acquire the ideas, beliefs, values and the like of their society, and that these cultural features provide the basic materials by which they think and perceive."[11]

Finally, the word culture underwent one other change in definition during the middle part of the twentieth century. Schools of thought on explaining culture, and thus the definition of it, grew into rival realist and idealist camps. The former focuses on "observed manifestations, behavior, and the products of behavior" and the latter on "the researcher's interpretation of the culture bearer's ideas of societal values and norms."[12]

Realists believe culture is an observable phenomenon while idealists infer it. The realist school of thought believes that culture is best understood through observable, tangible artifacts, rituals, and customs. Alternatively, the idealist defines culture in a way that includes customs, norms, values, and other criterion, yet excludes "all the man-made socially meaningful objects."[13] A middle ground definition would include those learned cultural attributes noted by the idealist camp as well as those "man-made material goods that have a social meaning."[14] The approach to culture in this book takes this middle ground and defines culture as: "a coherent system of values, attitudes, and institutions that influences individual and social behavior in all dimensions of human experience."[15]

The word culture, even when used as a noun, continues to evolve and is now moving from connoting an "informing spirit" to a "lived culture." The shift in meaning mirrors a change in the social interpretation of culture that has become more realist than idealist and more focused on products of cultures than on the processes in them.[16]

Technological advancement does not necessarily lead to cultural progress. "Clearly, cause and effect run in both directions in the relationships between culture and progress."[17] In the short term, there is invariably some impact and it is usually negative because technological advancement often leads to momentary declines in the coherence of culture.

WHAT IS ENVIRONMENT?

Like "culture," the definition and context of the word "environment" has undergone changes with time. What is now commonly referred to as environment was once thought of as "nature." Nature was often perceived to be more of a foe than a friend of the human being. In fact, most of human history epitomizes a struggle against nature for survival that, in turn, sets the tone for the cultural outlooks on it. The diversity of cultures thus represents a diversity of environments. "Ideas about what is nature, or what is natural behavior, are enormously divergent and quite culture-specific."[18] However, nature and humans follow differing paths in achieving diversity. Nature adapts to the environment by dividing into greater numbers of species that exploit distinctive resources. "In contrast, the single human species adapted itself to widely varying conditions on earth by means not of biological but of cultural differentiation."[19]

Nobel Laureate Herbert Simon's landmark work *Sciences of the Artificial* used systems theory to examine human behavior. Simon divides the realm of behavior into social and physical dimensions, or artificial and natural worlds.[20] Following this simple construct, the definition of "environment" here includes elements of the natural world, including its resources and biota. Defining environment, similar to culture, is not easy because it pervades our lives in so many ways. Nonetheless, environment is a general and a specific term. For civil society and average people, it is a general term that describes the physical world. For the individual, environment implies a local ecological context. A person has a natural bias and interest towards their own local environment because it most directly influences their immediate existence and quality of life. The locality of culture and environment produces unique micro-systems that are a blend of culture and environment.

Trade severs the context of the local environment from culture by separating producers from consumers in the process of creating macro-environments and large-scale production processes. Trade generally increases as a conjunction progresses, because it matches more producers with consumers in differing parts of the world. Due to economies of scale and their production advantages, trade tends to promote macro-environments over micro-environments. The result is that a disconnect develops between the human and the environment the more macro one's environment becomes since the human is naturally disposed towards a local environmental context for their culture.

The definition here intends to discriminate human or anthropogenic impacts on the environment from natural processes. Insofar as history does provide some earlier examples, it is possible to trace the pattern of human intrusion into the natural world over time. This tracing, as part of a search for patterns, then can help in providing a basis for understanding the role of the environment in the social context.

A system has some special features and this is especially important when the social context includes the environment as one aspect of it. From an environmental standpoint, one can think of the system in terms of what humans take from it (source impacts) and what they put back (sink impacts). Source impacts, often resource-related, have been the most important type of human impact on the environment throughout history. These source impacts mean the taking or harvesting of mammals, birds, ores, waters, or forests that have some level of finite or infinite depletion. Human environmental impacts were initially very species-specific, and over time have become more generalized and habitat-focused because of the growing macro-level influences of trade policy.

The appearance of culture and trade led to a key change in human behavior in prehistoric times and in the human relation to the environment. The Tool Conjunction began about forty thousand years ago, a time in which humans created new technologies (stone points and chippers) that shifted their subsistence patterns (early economies). The Tool Conjunction led to a tremendous innovation in the human social context by turning the human into the most effective predator on the planet.

After the Tool Conjunction, it was not the hunter but the gatherer that became the focus of progress. Plant and animal domestication, human population growth, and technology advances transformed environmental impacts from being species-specific to habitat-general in the Agricultural Conjunction (starting perhaps ten thousand years ago). These impacts include major deforestation (in Europe) and desertification (in the Middle East). These historic acts prove that large-scale environmental impact is not solely a modern phenomenon and limited to societies possessing advanced technologies. The Phoenicians, who built a thalassocracy (maritime empire) before the birth of Christ, did not require modern technologies to cut down the cedars of Lebanon to build the ships that carried them throughout the Mediterranean Sea. By 1600, most of China's forests were gone.[21]

Large-scale sink problems are of a relatively new vintage. They result from human outputs placed back into the environment, such as pollution and waste that accompany processing and disposal of end-use products. There have always been small-scale sink problems, but in the past, there were fewer people using lower-level technologies that minimized serious environmental impacts. The amount and type of waste and pollution now put back into the environment by higher technology and more people are much greater than in earlier times. This problem became evident during the Industrial Conjunction that began around the year 1750.

Human impacts produced both long and short-term environmental changes. Long-term change ordinarily relates to altered land-use patterns and short-term change to species extinctions. Certain species can become extinct in a matter of a few years, but changing a habitat is a much longer process. There is obviously a link between the short and long term, since all species together make up a habitat. Nevertheless, the sum is quite different from the mere total of the parts. Once the intricate relationships in the habitat are unraveled, then it is impossible to reassemble them.

WHAT IS TRADE?

The term "trade" indicates international trade, which today refers to an economic transaction that involves parties in more than one country. Trade theory suggests that through specialization there is a general welfare gain for countries and that these gains are greater under conditions of economic competition. Of course, trade is much more than just economics. Through trade, products from one country become a part of another country's social and environmental fabric. Trade policy acts as a regulator to the rate at which trade occurs and by inference change. Given this important role, trade policy has become a process of "determining how to find the optimal point along the policy continuum."[22]

Trade is an exchange of perceived worth between entities in differing geographic (environmental) systems that often also demarcate differing economic and cultural systems or countries. Diametrically different environmental situations produce different perspectives on value and worth. Thus, the value or worth of a product in one country and culture may differ radically from another one. Just as there are differences in production and specialization, there are differences in environments and culture that determine worth.

A separate issue relates to the nature of the country or nation-state itself and the implications of globalization for national sovereignty. It is clear that borders have become more porous and are somewhat arbitrary cartographic assignments based on political realities that change over time. The implication is that trade is international and involves parties between two far-off places, but this is not always the case because political jurisdictions differ in size and reach. It is farther from San Diego to Boston in the United States than it is from Madrid to Moscow, travel that requires crossing the borders of several countries. While political boundaries (nearly two hundred of them) define what constitutes trade, environments expressed by ecosystems ignore politics. Therefore, nation-states do not provide exact, or even approximate, replicas of natural environments. This ambiguity naturally complicates the understanding of trade from an environmental context.

The historical content of trade has always included aspects that are decidedly cultural and environmental in nature and rooted in place. This multipurpose utility in products has always existed but mostly been relevant to trade in goods. This prior focus is changing in two ways. First, the increasing trade in input products means that the connection between a product and a place is now much weaker. Now, more than one-half of world trade is in inter-industry trade of input products, mostly between multinational corporations. Second, the definition and institutional reach of trade is expanding and now includes and incorporates other forms of economic interchanges, such as services trade (including entertainment, telecommunications, tourism, transport, and others). Trade continues to extend to new product areas, including international financial transactions, trade in electricity (for example, the Great Whale project in Canada) or in water (Lesotho plans to export water to South Africa). The sale of weather data collected by satellites is another form of trade, as are communication and broadcast satellite transmissions. E-commerce is of course an important new trading medium with a whole range of cultural and environmental impacts. International investment is arguably a form of trade. Therefore, trade includes any economic interactions that flow across political borders that demarcate countries.

CULTURAL PERSPECTIVES ON THE ENVIRONMENT AND THE ROLE OF TRADE

Culture reflects human adaptation to the environment.[23] Today, humans in many respects are the masters of the environment, having tamed it and linked it to human culture. In pre-history, the human was subservient to the environment and human survival was a shaky proposition for millennia. In some sense, the defining of the human occurs at the point when people are able to control their survival in the environment rather than be under the control of it. With the advent of modern humans, culture grew closely linked to the environment through the rituals and customs of society and these relations evolved into systems of subsistence.

> The assumption . . . is that on the one hand culture can be understood primarily only in terms of cultural factors, but that on the other hand no culture is wholly intelli-

gible without reference to the non-cultural or so-called environmental factors with which it is in relation and which condition it.[24]

There are ways in which the culture and environment relationship differs or results in differences. Culture does not change at the same rate as the environment, producing a time lag between cultural and environmental behavior. Cultural habits, because of this lag, can lead to a historical "footprint," meaning that there is a social inertia and a tendency to repeat behavior in the future. The cultural legacy is the imprint of ancestral lifestyles onto more modern lifestyles and modern subsistence patterns. Here are two examples in which these cultural lifestyles persist despite the fact that the world changes in both economic and environmental terms.[25]

First, even after the woolly mammoths were nearly extinct in Eurasia and North America, people continued to carry out rituals associated with the mammoth hunt. When environmental change occurs, such as the extinction of certain species, people do not eliminate cultural practices associated with a subsistence pattern, but rather, focus their efforts on a substitute species that allows the cultural pattern to continue. After the mammoths died, buffalo eventually became the dominant resource for Native Americans and the mammoth rituals evolved into the buffalo rituals.

Second, the custom of abstaining from meat is a two-thousand-year-old Christian practice. However, the human devastation and subsequent labor shortages brought on by the bubonic plague (spread through trade) during the Middle Ages made the Roman Catholic prohibition of eating meat on Friday not merely the ideal, but a practical necessity. The Dark and Middle Ages resulted in fewer beef and grain producers, abandonment of many farmlands, and incredibly high meat prices. The "fish option" thus reflected economic reality. Under a Papal ukase in the Middle Ages consumers switched one-seventh (days in a week) of their meat consumption to fish. The meat ban also served to benefit communities that were more dependent on catching and exporting fish (especially Italian coastal cities loyal to the Pope).[26] Five hundred years later, many Roman Catholics still eat only fish on Fridays.

Every culture changes with time. The fact that many different cultures exist today illustrates the different ways that societies have adapted to their environments and the divergent ideas and ideologies that emerged in various environments in the world. The point here is that explaining culture is more than translating a topographical map to a set of corresponding cultural features, as "cultural determinism" theory would suggest. Anthropologists and sociologists identify three relevant environmental factors that explain differences in a peoples' cultural evolution:

1. the mode of adaptation to a changing environment via culture,
2. the technology that accompanies this adaptation, and
3. the diffusion of cultural practices and introduction of new technologies through trade.[27]

The approach to explaining the culture-environment link used in this book has a realist orientation, relying on intellectual fragments from Julian Steward, Clifford Geertz, and Marvin Harris. Julian Steward and other realists, for example, use a "multi-linear evolution" framework to explain culture, an approach that focuses on how societies share cultural values over time and how those values influence the environment. This conception is a constellation "of features which are most closely related to subsistence activities and economic arrangements. The core includes social, political, and religious patterns and are empirically determined to be closely connected to the arrangements."[28]

Julian Steward looks at population density and settlement patterns, the course of adapting to the environment and how humans introduce innovations into culture.[29] Clifford Geertz's realist approach is cybernetic in nature: using demography to explain culture and focusing on "a complex network of mutual causality," including energy flows and materials use cycles.[30] Critics of this approach, however, believe cybernetic interpretations tend to overemphasize energy flow models and other functionalist explanations, while neglecting historical and unique cultural factors.

Marvin Harris's viewpoint of "cultural materialism" is decidedly deterministic and realistic in approach. Harris suggests that the population pressure causes differential cultural approaches to using available environmental resources.[31] Harris ascribes to a view of anthropological behavior known as "cultural materialism."

Harris describes the material roots of culture in a variety of environmental settings. These settings in fact determine the cultural responses that achieve the greatest subsistence utility. Thus, cultural materialism can explain the particular role of cattle in Hindu cultures (it is far more efficient to keep cattle for dung and dairy products than to eat its meat), to the lack of pork in Muslim countries (pigs do not do well in arid climates and the meat turns bad quickly there). Cannibalism, according to Harris, is a systemic manifestation (in Papua New Guinea, Central America, and elsewhere) of overpopulation and scarce food resources. Given the different resources that shape culture, there are naturally ethical contradictions between people's cultures.[32] Harris points to several contradictions: Chinese detest cow milk, but like dog meat; Western peoples are lactophiles, dairy-product consumers, but the thought of consuming dog meat repels them.[33] Hindus not only avoid dog, but also would never eat the meat of the sacred cow. In the United States, on the other hand, beef has taken on an almost "holy" quality among consumers. This idolization differs in that the Americans love to eat the cow.[34]

> The possession of the same domesticated animals does not produce the same utilization. While the Tungu rides his reindeer, other Siberians harness their animals to a sledge; the Chinaman will not milk his cattle, while the Zulu's diet consists largely of milk.[35]

The role of the pig also varies across cultures and environments. There are "pig lovers," such as the indigenous populations of New Guinea, and "pig haters," such as the people of the Middle East.[36] The pig to the Tsembenga of New Guinea is a form of wealth. Pigs are capital accumulated by individuals and later disbursed back to the community in ceremonial feasts occurring in seven-year cycles. The Tsembenga cycle of pig production is closely linked to the societies' cultural, economic, and environmental cycles.

Some regard trade as an end to itself. World War II hastened interaction between Western and New Guinea peoples, and Allied nations sought their support in the jungle war against the Japanese. The initial interactions between the two groups involved the exchange of gifts. The gifts fascinated and astounded the peoples of New Guinea who came to regard the Allied largesse as holy. The tribes assumed that the makers of the fantastic products must be deities of some sort and waited in vain for their gods to return with more trade products, thus spawning the "cargo cults." Goods became a focus of worship simply because they were traded.

Trade is a critical factor in the relationship between the environment and culture. The material diffusion of goods and technology through trade alters the culture-environment relation. With trade, resource demands on the local environment no longer exclusively reflect and relate to the local culture and environment conditions. Trade separates the subsistence pattern (the economic survival strategy) from the culture and the environment.

Prehistoric humans were "autochthonous," or native to a home area considered by them to be "sacred geography." The immediate geographic area was sacred because of subsistence dependence that was rooted in cultural knowledge. The culture "consisted of a complex knowledge of the place, terrain, plants, and animals embedded in a phonology of seasonal cycles."[37] Culture, therefore, was specific to the geographic locale in which it existed because culture embodied the subsistence strategy of the society that lived in the sacred geography. Clearly, as a subsistence strategy incorporates trade, the product of other cultures' subsistence strategies in other geographies, the culture's relation to the local environment weakens.

The more trade proliferates, the more the traditional relationship between culture and environment, a local phenomenon that evolved over millennia, tends to erode. This is especially true as environmental resources lose their original form and become input products. Here are two examples of how a conceptual disconnect occurs between products and resources because of trade.

First, fur-bearing mammals have historically been a source of material for clothing. The extinction and near-extinction of many fur-bearing animals in North America in the seventeenth and eighteenth centuries (by the Hudson Bay Company and others), however, is more so the result of changing European fashions and the changing demands for furs (see the fur cases in Chapters 2 and 3). Economically speaking, the social aspect of the fur was much more powerful than the environmental aspect. Some fur-bearing animals became extinct due to changing European fashions that favored a certain look.

Second, throughout time Africans have killed elephants and rhinoceros for their meat. However, the current annihilation of these two animals is not the result of demands for meat, but of demands for the horns and tusk, which have cultural and medicinal values (see the ivory case study in Chapter 3). Extinctions can result from demands that are both economic and cultural in nature. Trade clearly alters the culture and environment relationship.

Differing types of trade policy produce differing environmental problems; often, this is the result of natural endowments and history. Cultures that are trade-oriented, such as the ancient Phoenicians and Venetians in the Middle Ages, or today's Hong Kong and Singapore, face a different set of environmental problems than countries whose economies are less trade-oriented. Countries that export resources may encounter environmental problems that are extractive or source-related, while those that import resources have problems that are waste or pollution-oriented. Furthermore, culture can act to prioritize trade and environmental issues, which can be very subjective. Indians could be major exporters of beef and Americans of bald eagle feathers. Both nations choose not to for cultural reasons. Culture can thus provide the parameters for possible trade.

Trade is one part of a culture's subsistence strategy and that strategy is determined in some part by the environment in which it exists.[38] This is not to say that the form and structure of a culture, as well as the psychological attributes of a particular group, are simply the product of a few environmental factors. A given environment can facilitate the emergence of certain subsistence strategies but not others. The environment, in this view, sets limits, but does not determine history (an approach known as "environmental possibilism"). This view includes other factors, such as a group's history, knowledge of techniques, and possession of material artifacts that together determine subsistence strategies.

With these definitions and a discussion of the links across culture, environment, and trade, it is now possible to discuss the three entities across time. The next part introduces the idea of a historic conjunction and explores it over several key periods.

CONJUNCTIONS THROUGH TIME

The factors of trade, environment, and culture do not cover all aspects of the human experience and human social context, but there are at least two good reasons to focus on them. First, trade, environment, and culture are particularly sensitive to technological change and thus are good markers of the pace of change. Together, these three entities form a powerful configuration for either positive or negative change in a society and thus the sensitivities magnify. Second, today's era of change has spread further than any earlier conjunction and produced a greater degree of globalization with more pronounced impacts. Thus, the disconnect becomes more widespread as it accumulates over time and this assertion can be analyzed by looking at trade, culture, and environment dimensions.

This section has two parts. First, it examines the concept of the conjunction with historic examples. Second, it studies the idea of a conjunction from anthropological, economic, and social viewpoints. It then puts these viewpoints in a historical framework.

The idea of a historic conjunction is an extremely subtle phenomenon: no newspaper headlines or ticker tape parades mark its inception; no decisionmakers suddenly integrate this factor into their policy calculations; and no catastrophic or special events occur in these times. Nevertheless, many scholars agree that an aggregation of small events eventually grow to epochal proportions in historic conjunction, a shift that becomes clearer in historical retrospect. Several authors refer to conjunctions by a variety of names, such as "stages," "epochs," "revolutions," "waves," "eras," and other terms. All, however, indicate that in certain historic periods, rapid and significant changes occur in human lives and lifestyles. These special periods arise from the introduction of new technologies and their interaction with unique social contexts.

Do conjunctions occur or do scholars define them? The answer is probably both. One need only compare people's lives today (at least in North America) with those of their grandparents to conclude that technology and the social context is substantially different. A largely rural, farm-based population is now urban and clustered around large cities. There is also little doubt that scholars shape and mold the description and explanation of change. Modern day scholars also have the luxury of a historic vantage point that earlier scholars obviously lacked. This is to say that it is easier to explain history if there is more of it.

While conjunctions have many similarities, they differ in several ways. Obviously, the level of technology is distinct and thus its ability to augment human powers. The type of technology associated with a historic conjunction may also produce markedly different trade, cultural, and environmental impacts. Because conjunction impacts are cumulative, there are more pronounced impacts with each successive conjunction. These additive impacts may not increase in a linear fashion, nor may the limits to the impacts occur at some fixed and immutable point.

The theory of how the conjunction occurs and makes its impact begins with an "agreeable" social context: a period in which a group possesses the basis for a new technology and one in which there is a social atmosphere which is willing (or forced) to accept and adopt the new technology. After meeting these new conditions, the new technology continues to evolve which in turn inaugurates another stage in the conjunction, one that focuses on the human condition and on changes in human culture and the environment humans live in. It is important that both the agreeable social context and the invention occur. The invention may not be new and may need to wait for an agreeable social context. To give an example with respect to one invention, "The first English patent for a typewriter was issued in 1714. But a century and a half elapsed before typewriters became commercially available."[39]

The types of forces, and therefore the types of change, that are set in motion by the conjunction have profound influences on the natural world (the environment) and the social world (culture). These two aspects are particularly inviting because they represent the outward and the inward foci of human society during times of great change. In simple terms, the conjunction tends to globalize the new social context and to impose new rules for interacting outside and inside the group. Naturally, there are some points where the outside and the inside overlap, like Venn diagrams, and these areas define the new social context.

New technologies that drive conjunctions do not occur in a vacuum. The techniques are part of a certain social context that both encourages its development and helps to implement it. The same technology in two differing social contexts may produce two entirely different outcomes. V. Harold Chile and Maurice Daumas, among others, therefore believe invention is a social product.[40]

> Whether it is due to progressive evolution or to invention, the development of technical methods is the result of a collective experience that is constantly being accumulated. Each generation continues to inherit the experience of all its predecessors; in the field of technology, progress is the sum total.[41]

Daumas describes technological change as the result of a social context occurring within a unique place and time. No particularly momentous events mark the period. In fact, the more important periods have perhaps been those with greater social tranquility. It is actually quite difficult to even trace an invention to a single person or place.

> Invention is never the product of a single man, but rather that of a period and a society; it is born in definite historical circumstances. This explains its simultaneity, since the circumstances required to make a given invention effective can be realized within a very short time interval in several places between which there was no exchange of information on the subject.[42]

Given the agreeable social context and a new technology, a conjunction is set into motion. It then begins a process of dynamic feedback with trade, environment, and culture that tends to accelerate the pace of the conjunction. A conjunction is a period of accelerated technological change, which produces an ongoing change in the social context. In the process, a new social context emerges out of the technological distance that the conjunction creates (see Figure 1.1).

Periods of high technological and social change are not always welcome because conjunctions cause changes in social structures, which then shift power relations. The losers in these shifts often resist conjunctions and their associated changes. The case of the Tower of Babel illustrated this issue in ancient times. Protests to the conjunction also occurred in the Agricultural Conjunction: "The traditional form of production (small-scale farming),

FIGURE 1.1 The Conjunction Model

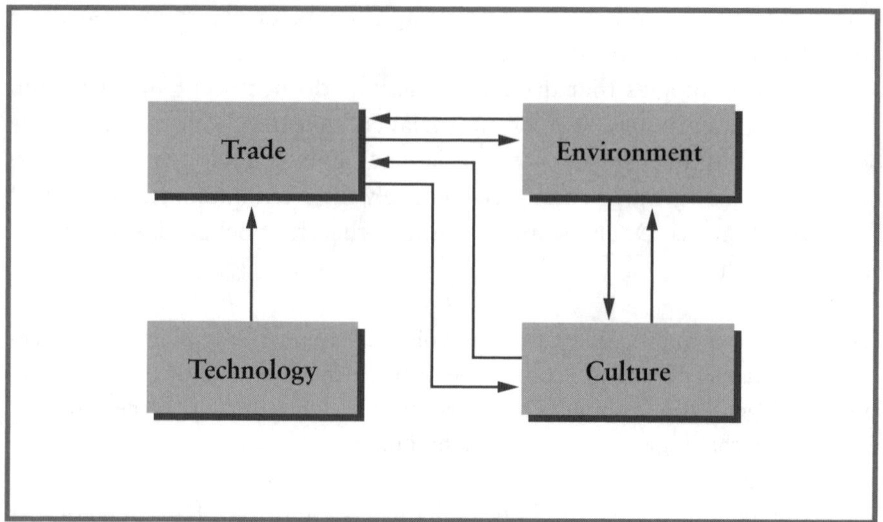

however, did not disappear easily under the pressure of modern techniques."[43] The Luddites, who opposed the Industrial Conjunction, are also examples of this resistance to change. The protesters in Seattle may appear only as modern day Luddites, but this is too simple a characterization. Today, the challenge of the conjunction is both the impact of a new technology but also a new and unparalleled degree of economic interdependence.

Despite the fact that conjunctions are inherently multidisciplinary in nature, the approaches to understanding them have not been. "While the history of technology has often been studied, most of these studies . . . are the work of economists and sometimes sociologists."[44] In general, conceptual frameworks for conjunctions fall into three disciplinary areas: anthropological, economic, and social history. From a review of these three fields, it is possible to compile a multidisciplinary conjunction history and thus a description of the changing social context over time.

ANTHROPOLOGICAL HISTORY

Anthropological historians approach conjunctions in terms of how, why, and when subsistence strategies change. Subsistence strategies underwent massive changes about forty thousand years ago during the Tool Conjunction. In this period, advances in technology led to economic and cultural

TABLE 1.1 Human Energy Sources from Food Types by Conjunction Period (Percent)

Energy Source	Tool	Agricultural	Industrial
Fats	20	15	40
Starches	60	65	30
Sugars	0	5	20
Proteins	20	15	10
Total	100	100	100

Source: Adapted from Charles L. Redman, "The Impact of Food Production: Short-Term Strategies and Long-Term Consequences," in *Pleistocene Extinctions*, ed. P. S. Martin and H. S. Wright (New Haven, Conn., and London: Yale University Press, 1967), p. 124, Figure 10-1.
Note: Sugars refer to refined products. Starches are minus sugar.

progress of incredible relative magnitude. Prior to this time, little evidence suggests use of bone, antler, ivory, and other related substances as formal artifacts that archaeologists call "points," "awls," "needles," and the like.[45] These tools fulfilled a variety of purposes, especially in making clothing and for hunting.

With the diffusion of superior tools and techniques, human diets and subsistence strategies dramatically changed over time. Table 1.1 compares the human diet in various subsistence patterns over the course of thousands of years. The table describes food energy sources for hunter-gatherer, agriculture, and high-energy societies. It reveals drastic changes in the sources of human energy over time according to the fat, starch, sugar, and protein content of human diets.

Food energy types grouped by subsistence patterns provide the basis for a timeline and underlie a story of huge changes in people and the environment. Over time, protein as a source of human energy from food has been somewhat stable, at about 10 to 20 percent of total human energy requirements. Fat, however, as a source of energy, has gone from about 15 percent in agriculture and hunter-gatherer societies to more than 40 percent in high-energy societies. Starch, minus sugar, which accounts for the bulk of energy in agriculture societies, is less than one-third the source of energy in high-energy societies. Sugar, which played only a minimal role in the hunter-gatherer societies, accounts for about 20 percent of total energy requirements in high-energy societies.

These changes in diets and the subsistence strategies related to them occur with great environmental consequence. High intakes of fat and sugar create stress on the environment through species extinction, land use changes, and pollution. The urge to consume fat and sugar is inherent in human chemistry and some believe a latent footprint existing over many millennia.

> Our Pleistocene genetic heritage [according to Edgerton] is maladaptive in post-Pleistocene environments. Our craving for salt, sugar, and fat, for instance, is healthy in wild environments where salt is not superabundant, sugar stimulates the appetite for fresh fruit, and saturated fats are limited and wonderfully balanced in wild animals.[46]

Cultural footprints are in some ways the path for the disconnect in a conjunction. Historian Charles Redman believes there are several elemental contradictions that inevitably arise in a conjunction and therefore can lead to a disconnect. The contradictions occur due to lags in impact between technological and other types of societal changes, precisely the same forces that inaugurate the conjunction. Thus, there is a disconnect between the short-term and the long-term in the subsistence strategy.

Subsistence strategies can also shed light on trade practices and patterns. Agrarian subsistence patterns led to a more settled lifestyle and subsistence patterns were originally very local. Urbanization acts as a catalyst for trade, since populations become more concentrated and stationary. As populations become concentrated and larger, so too do their demands extend to greater distances.

As these non-local demands intensify, the natural balance between the supply and demand of resources in the subsistence strategy becomes out of balance. Demands beyond a sustainable level often lead to the exhaustion of a resource. To a certain extent, these policies are rational and sound choices, but past some point they are self-defeating. Over time, a successful strategy in the short run becomes an unsuccessful strategy in the end.

> There are times in the long history of the human career when seemingly intelligent, productive enterprises—efforts that improve human life in the short term—have negative, even destructive, long-term effects. One of the most important transformations in human history, the shift from nomadic hunting and gathering to settled agriculture and village life, is an important example of the difference between short-term strategies and long-term consequences.[47]

Ester Boserup examined the relation between tools and the environment in the Agricultural Conjunction. She found several similar developmental cases and believed they represented a pattern. In many societies, population growth, combined with greater subsistence societies, eventually led to food shortages when suitable lands became limited. The inevitable response was to shorten fallow times for crops. As fallow times fell, so did the productivity of the often overworked soil. This change in turn necessitated a change of crops and tools to fulfill dietary requirements in the face of declining soil fertility. Technology was no longer simply the cause of the conjunction, but also the result.[48]

ECONOMIC HISTORY

Economists often view historic conjunctions in terms of factors such as supply and demand and therefore in how the periods influence economic systems. Arnold Toynbee, Karl Marx, and Simon Kuznets, among others, are well-known writers who describe conjunctions from such an economic perspective. Each in some way attempts to describe the attributes and characteristics of the period, but their interpretations are quite different.

Karl Marx lived and wrote in the mid-nineteenth century, during the early part of a period later known as the Industrial Conjunction. Marx recognized the momentous technological and socioeconomic changes underway at the time (he would no doubt call this period the Capitalist Conjunction) and saw this era as a seminal link in a chain of historic periods. "For Marx, the prelude of the revolution that laid the foundation of the capitalist mode of production was played out in the last third of the fifteenth century and the first few decades of the sixteenth."[49] Michael Albert and Robin Hahnel interpret Marx's theory of historical change to say:

> Human beings are both the subject and object of historical processes. We apply our powers and mold ourselves and our environments as subjects, and are in turn molded by them as objects. When this on-going process is sufficiently constrained by the contours of the status-quo to reproduce the defining features of those contours over and over, we have evolution. Details of life alter while core characteristics are reproduced essentially unchanged. But when the interplay between people and their social environments yields a change in at least one core characteristic, we call this social revolution.[50]

Marx views the Industrial Conjunction trends more in terms of changes in social structure than in technology changes. His outlook is almost that of an anthropologist in depicting the social stress resulting from a conjunction.

Marx suggests that the conjunction is a planned outcome and tool of economic decision-makers to further their control of the political system. "In the history of primitive accumulation, all revolutions are epoch-making that act as levers for the capitalist class in the course of its formation; but this is true above all for those moments when great masses of men are suddenly and forcibly torn from their subsistence."[51]

Arnold Toynbee was perhaps the first to conceive of a distinct historical period called the Industrial Revolution. His nephew, Arnold J. Toynbee, wrote in the preface to his work, due to his premature death at the age of thirty, that he was the "first economic historian to think of, and to set to describe, the Industrial Revolution as a single historical event, in which all of the details come together to make an intelligible and significant picture."[52] Arnold Toynbee saw a break point in history occurring around the year 1760 in England. "Previously to 1760 the old industrial system obtained in England; none of the great mechanical inventions had been introduced; the agrarian changes were still in the future." [53]

Along with the rise in population and manufactured outputs, enormous environmental changes were underway, especially in terms of land-use changes.

> There is no respect in which the agricultural England of today differs more from that of the period which we are considering, than in the greatly reduced amount of common land. The enclosure of the commons had been going on for centuries before 1760, but with nothing like the rapidity with which it has been going on since.[54]

Toynbee argues that these changes led to productivity gains: "For these reasons the connections between the practice of enclosing and improved agriculture was very close."[55]

Trade also exploded during this period, starting with the export of grain surpluses to Russia, Holland, and America. Agricultural advances also led to a greater supply of wool, and thus sheep, that provided inputs for the emerging textile industry (more on this in Chapter 2). Toynbee believed that "among the manufactures of the time the woolen business was by far the most important."[56] In 1770, woolen exports accounted for nearly one-third of total British exports, with a large part going to the American colonies. Toynbee felt that free trade was beneficial for improving the life of the average worker for three reasons: 1) it increases aggregate wealth, 2) it assures a steady, uninterrupted flow of goods and services, and 3) it provides for price and wage stability. Besides the material gains offered by free trade to the worker, Toynbee was optimistic in believing that social gains would result in the formation of trade unions and enacting of legislation to support worker rights.

Simon Kuznets examined the Industrial Conjunction to discover the elements required for industrial "take-off" in a society. His idea was a general theory about the appearance of new technologies in unique historical periods. Kuznets saw the new technologies as dominators of economies.

An epochal innovation may be described as a major addition to the stock of human knowledge which provides a potential for sustained economic growth an addition so major that its exploitation and utilization absorb the energies of human societies and dominate their growth for a period long enough to constitute an epoch in economic history.[57]

Kuznets identifies four aspects of a conjunction that make it notable. First, "social invention" drives change in a context that exploits new technology. Social invention is, in turn, the source of nascent technological and institutional changes. The impact is thus not only one of degree but also of direction and the feedback in the process is evident. Moreover, the second "implication of technological and social change must be stressed: growth during any epoch is a matter not only of total change but also of structural shifts."[58] Third, although technology may spark a conjunction, "the exploitation of the potential of growth provided by it usually requires much social invention."[59] Finally, Kuznets adds, "the impact of a conjunction [revolution] can be distinguished at various levels of social life (political, economic, cultural, etc., all of which are interrelated)."[60]

Kuznets's focus is on the economic aspects of what he calls a "scientific" conjunction, or the systematic application of technology to industry, a period that began in the late eighteenth century. Therefore, he examines the last two hundred years. Kuznets compares the Industrial Conjunction to earlier conjunctions and systems including nomadic hunter-gatherer societies, agricultural domestication systems, feudal organizations, medieval city-economies, and merchant capitalists. He finds they build on similar principles, although the rules of the systems differ.

SOCIAL HISTORY

Social historians view conjunctions from the standpoint of the individual through time. Alvin Toffler, Fernand Braudel, and Geoffrey Barraclough all examine economic development in terms of attendant social changes, especially changes in average lives. These authors are less interested in specific inventions and events than in general trends and lifestyles.

Futurist Alvin Toffler's view of history is both popular and academic. Toffler divides human history into three conjunctions and refers to conjunctions as "waves," or periods that provide widespread bursts of extraordinary social and technological change. Toffler recognizes that such an approach can also lead to broad generalizations.

> In attempting so large a synthesis, it has been necessary to simplify, generalize, and compress . . . As a result, historians may take some issue with the way this book divides civilization into only three parts—a First Wave agricultural phase, a Second Wave industrial phase, and a Third [Electronic] Wave phase now beginning.[61]

For Toffler, the Agricultural Conjunction began about 8000 B.C. and the Industrial Conjunction between 1650–1750.[62] The generality in these dates is non-specific for a reason. It is impossible to think of conjunctions in strict terms: they only serve as general benchmarks in time.[63] The Electronic Conjunction, driven by computers, arrived in the mid-1950s in the United States, concentrated in areas such as California's Silicon Valley and Boston's Route 128.[64]

Toffler surveys a range of authors who compare today's Electronic Conjunction with others in history. Nobel winner and physicist Sir George Thompson believes that the Electronic Conjunction is less like the Industrial Conjunction and more like the Agricultural Conjunction and its beginnings in the late Neolithic Age.[65] Philosopher Sir Herbert Read adds "possibly the only comparable change is the one that took place between the Old and New Stone Age" (the Tool Conjunction).[66] Kenneth Boulding can find no historic link to today's events, declaring it a time that will divide human history.[67] Julius Huxley believes that the human social context is changing 100,000 times as fast as it did in pre-history (before the Tool Conjunction). "Inventions of a conjunction magnitude that took 50,000 years to accomplish in the Paleolithic times has been reduced to a single century."[68]

Toffler is careful to point out that conjunctions are less the result of what leaders do and more a result of changing individual lifestyles. It is necessary to view a conjunction within a larger social context, especially in the process of social acceptance of new inventions. Technology creates the condition for change in the conjunction only when a proper social context exists.

For the individual, the conjunction provides "necessary inventions" (for example, the hoe in the Agricultural Conjunction) and "systematic inventions" (for example, the assembly line in the Industrial Conjunction) that exist in a distinct techno-sphere (the social integration of technology). From a small techno-sphere, the conjunction starts with a limited number of participants and matures into a general phenomenon. The new technology is only one part of the overall change in a social context. Critical inventions too are important components and it is important to remember "technology, by itself, is not the driving force of history."[69]

Toffler describes today's Electronic Conjunction, its components, and how the components relate to each other. He is generally optimistic and believes, for example, that the Electronic Conjunction will breach the gap between producer and consumer. Toffler is confident that this conjunction will inaugurate new types of socioeconomic systems, creating new economic realities and opportunities.

Toffler recognizes that the conjunction may also lead to social change and tension. Social tension arises partly from resistance to change because of stakes in prior conjunctions.[70] Violent conflict often emanates from the collision of interests between conjunctions. For example, conflict arose in many countries in the collision between the Agricultural and Industrial Conjunctions. This tension is evident in events such as the U.S. Civil War, the Meiji Restoration, and the Russian Revolution, among others.

Besides conflict, conjunctions can produce substantial environmental impacts. "Nothing more clearly illustrates the clash of ideas than our changing view of nature."[71] Prior attitudes focused on "taming" nature. While achieving enormous progress, the Industrial Conjunction also resulted in "rampant, perhaps irreversible damage done to the earth's fragile biosphere."[72] Toffler suggests tomorrow's technologies should be "subjected to tighter ecological constraints than those of the Second Wave era."[73]

In Toffler's view, the Electronic Conjunction will push forward the pace of human change. As these incremental changes evolve into broad changes in lifestyles, there may be a global "culture" shock, as people must quickly readjust to new social inventions.

> We may define future shock as the distress, both physical and psychological, that arises from an overload of the human organism's physical adaptive systems and decision-making process. Put more simply, future shock is the human response to over-stimulus.[74]

The eminent historian Fernand Braudel discusses historic conjunctions and, similar to Toffler, focuses on the changes in individual lives. His interest is in the growth of merchant capitalism and the development of a world trading system, which formed between the fifteenth and eighteenth centuries.

The lives of average people, Braudel believes, is the best representation of the impact of the conjunction. For Braudel, the technology itself only contributes to a change in an individual's overall social context.[75]

Philosopher Geoffrey Barraclough looks at conjunctions in sociological, economic, and technological terms, believing these are the key elements in the overall social context. He focuses on the intellectual underpinnings of a conjunction, which he credits with creating the "contemporary era." The onset of this period occurred during the latter part of the Industrial Revolution (late nineteenth century), distinguished by mechanical power.[76] Barraclough differentiates between the industrial revolution of the eighteenth century and the scientific breakthroughs of the nineteenth century. "The age of coal and steel was succeeded, after 1870, by the age of steel and electricity, of oil and chemicals."[77] Similar to Toffler and Braudel, his unit of analysis is the individual.

> There is a good deal of evidence . . . the cumulative effect of which is to suggest that the years immediately before and after 1890 were an important turning-point; but we shall do well to be aware of precise dates. Contemporary history begins when the problems which are actual in the world today first take shape; it begins with the changes that enable, or rather which compel us to say that we have moved into a new era—the sort of changes . . . which historians emphasize when they draw a dividing line between the 'Middle Ages' and modern history at the turn of the fifteenth and sixteenth centuries.[78]

CONJUNCTION HISTORY

The three conjunction viewpoints show a surprising degree of similarity in two respects. First, there is agreement across the disciplines on the existence of conjunctions and their periods. Admittedly, there are differing viewpoints on the conjunction's social causes and impacts. Often the interpreter's academic discipline directs the analyses and conclusions. Second, most agree that academic research into conjunctions, and the reality that this research exposes, covers many areas. The anthropologist also sees the impact of economics in the conjunction and the economist the impact of culture. Understanding these unique periods requires a general approach to historic conjunctions across disciplines.

Table 1.2 shows the conjunctions relevant to this discussion and their general time of onset. The timeline begins with the Tool Conjunction, followed by the Agricultural and Industrial Conjunctions. Some parts of the world are now undergoing the Electronic Conjunction. These general con-

TABLE 1.2 **The Historic Conjunctions**

Conjunction	Rough Year of Onset
Tool	40,000 B.C.
Agricultural	5000 B.C.
Industrial	A.D. 1750
Electronic	A.D. 1975

junctions accommodate the common views regarding major epochs according to social, economic, and anthropological historians. Conjunctions, of course, can be decomposed into inter-periods and have mini-conjunctions within them. "Much of history can be fruitfully considered as sequences of 'mini-globalization,' in the sense that, for example historic empire formation involved the unification of previously sequestered territories and social entities."[79]

The spread of the conjunction throughout the human community occurs at differing times and places. What is surprising is the lack of uniformity in its spread. Rather, if one were to plot the adoption of new technologies over time and space, it would look more like the spread of disease. Such diffusion is along certain limited pathways (in this case, roads and transportation networks) and thus, to use the human anatomy as an exemplar, occurs in arteries (networks) rather than organs (nations). What is different about the Electronic Conjunction from earlier periods is the difference in the rate of its spread to civil society and to business.

> It is something that practically no one foresaw or, indeed, even talked about ten or fifteen years ago: ecommerce—that is, the explosive emergence of the Internet as a major, perhaps eventually the major, worldwide distribution channel for goods, for services, and, surprisingly, for managerial and professional jobs. This is profoundly changing economies, markets, and industry structures; products and services and their flow; consumer segmentation, consumer values, and consumer behavior; jobs and labor markets. The impact may be even greater on societies and politics and, above all, on the way we see the world and ourselves in it.[80]

It is important to note that conjunctions do not always result in progress. There are two reasons why the environment often suffers during and after a conjunction. First, tremendous improvements in technology and changes in subsistence patterns characterize such periods. These improvements often have adverse environmental impacts because they usually increase resource extraction efficiency. Second, trade in technology tends to globalize impacts. Technological changes internationalize the trade network, which creates global demands and in turn harms the environment. Culture and environment have a dynamic relationship. Harm to the environment therefore must cause some harm to cultures and their underlying values.

The most important reference point for the current conjunction is the first one—the leap in human technology that began about forty thousand years ago. The forces propelling the Tool Conjunction significantly changed the lives of many peoples, including those living in relatively isolated areas. The next chapter describes the first three conjunction periods via the use of case studies, starting with the Tool Conjunction.

THE CONVERGENCE OF TRADE, ENVIRONMENT, AND CULTURE IN A CONJUNCTION

THIS CHAPTER SYNTHESIZES the role of trade, environment, and culture through selected case studies in the Tool, Agricultural, and Industrial Conjunctions. The purpose in a focus on these three periods is to later compare them to the Electronic Conjunction. In this comparison, there is a somewhat greater devotion to describing the Tool Conjunction and the early part of the Agricultural Conjunction rather than on the later Industrial Conjunction. One reason for doing so is that there are compelling contrasts revealed when comparing two eras separated by long periods. It is natural for researchers to compare today's Electronic Conjunction with its Industrial predecessor, but there is no reason to believe that these two periods are similar simply because they are in historical sequence. It may well be that today's Electronic Conjunction is more comparable to the Tool Conjunction for two reasons.

First, many scholars believe that these two periods are *revolutionary* in the development and application of new tools. The Agricultural and Industrial Conjunctions were in many ways *evolutionary* progressions in systematic tool use. The Tool and Electronic Conjunctions, however, exemplify the introduction of innovative tools that produce drastic changes in the social context.

Second, the role of the environment in the Tool and Electronic Conjunctions was and will be critical to human survival. Hunter-gatherers depended on the environment for survival in the Tool Conjunction and people will continue to depend on it in the Electronic Conjunction. People need resources for survival and the acquiring of those resources today is a profound issue.

Excess resource exploitation has long been a problem. In the Agricultural and Industrial Conjunctions, the approach to the environment was as something to be "conquered" to abet human development. Thus, taking resources was a goal almost unto itself. In the Tool Conjunction, however, the approach to the environment was more of compatibility between humans and the world in which they lived. One approach to the Electronic Conjunction would be to return to a search for compatibility with the environment, for both moral and survival reasons.

The case studies show the gradual disconnecting of the elements in the social context over each successive conjunction. Beginning with the Tool Conjunction, the cases show how interdependent and interrelated these three factors were in the social context. As the Agricultural and Industrial Conjunctions cases reveal, there has been a tendency to disconnect trade, environment, and culture over time in the interests of economic efficiency and a stable subsistence strategy. This disconnect had become common and widespread by the time of the Electronic Conjunction.

One problem is that globalizations are not universal and that differing pockets of lifestyles exist in differing parts of the world. At the same time that there is now an Electronic Conjunction underway, there are also people on the planet who live in Tool, Agricultural, and Industrial Conjunctions. The problem is thus not only one of place but also of time. Moreover, many of the cases resonate through several periods of time and up until today. Some remain, at their core, unresolved issues over thousands of years.

In the discussion that follows, there is no intention to suggest that new tools in a conjunction directly fuel the changes in trade, environment, and culture or the relationship between them. Rather, the tool sets in motion a series of events that may influence these entities in a variety of ways. In fact, with each successive conjunction, the tool and conjunction link has become more indirect as the application of new tools to existing interaction systems and their role in a society's subsistence strategy becomes ubiquitous. The scraper, during the Tool Conjunction, was of greater relevance to the environment (used for processing the meat of an animal) than the computer in the Electronic Conjunction (used for processing information). What follows are several case studies that trace technological developments in the Tool, Agricultural, and Industrial Conjunctions and the roles of trade, environment, and culture.

THE TOOL CONJUNCTION

The trajectory of human technological and cultural development evolved slowly over several million years. This development abruptly accelerated in the Tool Conjunction.

> In short, from the artifacts alone, we could conclude that human behavior changed qualitatively roughly 50,000 to 40,000 years ago and it was only afterwards that people possessed the fully modern human ability to innovate in response to changing environments or social conditions.[1]

Many researchers look at this period and see "an apparent quantum advance that occurred sometime between 60,000 and 40,000 years ago."[2] The major change was the relation between humans and the environment. The new tool-using human had the capacity to reap environmental resources in greater volumes than ever before. This was the first conjunction—in the sense of mutual interactivity between trade, environment, and culture—and the first time that scholars recognize the fully modern human in both a cultural and a biological sense.[3]

During the Tool Conjunction there was limited but important trade between peoples. Given the difficulty of travel in early times, the role of trade was marginal to people's subsistence and survival needs. Trade in bulk commercial items was still thousands of years in the future. Trade in capital goods, often in the form of new technologies, was important in the Tool Conjunction; products ranged from bow and arrow to boat technologies (including the tools to make them). Trade in agricultural products was rare, save for specialty fragrances and like products.[4] The actual trade process, however, may have been as important as the traded items. "Contact of peoples is thus an extraordinary promoter of cultural development."[5] It was this contact that led to the introduction of new social ideas and changes in social structure. In prehistoric societies "these exchanges do, however, play an important role in the evolution of techniques and institutions."[6]

The paradox of the Tool Conjunction, and later conjunctions as well, is that the new technologies, which provided short-term leaps in survival ability, often led to long-term consequences that made societies and their environments worse off. Technological advances resulted in elevated resource extraction levels that become unsustainable. Even as hunters developed better weapons in the Tool Conjunction, they often caused a species' eventual extinction. No doubt, there were ecological repercussions to an animal's removal from its habitat that produced a variety of system-wide changes and feedbacks.

The process of technological advancement illustrates how a particular need will ultimately result in a particular tool, thus imposing an evolving subsistence strategy. Thus, the tool emerges as an "optimeter" in the social context, a device that is the most efficient technology for taking resources in a given environment. Walter Truett Anderson argues that the tool is a device that propels the human being to the status of an "augmented animal." This idea of augmenting the natural physical and mental abilities of humans with tools echoes in the writings of Marshall McLuhan, Richard Dawkins, and Merlin Donald. Donald's "thesis is that the human species pulled itself upward through a series of inventions."[7] As important as were physical tools, the concepts and representations in these new tools were also critical keys to evolution.

The problem is that there were no limits to the new tool use. The Tool Conjunction created more efficient hunting weapons, led to vast changes in human lifestyles, and resulted in numerous animal extinctions.[8] Historian J. Lawrence Angel argues that the Tool Conjunction led to a series of species extinctions.

> At the very end of the Upper Paleolithic period, the grassland game herds of bison, horse, cattle, mammoth, and reindeer . . . [effloresced], then suddenly began to decline under the combined pressures of human overkill and rapid environmental fluctuations ending with the spread of Boreal forests at the Pleistocene-Recent transition from about 12,000 to 7500 B.C.[9]

The following five parts describe trade, environment, and culture in the Tool Conjunction. The discussion focuses on the role of new technologies in five parts: the social context, the overkill hypothesis, ivory and culture, how mammoth hunters became buffalo hunters, and perspectives on the period.

THE SOCIAL CONTEXT

Humans made the first tools from stones. Stone tools evolved over the course of many millennia, but about fifty thousand years ago there was a sudden acceleration in their form and use.[10] "Stones, the first tools of agriculture, originally used for grinding gathered seeds of ocher for body painting, became important implements for grinding harvested grains, also flint sickles were used for harvesting."[11] Stone technology, because of its enduring construction and its tendency to survive over time, is a fundamental basis from which to reconstruct human history. "Despite the unusual nature of its system of reference, prehistory is nevertheless primarily a history of technology."[12] The use of stone technology was the basis for the Tool Conjunction.

The evolution of stone tools, and the techniques for creating them, occurred over five stages in the Upper Pleistocene period of human development. The first stage, carried out by *Homo erectus* peoples beginning about 500,000 years ago, was the development of crude "choppers" with tapered points, used to cut tree branches for fire and butcher animal parts for food and clothing.

The second stage was the refinement of stone tools in which the entire surface of the tool was flaked and tapered with a true cutting edge. The third stage, occurring perhaps 100,000 to forty thousand years ago, expanded this form and structure to a wide variety of cutting implements with very specific economic applications. This stage introduced the species known as *Homo sapiens*.

Stage three was "a major step in the history of the human race, a step as important as the invention of agriculture or artificial propulsion, for it served as the foundation for the conditions of technological development until the appearance of metallurgy."[13] This historic period coincides with the Tool Conjunction.

The fourth stage of the Upper Pleistocene was the full blossoming and institutionalization of the Tool Conjunction. From a technological standpoint, it added to the basic cutting implement a further set of innovations by creating "a basis for genuine implements . . . The blade was then carefully fashioned into scrapers, gravers, drills and thin knives." Materials other than stone, especially bone, were later used to fashion tools. Some types of tool forms increased dramatically during this time, followed by the application of new materials. The use of stone gravers and scrapers made possible the refining of bone products. The use of bone peaked around the Magdelanian period, from 12,000 to 8000 B.C.

> The fourth stage, on the contrary, is marked by the sudden explosion of bone implements. Beginning with the Chatelperronian period, we find many pierced teeth, bone pendants, javelins made from mammoth tusks, reindeer antler, or bone, and later harpoons with fine barbs and slender needles with eyes.[14]

The role of trade was small but critical to the evolution and spread of the Tool Conjunction. Outside of some limited technology and craft exchange "trade, even if fairly regular, would be confined to luxuries."[15] Technologies showed clear and consistent refinement over time despite incredible distances between them.

> During the ages when direct contacts were indispensable, the rapidity of progress continued to be linked with the frequency of these contacts . . . Aside from the difficulty of creating the first tools from nothing, the dispersion of the human race suffices to explain the slowness of these early stages. The miracle is that they were accomplished.[16]

The fifth stage of the Upper Pleistocene period (sometimes referred to as the "Neolithic" era) was short and worldwide and introduced new technologies to the production mix. The stage also added new polishing techniques and the development of bigger tools such as axes and adzes. Not only had the tool been introduced, variations on it began to sprout up. As a result, the tool became a key part of the subsistence strategy in society.

While this period was becoming entrenched, the seeds for the next period were being laid. Early metallurgical development began during this period as well. "The significance of this evolution emerges in the relationship . . . between the manufacturing process and the technical efficiency of the implement obtained."[17] This growth in efficiency equaled growing output, but also led to the creation of smaller and more delicate tools. "Descending from the beginning stages down to the Neolithic period, the average size of the implement diminishes."[18]

Trade played a minor yet critical role at this stage as well. Through trade, "tool technology also continued to change. Conservation of raw materials was carried to a new extreme by the development of cutting edges made from tiny blade flakes known as microliths."[19] The new technology spurred the development of flaking and grinding techniques, which in turn provided the means for perfecting fishhooks and spears, fish nets, bark boats, and other new tools. Entire tool kits, "containing microliths, barbed harpoons, bone needles and fish hooks" were available to hunters.[20]

The Tool Conjunction is historically a part of the latter Upper Pleistocene period of human development. This period can be broken down into more discrete parts than the five noted here. Improvements in tool making no doubt occurred in very tiny increments. "Tiny technical advances, hardly more than 'tricks,' have a huge impact on biological success, as can be seen in any group of animals. The particular trick of humans is not to forget but to *accumulate*, over time, all the tricks of other people and of previous generations."[21] The tools were representative markers of progress as instruments for dramatic cultural and social changes. These changes propelled the Tool Conjunction. Culture changed when there were dramatic shifts in human subsistence strategies that these new tool technologies launched.

> The close relationship between the cultural "take off" and the emergence of archaic *Homo sapiens* lends additional support to the view that the distinctive characteristic of our species must be sought in our unique capacity for adapting to nature by means of cultural rather than biological innovations.[22]

As part of this historic shift in culture and technology, tools played a critical role in several ways. A first step was an increase in dietary efficiency. Before this time, humans were largely vegetarians and meat consumption was heavily dependent on scavenging. Eating meat is more efficient than eating plants, at least from the predator's point of view. "The Upper Paleolithic is characterized by a sudden increase in blade tools and by a great fluorescence of ivory, bone, and antler implements," the advent of which led to meat as a regular part of human diets.[23]

Out of this increase in the efficiency of the economic system, a social surplus emerged and spurred the Tool Conjunction. During this time, humans invented a social context that gave rise to new technologies and true human cultures. Around forty thousand years ago, evidence of greater technological refinement appeared in abundant cultural artifacts that are still found today in carvings and rock paints.[24] Clothing no longer was simply the wearing of the skins of dead animals to provide warmth. Clothing became much more efficient vehicles of warmth but were also much more expressive in a cultural sense. Personal adornments suddenly appeared in this period and soon became widespread among ancient peoples. At the personal level, this was a change of massive cultural proportions.

The cultural changes that came from the Tool Conjunction appeared first in symbols as a form of expressing identity. "Among the oldest types of art is personal decoration; ornaments such as beads, bracelets, pendants and necklaces."[25] This ornament-based identity was both intra- and extrapersonal. Richard Klein adds that this unique historical period also assimilated cultures over great distances, thus attributing an importance to the role of trade.

> Perhaps most important, the artifact assemblages that antedate 40,000 years ago commonly exhibit far less variability through time and space than later ones, whose remarkable spatial and temporal heterogeneity has allowed archaeologists to recognize numerous distinctive artifact 'cultures,' even within relatively small regions of short time spans.[26]

Culture, trade, and environment came together in this period through the invention of portable art. At several sites throughout Europe and Asia,

FIGURE 2.1 **Milestones in the Tool Conjunction**

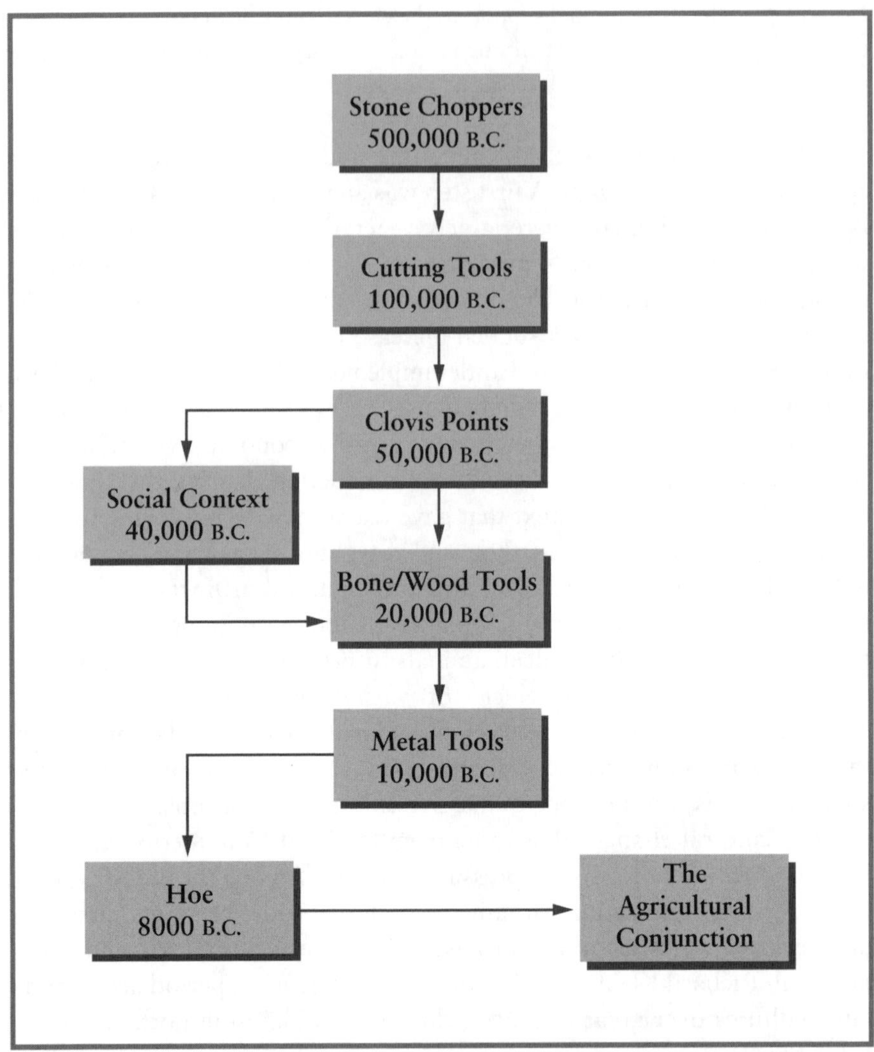

there have been archaeological finds of goddesses carved from woolly mammoth ivory (although the animals were killed primarily for their meat and not for ivory).[27] Such goddesses or "Venus" statues dating back thirty thousand years "may have possessed some ritual significance associated to women's fertility."[28]

In short, from the artifacts alone, we could conclude that human behavior changed qualitatively roughly 50,000 to 40,000 years ago and it was only afterwards that people possessed the fully modern human ability to innovate in response to the changing environment or social conditions.[29]

This distinction between modern and pre-historic humans is critical in explaining the human relationship to the environment. Before this time, changes in the environment led humans to change their behavior. After this time, changes in human behavior caused changes in the environment. Figure 2.1 shows the lineage of the tool conjunction and its major milestones.

THE OVERKILL HYPOTHESIS

The Tool Conjunction created a lifestyle largely based on killing. This killing focused on the culling of large mammals for food, clothing, and other human survival or subsistence needs. "By the time we had turned ourselves into culturally modern people, about thirty thousand years ago, we had already become the most proficient predators ever seen."[30] This proficiency eventually led to widespread changes. The "overkill hypothesis" posits that the mass extinction of megafauna in the Pleistocene era was largely due to human over-hunting brought on by the invention of these new tools. The development of better hunting tools during this time created a subsistence strategy highly dependent on killing, often focused on a single species.

One technology of substantial advancement was the development of the spear: the result of attaching a large carved stone (essentially a big arrowhead called the Clovis point) to a long, straight tree branch. Thrown by the human, it allowed the predation of larger mammals and thus expanded the scope of available food sources. Despite the importance of this technology, there were multiple variations on it in an effort to target animals other than mammoths. All of these variations contributed to the progress in the Tool Conjunction. In the overkill hypothesis, spear technology, specifically designed for killing, was the chief instrument in the demise of many large mammals.

For too long, archaeologists interested in this period focused myopically, if understandably, on one type of technology referred to as *Clovis*, whose archetypal artifact is an impressive spear point from three to six inches long and supremely adapted to wounding or delivering the coup de grace to large animals . . . For some years now the evidence has mounted for very different Paleoindian technologies and adaptive strategies in North America (indeed throughout the New World) . . . Undeniably, some Paleoindians many have been deliberate or opportunistic hunters of megafauna that became extinct, but others were probably hunters of caribou, deer, beaver and smaller animals."[31]

The mammoth culture is not the only example of a single species focus in a society's subsistence strategy. No doubt, many cultures showed similar singularity in their subsistence strategy, the only real difference being their available food sources. For example, "Here was a mammoth culture comparable with the 'moa culture' of New Zealand—and, as in New Zealand, the apparent profligacy implies carnage."[32]

Subsistence was not the only reason for killing some animals. In some cases, hunters would kill certain animals for cultural reasons. Paleolithic hunters also killed some large mammals for prestige. "There would be kudos indeed in killing a creature that was not only huge and powerful but also hard to find."[33]

For all of these reasons and more, about eleven thousand years ago there was a substantial but slow warming of the climate which coincided with human predation of large mammals. In Eurasia, the woolly mammoth, woolly rhinoceros, and the giant (Irish) elk became extinct around this time. North American fauna were particularly devastated and eight large mammal species became extinct. These extinctions paralleled the introduction and spread of Paleoindians to the Americas from Asia.[34] By 7000 B.C., thirty-two genera of New World animals became extinct, including the horse, giant bison, oxen, elephant, camel, antelope, pig, ground sloth, and giant rodent.[35]

Scholars debate the causes of megafauna extinction in North America and elsewhere. Some scholars argue "climatic and environmental change was very important to the extinctions."[36] Species extinction and the entrance of humans, in fact, coincided at many times and in many places. In Australia, the archaeological and fossil record suggests some striking parallels with North America. The colonization of Australia, and subsequent extinctions, may have occurred as early as forty-five thousand years ago.[37] Mass extinctions followed the arrival of humans on islands such as the Galapagos, Hawaii, New Zealand, and Tasmania.

The first human arrivals in North America were woolly mammoth hunters, whose annual hunts were very important events in their lives.[38] Archaeological finds indicate a fixation on the mammoth in painting and in sculpture. The finds indicate rituals that consistently reference the mammoth because the people depended on it not only for food, but also for clothing, ivory, and even tent shelters made from mammoth hides and bones. Burning the animal's dung provided warmth inside the tent. Here was a subsistence strategy that was highly specific and carried a high cultural content.

> Hunting and pastoral peoples depended on animals for far more than food. Skins became clothing and shelter, bones became tools, fat became fuel and medicine. And the relationships have always been deeply psychological as well as utilitarian: in rituals and myths, with totems and symbols, primitive peoples drew on the strength of animals, sought their protection, sometimes made them gods.[39]

The mammoth hunters were successful in their craft due to efficient weaponry and a highly effective killing organization. The hunt not only met survival needs but also was part of a symbolic ritual and an initiation rite. The effective use of the mammoth in human lifestyles was ineffective for the mammoth. By 20,000 B.C., the woolly mammoth was largely extinct in North America. Although the warming climatic conditions were partly responsible for the mammoth's extinction, some conclude that human hunting hastened its demise by thousands of years.[40] Marvin Harris believes that humans were part of these extinctions.

> By 10,000 B.P. much of the so-called *Pleistocene megafauna* had become extinct in Europe. Upper Paleolithic hunters contributed to this ecological catastrophe, just as New World hunters probably played a role in the extinction of Pleistocene megafauna in the New World.[41]

With the loss of species such as the mammoth, tool technology again evolved to meet a new environmental subsistence reality. A new strategy focused on other environmental resources. "Thus Mesolithic people turned increasingly to a broad spectrum of plant foods and fish, mollusks, and other riverine and maritime sources of food."[42] Not only did new tools cause new diets and new extinctions, they changed art as well. After all, the pictures on cave walls could no longer show pictures of many large, wild animals.

Species extinctions also relate to the dynamics of the habitat. Key species can play a significant role in the health of habitats. Mammoths were grass eaters and it is possible that their foraging habits held back northward forest advancement after the end of the Ice Age by eating small trees and knocking down big ones. They alone, however, could not have halted the inevitable northward progression of forests in North America.

Perhaps the best source of information is the mammoth itself. The mammoth tusk is an indicator of the environmental changes. Abundant woolly mammoth tusk finds remain even today. The tusk shows stages of the woolly mammoth life, much as rings of a tree describe its life. Some scholars contend that mammoth and mastodon archaeological finds around the Great Lakes region of North America suggest the presence of intense human hunting pressure rather than evidence of climate change. Analysis of the tusk rings show that the animals ate properly and show no signs of a great climatic shift in their diets. The tusks also show normal gestation periods of four years for the mammoth, similar to elephants of today.[43] So there is little tusk evidence of climate stress that some claim led to mammoth extinctions. The evidence does not provide definitive proof for either side of the debate on the Overkill Hypothesis.

> The scientific community has failed to reach a consensus about the causal linkage at the Pleistocene-Holocene boundary of a major, climatic change, a dramatic number of faunal extinctions, and the expansion of humans into Northern Eurasia and, hence, the New World.[44]

Some scholars contend that the megafauna extinctions are the result of the extraordinary temperature changes that occurred over a rather short period at the end of the last Ice Age. Evidence from Arctic ice-core samples suggests that the mean temperatures many have changed by as much as 10 degrees Fahrenheit over the course of about a decade. This sort of climate change would far exceed the current rates of overall climate changes from anthropogenic sources.

> The climatic changes at the end of the Pleistocene alone must have been sufficient to overwhelm certain animals and plants unable to adapt under altered conditions. Desiccation by itself must of imperiled some animals or forced them to come to the remaining sources of water. Either animals moved to where conditions remained favorable, or they were left susceptible to a Paleoindian coup de grâce, or they were weakened to the point of eventual disappearance without helping human hands.[45]

Scholars often interpret changes in animal and fauna populations as extinctions, according to R. Dale Guthrie. To the contrary, he argues, changes in species' populations are natural consequences of climate change, but they do not constitute extinctions. Further,

> the community simplification at the Pleistocene-Holocene boundary was mainly due to regional isolation resulting from range retractions. Some threads were lost in extinctions, but many colors changed when the loom was rethreaded in a newer and simpler Holocene (later Pleistocene) pattern.[46]

Guthrie describes this transition period as one that transformed a "complexly patterned plaid to a much smaller set of stripes."[47]

Extinction without replacement is central to the overkill hypothesis. This assumption applies to a "disappearance of sloths, camelids, equids and proboscidean, which are clear extinctions without replacement."[48] However, the theory assumes a static rather than dynamic state of nature. Some species, or sub-species, may become extinct in one place but survive in another.

Paul Shepard overtly rejects the overkill hypothesis as a misinterpretation of the moral beliefs of distant human ancestors.

> The most strident of these theories [about primitive peoples and the environment] projects overkill onto the aboriginal inhabitants of the world by claiming that, being basically avid, they were responsible for the extinction of many large animals at the end of the Pleistocene . . . Studies of hunting-gathering peoples show that to hunt big mammals exclusively is bad strategy: generalized subsistence is more efficient and reliable; and indiscriminate hunting is inefficient and goes against long-term survival.[49]

Shepard also questions the timing of the overkill theory, arguing that the megafauna in North America were in decline for climatic reasons long before the arrival of Paleoindians from Asia. "Most of the documented extinctions brought about by primitive humans are associated with islands or with agriculture."[50] In addition to a lack of evidence for the theory, Shepard believes overkilling makes no sense in a subsistence strategy. "Overkilling was regarded with repugnance because it led to competition and territoriality between tribes and for these reasons was virtually unknown among hunter-gatherers."[51]

Shepard believes the problems of today actually are the fruits of seeds planted during the Agricultural Conjunction. The transition from this natural life in the Tool Conjunction to the domesticated lifestyle in the Agricultural Conjunction established the patterns of lifestyle today and began the process of widespread environmental changes.

> Domestication changed means of production, altered social relationships, and increased environmental destruction. From ecosystems at dynamic equilibrium ten thousand years ago the farmers created subsystems with pests and weeds by the time of the first walled towns five thousand years ago . . . Domestication would create a catastrophic biology of nutritional deficiencies, alternating feast and famine, health and epidemic, peace and social conflict, all set in millennial rhythms of slowing collapsing ecosystems.[52]

Shepard sees historical footprints that lead to today's lifestyles and traces their beginnings back thousands of years. He argues that the orientation towards human patterns of life and the material items they demand are driven by a life time plan which implicitly includes a desire for increase and technological progress. Shepard believes the lifestyle is part of the human genome.

I propose that our ontogenetic (a life time plan) agenda has been carried in our genome from Pleistocene times when our species made its debut. Furthermore, we have inherited from our primal ancestors an orientation to the world, a way of perceiving our place in the scheme of things.[53]

For Shepard, the genome, which led to this biological strategy, was certainly much more than a mere matter of chemistry.

The human part of our genome came into existence along with social patterns and skills. And these were followed, over hundreds of thousands of years, by different human cultures, each unique and yet appropriate to the human niche. In a broad sense there is a Pleistocene way of life that encompassed the many human primal cultures, all of which were consistent in certain ways and are shared even today among recent hunter/gatherers.[54]

Shepard describes the Tool Conjunction as a fundamental change in the relations of the human to the natural world. Adoption of new technology did indeed contribute to the disconnect in the social context.

The transformation of the ecosystem of hunter/gatherers to the controlled monocultures of agrarian communities was accompanied not only by a change in cosmic view, but by social and political Zeitgeist as well. As agriculture became more complex, the importance of kin connections was subverted by politics, spiritual connections to the landscape were disrupted, and ecological relations to the land and animals were forgotten.[55]

This book adopts the idea that historical footprints exist by examining specific case studies. As a starting point, the focus is on ancient problems and how they are relevant to today's lifestyles and behavior patterns. This book takes the viewpoint that many of today's problems emanate from seeds planted long ago. Thus, just as there is "biological DNA" handed down from generation to generation, so too is there "cultural DNA."

IVORY, TOOLS, TRADE, AND CULTURE

Archaeologists have found considerable stockpiles of worked and raw mammoth ivory, which provide insight into the ivory manufacture process in ancient times. To make the ivory more workable and malleable for carving, the first step was to soften the (Siberian) mammoth tusk. Carving began with stone and later with metal tools. These ancient technologies created products that were extremely durable and the finds are evidence of their lasting quality. "Ancient carvers of ivory may not have realized how durable their works would be. Some surviving examples have endured for thousands of years, outlasting most of the ancient works of art that used such materials as paper, cloth, or wood."[56]

The first traded product in modern history was probably worked ivory.[57] Ivory is a modified dentine or tooth, often manufactured from animal horn and tusk. This first-traded ivory, however, came from mammoths and mastodon, at first in Eurasia and later in North America. No doubt, trade in elephant ivory was underway around this time in Africa and East Asia.[58]

Ivory had little to do with the demise of the woolly mammoth because the mammoth supplied so many human demands essential for survival. The killing of these enormous animals for their ivory, at considerable risk to the hunters, seems unlikely. Ivory may have been a by-product of hunting, but more likely it was scavenged from dead animals.[59]

Ivory was not only the first traded product but also perhaps the first portable human cultural art form. "Prehistoric sculptors also recognized the beauty of ivory and fashioned it into highly original and sophisticated carvings, which are among the first of their kind created by human hand."[60] (Of course, there were also earlier cultural expressions through cave paintings, but this art was not portable.)

There was extensive use of ivory by the Gravettian culture in 22,000–18,000 B.C. Archaeological finds reveal artifacts such as clothing and ivory included in graves, presumably part of burial customs. Ivory beads usually accompanied buried children. At one find spread out over several sites, there were "about 3,500 beads of mammoth ivory each."[61] The number of beads implies an underlying system of mass production. There is also some indication that humans carved musical instruments out of mammoth bones. The simple, representational art of Gravettian culture left behind many carved ivory figures of mammoths.[62]

The Magdalenian culture (15,000–8000 B.C.) also produced sophisticated animal art, both in depicting animals and in using them to create products. The art includes mammoth paintings and carved ivory objects, such as a carved ivory horse found in the Pyrenees. Finds of similar carved horses were unearthed in Siberia, in the Anara valley near Lake Baikal, six thousand miles away from Spain. Archaeologists found ivory "Venus" statues in southwestern France, Ukraine, and Siberia.[63] Through trade, the breadth of the mammoth culture may well have exceeded the mammoth's geographic range at that time.

Mammoths may have become the singular focus of many people's subsistence strategies. In North America, the "Clovis Cultural Context has been associated with mammoths" (12,000 to 10,000 B.P.).[64] This focus has been interpreted variably to include strict reliance (hunting), casual utilization (scavenging), and conceivable intermediate stages of evolution (mixed utilization).[65] Clovis period excavations at the White River Badlands in South Dakota [in the United States] date back about eleven thousand years. The finds show significant evidence of mammoth bone and animal butchering.[66] Clovis peoples in modern South Dakota rapidly buried "disarticulated, butchered remains of the adult and juvenile elephants," no doubt to prevent attracting predators or scavengers.[67] Stone, specifically quartzite, tools may have been used to cut the hide. Humans used stone tools to butcher mammoths in the Clovis period and then developed new tools from the mammoth bones. These new tools included "blades, end scrapers, shaft straighteners, cylindrical point and ivory points, flaked bones, unifacial flake tools, mammoth-ivory semifabricates, and the use of red ocher."[68]

Why focus on mammoths in early human culture? Mammoths were not the only major food source for these peoples. Reindeer, for example, were also a major food source but they were not as conspicuous in human art. Outside of the workability of ivory, perhaps it was the great size of the animal that attracted humans or perhaps recognition of their spirit and intelligence. The disappearance of megafauna such as the mammoth, however, led to a decrease in some types of bone working. Tools based on bone did not disappear, but changed. Moose-antler horn replaced mammoth bone and became the basis for constructing hoe blades. The end of the mammoth and the Tool Conjunction laid the seeds for the future. The hoe was the key tool invention in the Agricultural Conjunction.[69]

HOW MAMMOTH HUNTERS BECAME BUFFALO HUNTERS

The focus of tool technologies, cultural artifacts, and subsistence strategies with respect to mammoths changed when the mammoths became sparse and later extinct. Over time, these Clovis cultures evolved into the modern Native Americans. "The Plains Indians are indicated to be descendants of the Clovis people."[70] This descent was not only genetic but a social and cultural footprint. After the mammoth's extinction, the buffalo replaced its central role in the human subsistence strategy and social context.

The Agate Basin Site [in South Dakota] strongly suspects repeated use during the winter as an area favorable for arroyo bison trapping and camping alongside the frozen carcasses during Folsom, Agate Basin and Hell Gap times. It would have been a subsistence strategy not unlike that at the Colby site, where the bison replace mammoths.[71]

As the subsistence strategy changed with the disappearance of the mammoth, the increasing reliance on the buffalo had the inevitable effect of changing the cultural customs and rituals to suit these economic changes. "Ritual was often important for the success of the planned hunt, and marked the entire effort from beginning to end. The Mandan [a Native American Plains tribe] and others danced to call the bison near."[72]

With the decline of the mammoth, North American peoples focused on new subsistence sources. Over time, the buffalo replaced the mammoth by becoming the Native American Plains Indians' chief source of food, clothing, and other materials. Besides using the meat, hides, and bones, the Plains Indians carved buffalo horn for significant ceremonial purposes (horn was also employed as a waterproof container). The woolly mammoth and the buffalo appeared to serve similar roles in evolving environments and cultures. "The Clovis mammoth interdiction example suggests that many of the same challenges of, for example, geography, season and herbivore behaviors, were encountered by both (ancestral) mammoth and (descendent) bison hunters."[73]

Another species that became extinct during the Upper Pleistocene was the horse. Humans more than likely played a role in its demise. The horse actually originated in North America millions of years ago and from there spread throughout the world. The horses' extinction in North America may have been in part due to demands of early Native Americans for food and clothing.

"Horses died out in the Americas some 8,000 to 10,000 years ago, and returned again only when Columbus carried several to Hispaniola in 1493."[74] When Native Americans again encountered horses, the beast's appearance frightened and disoriented them. Their fear of the horse, an animal known to their ancestors, contributed to Spain's quick conquering of the Aztec and Inca Empires.

The lack of horses had a significant impact on North American lifestyles, compared to evolution in similar environments such as Central Asia. Without horses to hunt buffalo, North American tribes lived near the forest fringes because there were few resources and shelters available in the middle of the Plains. On foot, Native Americans traveled long distances to reach buffalo hunting sites. One method for hunting was to camouflage themselves with buffalo hides, sneak up on the buffalo, and then attack with spears and arrows.

Another method of killing buffalo used an ecological weapon. "Buffaloes driven over grassy bluffs seventy feet high, as many were, would be stunned if not killed in the fall, and likely to break their legs or backs."[75] The hunters started large prairie fires that meant to orchestrate a stampede of buffalo in a certain direction that happened to include a cliff or a man-made pit with upturned spikes on the floor. "Hunters rounded up their prey by setting fires, drove them over cliffs, and dispatched them with an arsenal of stone and bone projectile points, spears, darts, long knives and bows and arrows."[76] This practice was especially hard on the environment for two reasons. First, the practice killed large numbers of buffalo. Second, the prairie fires usually burned out of control until rain came.

The domestication of the horse in Eurasia provided a critical step in both political and technological development. Originating in the steppes of Asia, the horse with a stirrup provided a considerable economic and military advantage. Some scholars believe that the horse was the key to the Mongols' ability to create the largest empire in human history in the thirteenth century. Much of the later military domination of the New World by the Old World

> can be attributed to the differential natural endowments of the Middle Eastern and nuclear American regions. The extinction of potential animal domesticates among the Pleistocene megafauna rendered the American Indians vulnerable to military conquest by European adventurers mounted on horseback.[77]

Then in the mid-seventeenth century, Spanish settlers brought the horse back to the Americas. Some horses escaped from townships, and Native Americans bought and bartered for them. The horse drastically changed the lifestyles of Native American tribes that lived on the plains when it again became widely dispersed in North America. The Apaches were among the first tribes to adopt the horse, which then traded it to other tribes. The horse brought at least three advantages to the Native Americans. First, they provided a significant military advantage. Second, unprecedented mobility allowed for more efficient buffalo hunting techniques. Buffalo became available to the Native American throughout the year because they could migrate with the herds. Third, the horse enabled the people to spread out across the plains, even during winter, because they could carry more equipment and move faster.

The environment was still favorable to the horse. The horse was reintroduced into North America (and introduced into South America) and the animals thrived in captivity and in the wild because they were valuable "bio-machines" and an intelligent source of energy.

In 1800, Indians on the Northern Plains had to find forage for thousands of horses when they moved from one camp to another, and through time herds of wild horses increased in size throughout the Plains . . . Each million horses—Flores estimated as many as 2.5 million on the southern Plains alone—meant a million fewer bison that could be supported.[78]

Each of the thirty tribes from the Great Plains, such as the Sioux, Cheyenne, and Comanche, came from different geographic areas and had different backgrounds, languages, and customs. Once they adapted to life on the Plains with the horse, their cultures became more homogenous.[79]

The horses added considerably to the real incomes of the North American Plains Native Americans. The horse became the basis for several new technologies in transportation and hunting.

The impact of the horse on Indians' lives can be measured in terms of increases: in possessions, because four times more could be transported, because horses others owned became intensely desired, in economic and social stratification, because horses were private property and unequally possessed; and in the emphasis on like values like individualism.[80]

PERSPECTIVES ON THE TOOL CONJUNCTION

Trade, environment, and culture underwent critical changes during the Tool Conjunction. The inherent relationship between the three factors ushered in new patterns of human behavior and provided some of the key building blocks for modern human society. The culture and environment interaction dominated the system at this time, with trade occurring as a marginal afterthought, despite its critical importance to the spread and intensification of the conjunction. Most of the trade impact was, however, indirect through ideas and institutions and therefore of more importance to the process of society rather than its products. (This distinction between a trade product and a trade process is a critical issue for today, as discussed later in Chapter 4.)

The level of trade dependence in the culture's subsistence strategy was low in the Tool Conjunction. Trade was mostly a conduit for a limited amount of cultural artifacts, ones that helped introduce the idea of religion, or new tools that allowed for more efficient environmental resource extraction. What was more important than the tool itself was the idea behind the product, because it allowed the importer the chance to copy the icon or the tool.

The degree of dependence on trade in a subsistence strategy is important to understanding its strength during a conjunction or any period for that matter. Ivory trade forty thousand years ago had little to do with a society's subsistence strategy. Ironically, the early twentieth century may have marked the period with the highest reliance on the mammoth, since mammoth ivory was one of the key sources of foreign exchange earnings for the Russian government up until World War I. Nonetheless, the inexorable historical pattern shows an increase in the role of trade in subsistence strategies over time that changes the relations with and between environment and culture. This is not a linear relationship but probably more of an exponential pattern.

Despite steady progress in the Tool Conjunction, there was also a decline of some species—the result of unintended consequences related to overhunting. As the cruder tools were the first to develop, the first environmental resources were those that were the easiest to extract. This social context existed until the resource was nearly fully exploited, which then forced the development of new tool technologies to extract other resources that were more difficult to obtain.

The chain of events is conceivably a virtuous or a vicious cycle, depending on one's perspective. As a virtuous cycle, the continuing improvements in tool technology created long-term food surpluses despite some short-term deficits. Forcing a people to change created a positive pressure for the advancement of civilization. The vicious cycle perspective cites a path of progress built on extinctions and over-use of resources that will eventually reach a dead end.

The lifestyles that evolved during this period stamped future generations and created the basis for today's society and the modern relationship between trade, culture, and environment. Socialization also led to cultural conditioning on a scale never before seen. Lewis Mumford believes that "the instruments of mechanization five thousand years ago were already detached from other human functions and purposes . . . Mass culture and mass control made their first appearance."[81]

The mass approach to subsistence strategies even during this time showed the propensity and power of macro systems to overwhelm and eventually replace many smaller, less integrated micro-systems. With more trade, there are more general welfare gains but also more losses specific to certain peoples and places. Now magnify this trend many times and the implications of today become clear. The total victory for the macro-systems may well be at hand due to the small set of changes set in motion thousands of years ago.

What is striking about the cases in the Tool Conjunction is the integration of trade, culture, and environment in the products of the time. The trade in ivory carvings inevitably related in some way to a culture or an idealized view of some part of the world. At the same time, the carvings came from real animals and held a meaning far more tangible than the often-used inorganic plastic molding that is common today. The figures were an organic edifice that had come from a living creature well known to people and carved by human hands. It was easy to identify with the cultural and environmental implications of the product. The Tool Conjunction created patterned transactions between people that spread ideas in a new way. The role of trade was critical in many respects to the events in this period, but not yet a part of a culture's subsistence strategy. The transition from a direct to an indirect relationship between the environment and the subsistence strategy intensifies in the Agricultural Conjunction.

THE AGRICULTURAL CONJUNCTION

Building on the Tool Conjunction, the Agricultural Conjunction created new trade, environment, and culture interactions as well as new patterns of behavior. Did a sudden agreeable social context and a convenient invention suddenly occur or did changing environmental conditions force people to change? Why did the peoples of the Tool Revolution switch from the life of a roaming hunter-gatherer to that of a sedentary agriculturalist? Some suggest that what pushed them were the environmental changes that severely reduced the amount of large mammals and thus meat available to them, especially after the end of the last ice age of eight thousand years ago. "Such shifts from hunter-gatherer life to agriculture were leaps in human cultural evolution that would set in motion an ongoing series of further changes."[82]

The great melt off that followed the Ice Age may well have provided the impetus for changing human lifestyles. The great speed of the warming led to floods and stories that echo in many ancient texts. In the Epic of Gilgamesh, Utnapishtim, like Noah, warned of and survived a tremendous flood. Historical records on such floods are mixed. Archeological digs at the ancient city of Ur (in modern Iraq) show a layer of sand and silt that settled about 5000 B.C. by the flooding of the Tigris-Euphrates.[83] A newer theory is that the flood occurred in the Black Sea and led to the breaking of a natural land bridge in the Bosporus Straits.

The warming trend that ended the Ice Age did not stop there but proceeded, turning the temperate climates of the Middle East into dry ones. With the end of the ice age, climate changes had different impacts on different parts of the world. "The retreat of the glaciers and the intensification of big-game hunting did not have precisely the same consequences in Europe and the Middle East, but both regions probably suffered similar environmental problems which raised the costs of obtaining animal proteins."[84] In the Middle East, as in other areas, some of the first human settlements arose during the Agricultural Conjunction. With these settlements came language and the peoples of the Tigris-Euphrates area produced some of the earliest known writings in human history. These settlements also demanded resources that a hunting-gathering lifestyle could not provide.

The Natufian, an ancient people of the Middle East, may well have discovered or invented agriculture about ten thousand years ago. "They had well-built houses and a sophisticated social structure, and tools such as flint sickles and stone mortars and pestles that they used to harvest and process grains." The technological breakthrough was in learning to plant the grains and cultivate them, in addition to the gathering of wild grains. "The innovation was the result of a 'convergence of accidents.' Four elements had to be present at the same time: genetic resources, technology, social organization and need." The need was a declining wild food base due to the drying climate in the Jordan Valley and the Fertile Crescent in general.[85]

Trade evolved from small-scale interactions in specialty goods to large-scale interactions that included bulk items. Jane Jacobs makes the case for a regular trade system functioning in the Middle East ten thousand years ago. Through this trading system newly invented farming techniques spread throughout the eastern Mediterranean.[86] Greater tool efficiencies led to improvements in the human diet, which in turn increased stress on the environment.

The Agricultural Conjunction introduced the domestication of plants and animals and inaugurated massive land use changes. Over time, land use changes resulting from domestication have transformed large parts of the earth's land area. The portion of the world's land area now devoted to human purposes (mostly agricultural) stands at about 25 percent. Land use changes are perhaps the most pervasive form of environmental change because they transform entire habitats.

As the Agricultural Conjunction accelerated, new environmental impacts ensued that focused on habitats rather than the species targeted in the Tool

Conjunction. Humans accelerated this trend. With the cutting down of many trees, the limited rainfall trickled off the land. With the introduction of large numbers of ovines (goats and sheep), the fragile vegetation became overgrazed. Without the vegetation and trees, the soil retained less water and this in turn led to further vegetation loss. Over time, fertile areas became deserts. Many species were unable to survive in this new and less fertile environment.

The Agricultural Conjunction completed the revolution of the hunter-gatherer lifestyle. The Tool Conjunction focused on the hunter. This period focused on the gatherer and the introduction of agricultural systems. This section has five parts that trace culture, environment, and trade in the Agricultural Conjunction: the social context, amber trade, the Epic of Gilgamesh, the Cedars of Lebanon, and finally perspectives on the Agricultural Conjunction cases.

THE SOCIAL CONTEXT

Pinpointing the precise onset of domestication and the beginnings of the Agricultural Conjunction is very difficult. The actual process of domestication was no doubt a slow evolution over a long period. John Yellen suggests that agricultural domestication began perhaps thirty thousand years ago in tropical forests of Africa, by the planting of favored fruit trees.[87]

> Between about twelve thousand and eight thousand years ago this transformation in human culture took place in the eastern Mediterranean and Near East. We begin with small, semimobile groups living in what we would now call "wilderness" upon which their impact was small. Then, here and there, little patches of wheat grasses, intensified monitoring of some wild goats or sheep, and hangdog shadows of scavenging wolves whose offspring were sometimes captured and tamed, all made little pockets of the first agriculture.[88]

The Agricultural Conjunction probably occurred in two phases. First, there was a period of plant domestication and then a period of animal domestication. The cumulative impact on the human subsistence strategy and the environment was that there was "domesticated barley, wheat, goats, sheep, and pigs, dating from 11,000 to 9,000 B.P." which slowly "became larger parts of diets, especially [the] grains."[89] The original purpose in growing grains was for human consumption, but with animal domestication, humans began growing grains for these captured animals.

Domestication may have actually reduced the enormous pressure on wild animals. Because of the success of the Tool Conjunction, some large mammals

TABLE 2.1 **The Timing of Domestications in the Agricultural Conjunction (earliest date)**

Plants	Year	Animals	Year
Trees	30,000 B.C.	Sheep	9000 B.C.
Grasses	9000 B.C.	Dogs	8400 B.C.
Barley	9000 B.C.	Goats	7000 B.C.
Wheat	9000 B.C.	Pigs	6000 B.C.
Legumes	9000 B.C.	Cows	6000 B.C.
		Bees	3000 B.C.
		Chicken	2000 B.C.
		Cats	1000 B.C.

Source: Data from Marvin Harris, *Culture, People, Nature: An Introduction to General Anthropology* (New York: Harper and Row, 1980), pp. 147–48.

at this time were nearly extinct. The domestication of certain animals perhaps was an effort that consciously prevented the extinction of those wild animals.[90] Some animals were favored and domesticated precisely because they were rare. Other scholars attribute animal domestication to the development of sedentary lifestyles. Humans settled and no longer migrated with herds, so the role of these animals in human subsistence changed. Their domestication, or imprisonment, may have been simply to prevent their migration.

Domestication of sheep occurred around 9000 B.C., followed by dogs in 8400 B.C. and shortly thereafter goats, pigs, cattle, and in Peru, guinea pigs (all about 6000–7000 B.C.). The domestication of the silk moth took place in 3500 B.C. in China and of the honeybee in Egypt in 3000 B.C. The chicken and the goose were not domesticated until about 2000 B.C. and cats not until about 1600 B.C. in Egypt (see Table 2.1).[91]

Urbanization brought on by the Agricultural Conjunction increased the scope and type of environmental problems. According to Paul Shepard, it was in this time that the disconnect between the person and the environment first began. The building of artificial city environments further removed, both socially and geographically, these people from their natural environment, especially when compared to hunter-gatherers.

Bernard Campbell describes how, as urban centers develop, trade and manufacturing activity increases.[92] Urban centers needed "immense quantities of food, raw materials, minerals, timber . . . peat, coal, cattle . . . and manufactured products from other places."[93] Urban centers also produced an entirely different mode of trade. Trade in bulk commodities began, especially trade that used domesticated animals for the source of energy. Perhaps trade came about not because of surplus production but, rather, shifting subsistence strategies.

> Trade among agriculturists probably was not induced by the development of surplus but rather by the narrow range of subsistence activity, the development of storage facilities, and the settled mode of life, which not only limited the farmer's access to distant resources but also must have encouraged the establishment of fixed trade networks.[94]

Urbanization almost immediately had adverse consequences on ecosystems. Massive erosion occurred in the old city of Teotihuacan in Mexico, and chemicalization became rampant in Mesopotamia, Tigris-Euphrates, and Sumerian and Akkadian (Babylonian) cities. "One of the main factors for the collapse of the system was the excessive accumulation of sodium chloride [salt] which was brought into the system in dilute solution in river water and was left behind as the soils evaporated."[95]

This process of conjunction starts from a set of simple tools because inventions drive conjunctions. Hunting tools shaped the Tool Conjunction. One tool, however, is only the beginning of a process of conjunction and the Tool Conjunction evolved out of a series of tools that built on and complemented one another. This incremental process was also evident in the Agricultural Revolution, where a chain of related inventions culminated in dramatic progress and the invention of the hoe.

The hoe, and variations on it, allowed people to alter their habitat. Its fundamental design derives from an earlier invention, the spear. The spear combines a piece of wood (for leverage in throwing) with a deadly weapon (the arrowhead). The agriculturalist transformed the stone spear by pointing the enlarged arrowhead not out but down, thus symbolically attacking the ground, not the prey. The hoe provided a means to till soil, plant crops, and weed out competitor plants. With the hoe, humans were now plant domesticators and not just plant gatherers. Variations on the hoe came later, such as the plow (or plough), which is essentially a huge hoe. At first, humans pulled plows. Later, domesticated animals (ox, horse, or donkey) pulled them. Teamed with animals, "the plough was the first application of non-human power to agriculture."[96]

The plow provided a huge impetus to developing systems of cultivation.

The use of animal power to pull the plough was a natural extension of the technology, but required the invention of some kind of yoke or harness. The widespread use of the plow began in Northern Europe. The yoke strap or collar, which evolved into a harness, is an invention dating back to Roman finds from the third century A.D. Turks and Slavs developed the basic yoke idea and passed it to the Germans during the "great Slavic Diaspora of the sixth century."[97] The yoke was an invention across several cultures and environments.

The plow had an enormous impact on the development of social systems. The plow transformed the structure of Northern European society from a loose collection of farms into a manor-based system of organized production and administration. The hard, compacted soil required the use of a deep-tilling tool for which an even bigger plow was required. In turn, teams of animals, usually large horses, were required to pull the plow. South of the Alps, "the climate encouraged the older method of scratch-plowing [and] the social structure was quite different, and more individualistic."[98] The soil, the tools to till the soil, and the social structure all were part of the type of subsistence strategy that ensued. Was this simply evolution or was it a new system of political economy? Heinrich Brunner characterized the feudal manor system as a military structure designed to support cavalry. This horse-based system of mechanization rests on the invention of the stirrup.

The stirrup is itself a by-product of the yoke-harness invention. People had long ridden horses (and many other animals) during combat, but not with much effectiveness. "Before the introduction of the stirrup, the seat of the rider was precarious."[99] Those fighting from horseback, whether against man or beast, did not have a stable basis to throw a spear or shoot an arrow. "The stirrup . . . effectively welded horse and rider into a single fighting unit capable of violence without precedent."[100]

The foot-stirrup allowed for other useful socioeconomic applications such as transportation and hunting game. The stirrup arrived in Europe via technology transferred through trade. The foot-stirrup was probably a Chinese invention that passed to the Turks and other peoples. Chinese representation of stirrups appeared in the fifth century A.D. Others contend that the rudimentary idea of a stirrup appeared in India in the second century A.D.

The harness-stirrup was itself part of a larger invention, the saddle. Barbarians brought the saddle to Europe about the first century A.D. Innovations in this techno-sphere extended beyond the saddle to the animals themselves. The breeding of heavier horses occurred, albeit much later, not only to pull the huge plows but also to carry the warriors clad in the metal armor favored by European military leaders.

There was another important invention besides the harness, stirrup, and saddle: the horseshoe. The nailed horseshoe prevented a variety of hoof maladies that struck horses with and without mounts. The nail, upon which empires stood, was the key invention. "There is no present firm evidence of the nailed horseshoe before the end of the ninth century."[101] Others put the date for the nailed horseshoe's introduction in the fourth and fifth centuries A.D.[102] or perhaps earlier.[103]

Paul Shepard argues that the Agricultural Conjunction completed the subjugation of environmental and human rights by the development of warrior kingdoms. Usually, these kingdoms had exhausted much of their own environmental resources and used war to make up for that deficit. The warrior was originally the herder of domestic ungulates: the person who tended the horses and oxen learned how to ride them in battle. Thus, a fusion of Tool and Agricultural ideals followed; the desire for the hunt combined with the efficiency of modern social systems. The warrior restored the hunting ethos by changing the focus from animals to humans. These warrior societies, often built on conquest and slavery, were essentially farming farmers. "The hero, the warrior, and the cowboy are almost inextricable. For the most part of history they are all connected to horses or boats, although the Indo-European tool looks especially to the horse."[104]

The pragmatic invention of the hoe in the Agricultural Conjunction was a great juxtaposition to the innovative nature of the chipper stone in the Tool Conjunction. In the Tool Conjunction, inventions largely focused on better methods of killing animals and the development of stone, bone and metal industries to process the kill. In the Agricultural Conjunction, the tool focus was much more on plant sources than animal sources in human diets. The meat intake of humans actually fell dramatically during this period. Thus, humans turned their literal swords (spears, etc.) into ploughshares! Figure 2.2 shows the milestones and lineage of the Agricultural Conjunction.

AMBER TRADE

Ivory was perhaps the first traded product in history and was in demand for a variety of religious and spiritual reasons. These same reasons were also the cause for the amber trade.[105] Amber may have been the second traded product in human history and the first product traded in bulk: it was a "raw material which played an important part in the economy of the

FIGURE 2.2 **Milestones in the Agricultural Conjunction**

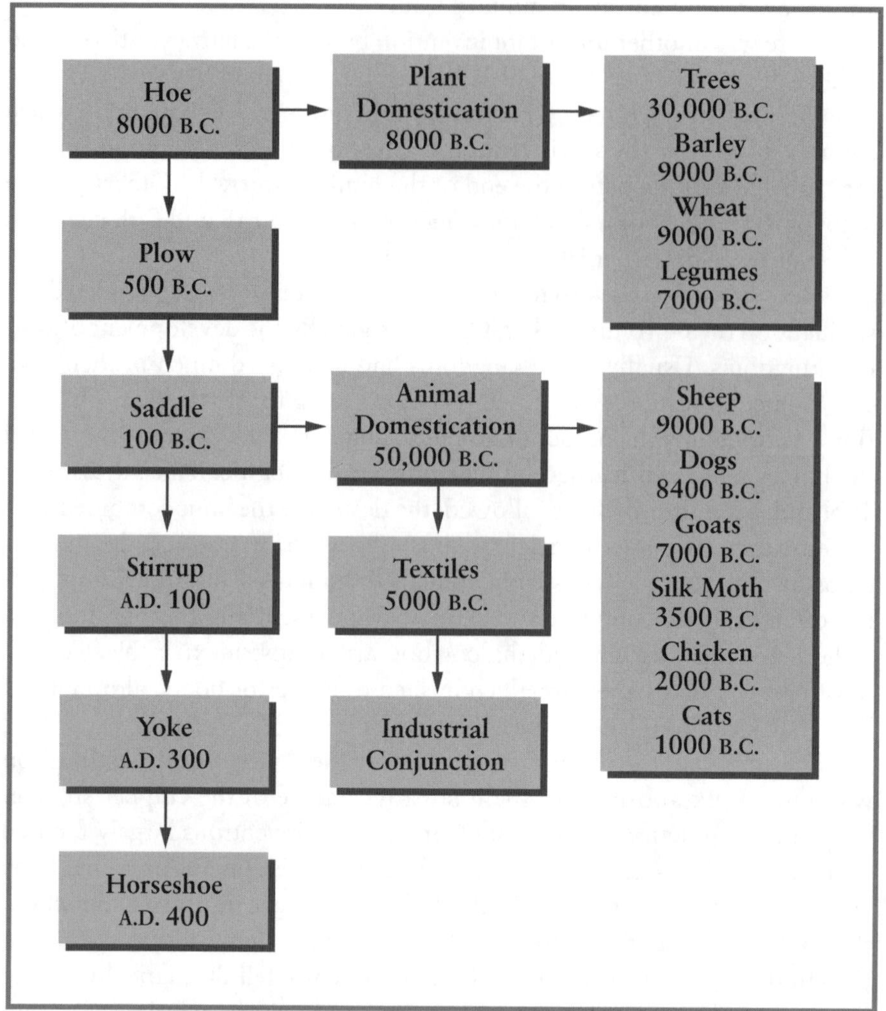

early Neolithic communities" and W. A. Buffum believes that "the development of civilization was stimulated and furthered by the trade in amber."[106] Similar to mammoth ivory products, it is possible to find amber products in areas containing no natural amber. Jensen believes that amber and flint were two of the earliest traded products.[107] Although amber trade probably began much later than ivory trade, it was in greater quantities with more geographic diversification.

> One of the most powerful stimuli of commercial relations between northern and southern Europe was the desire of the southern populations to secure amber, a material confined to the Baltic region and occurring particularly about the Jutland and the mouth of the Vistula. Amber beads have been found in Swiss pile-dwellings but also in Mycenean graves of the second millennium B.C.[108]

Amber has a long history. About forty to fifty million years ago, temperate fir forests covered what is now Northern Europe and produced considerable amounts of amber. Amber results from normal secretions from fir trees that harden with exposure to wind and water, trapping and encasing both plants and animals. Over time, many types of geologic formations overlay the secretions, which fossilize, to make amber.

The largest concentration of amber is in former East Prussia, now the border area between Germany and Poland. Large quantities are found in Russian Kaliningrad, Latvia, Lithuania, and Estonia. In 1934, this area produced 88 percent of the world's amber but the ratio has declined over time. Other significant deposits exist in Southeast Asia and the Caribbean. The Jutland region of Denmark is the second largest amber reserve, although its remaining stocks have seriously declined over time. Peoples from these areas, especially from Jutland, have exported amber for at least five thousand years. The most sought after, and thus valued piece, was red amber, although the belief was that white amber had a better odor.

> Already during the Stone Age amber was manufactured into ornaments which had a sacred significance. It was not until the Bronze Age that amber, in its natural form, became a commodity that was used for large-scale trade with the West and South. The culture of the Bronze Age in the Baltic regions was due entirely to the amber trade, for this product of nature—unsuitable for any direct practical usage—became the determining factor in the development of civilization along the Baltic shores.[109]

The great expansion of the amber trade was in part due to Phoenician navigators, who discovered a sea route to the Baltic. Much later, land routes were developed and tied to the expansion of the Roman Empire.

> With its subsequent development this commerce created a noteworthy precedent in the history of the world's discovery, by showing us how love for one single product of a foreign land can incite relations and discoveries among peoples and further the exploration of far away lands.[110]

The amber case shows how each conjunction increases the ability of people to acquire products in greater quantities over longer distances and how specialized cultures induce trade.

A limited amount of amber trade began even earlier in the Late Stone Age, reaching at least as far south as Crete. After a period of slow growth during the Iron Age, amber trade reached its peak under the Roman Empire. Roman emperor Nero loved adorning arenas such as the Coliseum with amber decorations for gladiator combat. Evidence of Roman metal (bronze, copper, and gold), and thus trade, began appearing in the Baltic region during this time, often found in coins and other personal items.

Amber had two other uses. Roman women carried balls of amber that emitted an "agreeable" odor when warmed in the hands.[111] Pliny the Elder, a Roman historian, in the *Natural History of Pliny*, Volume XI, noted that women were the primary consumers of amber. A second use of amber was for medicinal purposes. Hippocrates and Pliny describe its ability to cure a variety of ailments, ranging from a toothache to lung disease. For Homer, amber was a thing of beauty, but especially a talisman to protect small children. Amber was also effective in counteracting magic, particularly valuable against the "evil eye."

Pliny accurately described amber as the hardened resin of pinesap. However, wild myths were conjured to explain amber's origin. Demostratus called amber "lyncurion" and thought it was dried urine from a beast called a lynx (not the North American feline). Sophocles believed that amber came from beyond India, the result of tears shed by a bird called meleagrides, in tribute to the hero Meleagar.

The Roman Empire built a long-range trading system, but the products that merchants carried the farthest were specialty items. "Amber, ivory, incense, pepper and silk were the mainsprings of long-range trade" for Rome.[112] Thus, amber and other precious stones served an important role in Europe's development. In promoting development, amber was to Europe what jade was to China and Mexico.

Of course the story of amber did not stop with the end of significant Roman demand for the product. New demands arose. The Teutonic Knights controlled amber trade in the Middle Ages with a strict rigor: the penalty for illegal amber harvesting was hanging.[113] Eventually, amber trade came under the control of guilds and the 1477 Danzig guild still controls considerable amber trade today.[114]

In the Baltic, the easily accessible amber was gone by the mid-1800s, but the still powerful demand forced the beginning of dredging operations. By 1854, dredging activities had reached thirty-five feet below sea level in East Prussia and significantly increased amber outputs. Amber mines at Palmnicken produced 4,400 pounds of amber in 1862 and by 1895 the mine was producing one million pounds of output per year.[115] The huge increase in amber production also meant commensurate increases in environmental damage.

> In addition to the damage done to the environment by mining itself, the processing of amber also harms the local ecology. The Baltic Sea, which has been deteriorating at an alarming rate for the last 50 years due to rapid industrialization, endures most of the harm. In the last century, strip mining by the Yantarny [amber] plant alone, has discharged more than 100 million tons of waste into the Baltic. The mining and processing of amber produces matter which the Baltic's brackish water cannot dissolve. Sewage produced by the plant is discharged onto the recently built dam, over which it flows into the sea.[116]

The Baltic Sea Joint Comprehensive Environmental Action Program (BSJCEAP), approved in Helsinki in 1992, intends to restore the sea's ecological balance. One aspect of the treaty relates to point and non-point pollution into the sea and how this pollution impairs coastal lagoons and wetlands. As amber miners exhaust reserves in sea areas, they create ecological problems. The impact of amber mining on the environment is similar to that of gold mining, especially as it upsets natural eco-systems with the dredging and digging processes. The treaty therefore has some regulatory requirements over amber mining emissions or disturbances to the sea. Is this regulation similar to or different from the amber trade of several millennia ago? No doubt, some loose system of rules and regulations existed even then.

The footprint of amber trade has evolved along a path of production for a consumer market that is increasingly disruptive to the environment. Amber trade patterns that sprouted five thousand years ago have grown slowly into a worldwide web of distribution.

Today, most amber is not used for craft or ornament but is of such poor quality that 90 percent of the product is used for other purposes such as varnish, amber oil, and distilled acids. Jewelry and ornaments make up the remaining 10 percent.

THE BABYLONIAN EPIC OF GILGAMESH

Trees may have been the first domesticated plant and as a result, they have long been important to people's subsistence strategy. Some trees have been especially critical to that strategy and one is the cedar. The cedar is a key environmental resource whose value is noted early in human history, as far back as the *Babylonian Epic of Gilgamesh*, which pre-dates even the Bible. Written about 2600 B.C., the earliest stories in the Gilgamesh Epic occurred not long after the advent of the Agricultural Conjunction and the invention of writing (about 3000 B.C.). Many historical writings, including those of Theophrastus, Homer, Pliny, and Plato as well as the Old Testament of the Bible, document the (once) rich and luxuriant cedar forests of Lebanon. Equally well documented is the widespread cedar trade. The Epic of Gilgamesh, written on a series of tablets found in modern day Iraq, is a story of the conflict between humans and the environment, the opening of trade, and the incorporation of these events into culture via mythology.

Gilgamesh is a "modern" man by the standards of 2600 B.C. and the King of Uruk, a city-state that existed along the Tigris-Euphrates River in the Middle East. He is a super-human (two-thirds god and one-third human), the result of gods mating with mortals, and there is no person in Uruk who can match his strength and power. He is a cruel king who steals from and subjugates his people. Gilgamesh commands, for example, that every bride have sex with him before doing so with her own husband on her wedding night. The people of Uruk cry out to the gods for relief from the harsh rule of Gilgamesh. The god Anu answers their plea by creating Gilgamesh's *doppelganger*, Enkidu. Anu hopes Enkidu can match both wits and strength with Gilgamesh and therefore occupy and engage him and lessen the suffering of the people of Uruk.

Enkidu is a forest creature, but a human, living like and with animals (Tarzan may be a comparable image) with the strength of twelve men. The son of a trapper discovers him because Enkidu has been letting his animals loose from the traps. The trapper's father brings a priestess/prostitute called Shamhat from Uruk to lure Enkidu out of the forest and domesticate him. She seduces Enkidu and gradually civilizes him during six days and seven nights of lovemaking. After this period of human socialization, his animal friends will have nothing to do with him. They symbolically expel him from Eden!

Shamhat brings Enkidu to Uruk. As they enter the city, they find Gilgamesh on his way to interrupt another bride and bridegroom. Enkidu confronts him and stands in the doorway of the house, blocking Gilgamesh's path and literally standing in the way of the abuses of Gilgamesh. The two enter into a terrible battle that goes back and forth. Gilgamesh eventually gets the upper hand, but no man had even dared to fight Gilgamesh because of his god-like abilities. Because their abilities match, Gilgamesh and Enkidu become great friends.

The two comrades agree to challenge a formidable foe to test their friendship. They travel to the great cedar forest to the west (modern day Lebanon and Syria) to kill the protector of the cedar forest—Humbaba in Akkadian texts and Huwawa in Sumerian, Hittite, and Assyrian texts—and take the mighty cedars. This is, of course, a symbolic event.

> The defeat of the guardian of the forest may cast in mythic form an historical event, the capturing of valuable woodlands or the establishing of trade involving wood—a precious commodity almost totally lacking in the plain that constitutes Sumer (southern Iraq).[117]

Civilization's struggle with nature (epitomized in Humbaba the forest monster) portrays a battle of good against evil (light and darkness). Humbaba lacks the civility of humans: he lives in the wild in a giant cedar house and has never been seduced. Humbaba's death, the two think, would not only impress the gods (despite the fact that the god Enil appointed Humbaba as forest guardian, something which would later haunt the two friends), but also open the way for Gilgamesh to take the precious cedars and open trade routes. Upon reaching the forest, Gilgamesh and Enkidu eventually lure Humbaba to a confrontation with an act of environmental destruction.

> Gilgamesh took the axe in his hand
> [and] felled the cedar,
> [When Huwawa] heard the noise
> he became angry. "Who has come
> and slighted the trees grown on my mountain
> and has felled the cedar?"[118]

After felling seven cedars, and a not-so-epic battle with Humbaba, the god Shamash intervenes on the side of Gilgamesh and Enkidu. Humbaba sues for peace, offering all the trees in the forest and to become the servant of Gilgamesh. However, Enkidu argues that Humbaba will not keep his word (he can never be civilized) and an unfinished battle cannot lead to peace. Convinced, Gilgamesh strikes Humbaba with his axe and Enkidu follows suit and eventually beheads the beast. With Humbaba dead, the taming of nature is complete and the cedar forest and its riches are for the taking. Humbaba cries out as he dies: "Of you two, may Enkidu not live the longer, may Enkidu not find any peace in this world."

The two then commence cutting down the cedars, especially the tallest trees, and float down the Euphrates River on cedar rafts, returning to Uruk triumphant. The people use the cedar to build a huge wooden gate to the city. Gilgamesh is a hero and the gate is his monument.

This is only the beginning of the struggle of economy, environment, and culture for the city of Uruk and Gilgamesh. The goddess Ishtar, hearing of his exploits as the conqueror of Humbaba, offers to become the lover of Gilgamesh. Gilgamesh rejects her entreaty, in part because all of her previous lovers eventually turned up dead. However, he makes a mistake by insulting her. She then has her father, who happens to be the god Anu, let loose the Bull of Heaven on the city of Uruk. Gilgamesh and Enkidu battle the giant bull and eventually slay it.

The gods are not pleased with these events and the loss of the Bull of Heaven. He was a formidable beast whose breaths caused holes in the land that swallowed up hundreds of people. Slaying the bull is again symbolic. Human societies could withstand nature's most violent impulses (earthquakes, floods and the like) and were in the process of replacing natural law with a moral and legal code. As in the story of the Tower of Babel, the tension between technological advancement and religious beliefs is evident early in history.

The god Enil, specifically remembering Enkidu's rejection of Humbaba's pleas for mercy, calls for revenge. Enil subsequently turns the gods against Gilgamesh and Enkidu. Because of his role in the death of Humbaba, the gods decide to subject Enkidu to a slow demise ("the paralysis-demon"). Tortured by the events, Gilgamesh bitterly cries upon Enkidu's death.

Afterwards, Gilgamesh roams the earth like a homeless man, meets an immortal that had survived a great flood (Utnapishtim), receives the gift of immortality and then loses it to a snake. He finally winds up where he started: at the cedar gates of Uruk. Thus, through his story the reader sees the transition from the primitive to the civilized and from there the process of civilization in human terms.

THE CEDARS OF LEBANON: DEFORESTATION AND DEVELOPMENT

Other ancient monarchs, such as the Egyptian kings Thut-Mose III and Ramses III, as well as Babylonian King Nebuchadnezzar, also describe the taking of cedar as part of conquest. Nebuchadnezzar described his efforts as follows.

> I cut through steep mountains, I split rocks, opened passages and [thus] constructed a straight road for the [transport of the] cedars. I made the Arahtu [the trees] float and carry to Marduk, my lord, mighty cedars, high and strong, of precious beauty and of excellent dark quality, the abundant yield of Lebanon, as [if they be] reed stalks carried by the river.[119]

Contemporary writers of that time recognized Nebuchadnezzar's exploits as a pillager of wood and destroyer of forests. In the Old Testament of the Bible, the book of Isaiah is quite clear on the subject of Nebuchadnezzar's role in causing deforestation, noting on his death in 562 B.C. that:

> The whole world has rest and is at peace,
> it breaks into cries of joy,
> The pines themselves and the cedars of Lebanon exult over you,
> Since you have been laid low, they say,
> no man comes to fell us.[120]

From 2600 B.C. to A.D. 138, various cultures populated the Middle East including the Canaanites, Aegeans, Armenians, and Phoenicians. During this time, these peoples gradually finished the destruction of the famed Cedars of Lebanon that Gilgamesh earlier had begun. Perhaps most conspicuous in this role were the Phoenicians. In pursuit of their thallasocracy (maritime empire), the Phoenicians built enormous sea-faring fleets for exploration, conquest, and trade. For nearly three millennia, cedar and other timbers from Lebanon served a variety of needs: fuel, ship material, building material, and household usage. Through cities such as Sidon and Tyre, wood exports went to Palestine and Egypt, areas with large populations and relatively little forest cover. The result was large-scale deforestation. The scarcity of trees was so noticeable that, over time, the few remaining tall trees became objects of worship. Cedar was also the most prized wood because of geography.[121]

> Owing to the diminution of rainfall from north to south, from west to east, and from highland to lowland, these were exactly the directions in which the chief lumber traffic moved [along the Mediterranean in ancient times]. Exceptions occurred mainly where choice woods from a limited area of production gradually acquired wide use as in the case of . . . the unsurpassed Cedars of Lebanon.[122]

The cedar is part of ancient Egyptian mythology. According to Egyptian legend, a man named Amasis happened upon the god Osiris's barge at Thebes on the Nile and, noting its manufacture from weak acacia wood (the best Egypt could offer), ordered it rebuilt with Phoenician cedar.[123] Osiris was impressed and vast quantities of cedar and pine timber were made into rafts, which in turn were towed by boats from Byblos (now known as Jubayl in modern Lebanon) to Egypt in 2800 B.C.[124]

Demand from outside Phoenicia merely added to the pace of cedar deforestation. By 3000 B.C., Babylonia, along with Egypt, imported cedars and required it as a tribute of conquest. Egyptian and Mesopotamian records of military campaigns include information on "captured" timber brought back with slaves and gold. "Cedar was thought to be the prize which all states of the Near East coveted, and for which the empires of Egypt and Mesopotamia were prepared to fight."[125]

King Solomon of Israel signed a contract for the delivery of cedar logs from the Lebanon Mountains (as well as for some pine) for the construction of the First Temple, destroyed by the Babylonians about 500 B.C.[126] This transaction is noted in the Bible (II Chronicles 2:3): "as you dealt with David my father and sent him cedar to build himself a house to dwell in, so deal with me." Solomon also sent forced laborers to Phoenicia to help cut and transport the cedar.[127] Meiggs surmises that Solomon's effort to obtain cedar for the Temple was a show of extravagance for internal political reasons.

To build the temple, the Phoenicians exported their labor and engineering technology services related to wood exports. Phoenician contract labor built most of the Temple.[128] Phoenicia was also involved in the Temple restoration in 520 B.C. (Ezra 3:7) and in many joint ventures with Solomon.[129] Merchants shipped Lebanese cedar to Greece to build the Temple of Diana and to Egypt to create the famed temples of Seti I at Thebes and Osiris. Burial coffins used cedar and body mummification used resins from cedar, fir, and pine.

Ship builders revered Lebanese cedar for its strength, size, beauty, and workability. For Pliny, cedar was the standard by which to measure all other timbers and Diodorus documented its relative strength and beauty.[130] Around the time of Plato, deforestation was widespread in Greece and Athens began importing extensive amounts of Phoenician timber. Athenian timber imports thus contributed to the expansion of their city-state's naval capacity. Both combatants in a war used wood from the cedars. Phoenician timber was central to the construction of the Persian fleet that battled the Greeks during the fifth century B.C. Some suggest the motive for the Phoenician invasion of Cyprus (eleventh century B.C.) was to preserve forest resources at home. However, shipbuilding was the primary, but not the sole use of cedar.

> The demand for all products of resinous woods was relatively greater in antiquity than now. They were employed for the preservation of ship wood and all ship equipments, for coating the interior of earthenware wine jars, and for the preparation of volatile oils, salves and ointments, which were almost universally used in ancient times. Resin and tar were the chief basis for cough medicines prepared by Greek physicians, and were ingredients for salves for external use.[131]

Fuel was another use for the cedar. Theophrastus, the Greek historian, noted that cedar can burn at a sufficiently high temperature to make mortar or pitch from mined limestone. Temple builders used cedar to make lime. In Sidon and Tyre, the burning of cedar made possible bronze manufacturing. Sidon was renowned for its glass crafts, which required great quantities of wood fuel.

With the eventual loss of the cedars, the soils that lay underneath the trees washed away and there was a drop in biological richness. This led to the decline of many other native plants and animals in the ecosystem. Domestic sheep and goats that grazed in these areas destroyed ground level plants, new seedlings, and saplings. Eventually, the loss of the cedars changed the topography of Lebanon, resulting in its current semi-arid climate.

PERSPECTIVES ON THE AGRICULTURAL CONJUNCTION

The Agricultural Conjunction illustrates two new manifestations of the trade, culture, and environment relationship. First, because of trade in bulk items, contacts between peoples became more frequent and more necessary in a subsistence strategy. Products took on new commercial and cultural attributes in the process. Second, human-related impacts on environmental habitats were a significant part of the conjunction and these impacts had a significant influence on culture. The basis of the new culture was the conquering of nature and this philosophy led to changes in large-scale habitats, resulting in deforestation and other environmental maladies.

The success of the tools in the Agricultural Conjunction was spectacular, focusing on the ability to domesticate plants. The technology of hunting, starting way back with the stone scraper, evolved into a technology of digging, evident in the hoe. The digging technologies, while primitive, reaped huge benefits in food output. As agricultural production created huge trade surpluses the first urban centers grew and the first trade systems began. It is important to keep this in mind when considering today's debate on globalization. One of the reasons for the failure of the Seattle meeting was the lack of agreement on agricultural subsidies and their relation to environmental issues.

What is clear in the stories of amber, Gilgamesh, and the Cedars of Lebanon is the active embrace of the disconnect between subsistence strategies that involved trade, and traditional views on environment and culture. The dichotomy between trade and the environment in the story of Gilgamesh is abundantly clear. What stood in the way were the cultural barriers to assuming a new worldview, one that broke with the past and compartmentalized the social context. The killing of Humbaba and the Bull of Heaven emphasize the choice of trade over environment and of the separation of the social context into competing rather than complementary factors.

It was also during this period that the trade dependence ratio became significant and some areas became critically dependent on trade in their subsistence strategy. As a result, changing trade patterns led to a gamut of cultural and environmental impacts. During the Agricultural Conjunction there continued to be a strong relationship between trade, environment, and culture simply due to historical inertia. However, the formation of a new economic trading system was taking place. This formation coincided with the emergence of new networks and new products. Trade dependence grew in this time but was not yet dominant in the subsistence strategy of the average person. The beginnings of bulk trade were an indication of the direction that future trends would follow in the Industrial Conjunction.

THE INDUSTRIAL CONJUNCTION

Many agree on the existence of the Industrial Conjunction, but not on when it began. Leften Stavrianos explains the Industrial Conjunction in economic and scientific terms: "about 1870 the Second Industrial Revolution got under way, characterized by new mass-production techniques and by the systematic application of science to industry."[132] Karl Polyani sees the events earlier in time: "after 1815 the change is sudden and complete. The backwash of the French Revolution reinforced the rising tide of the Industrial Revolution in establishing peaceful business as a universal interest."[133] The Industrial Conjunction was reinforced by what Polyani calls the Hundred Years' Peace (1816–1914). The absence of conflict allowed commercial interests to prosper and take advantage of new technology, as well as creating an amenable social context.

The Industrial Conjunction originated in northwest Europe and fundamentally changed the lives of people. Before Industrialization, most people in England, for example, might have had a small plot of land and fished for dinner in the Thames River. After industrialization, they had jobs in factories and bought dinner on their meager salaries.

After some time, fish became somewhat rare as many species began to disappear from rivers, such as the Thames, due to human and industrial pollution. Until 1870, the Thames River in England supported a vibrant fishing industry, including salmon. The twin impacts of urbanization and industrialization so polluted the river that few fish remained in the area around London and downstream on the Thames River. Urbanization brought domestic waste from cesspools that eventually wound up in the river. Industrialization brought factories, tanneries, and slaughterhouses. As early as 1857, the Houses of Parliament, in part for personal relief, introduced the Thames Conservancy Act. No real improvements in the quality of Thames River water occurred until 1878 when tragedy struck. The *Princess Alice*, a pleasure steam ship, sunk near London and an inquiry into the sinking revealed that most died from the putrid waters, not from drowning. These efforts were not enough. By 1950, the Thames was a biologically dead river. Along with the deindustrialization of London, clean-up efforts began in the 1960s. By 1974, salmon had returned to the Thames River, but only after great cost.

Trade in the Industrial Conjunction also facilitated exchange of plants and animals over large distances. During the Industrial Conjunction, crops spread throughout the Old and New Worlds; for example, by the 1750s, Portuguese and Dutch traders were importing large amounts of nutmeg. Trade in tobacco, corn, potatoes, peppers, sugar, and tea soon became worldwide. The intentional and unintentional spread of plants and animals subjected many fragile habitats to enormous biological invasions.

The Industrial Conjunction began with changing energy sources. Energy machines powered first by water and then by combustion replaced animal energy, discovered in the Agricultural Conjunction. This energy allowed for greater mass production and thus an impact on many more people and bigger macro-systems than in earlier periods. Today, a new and major environmental problem is the problem of residues from energy use. This section has five parts that describe the Industrial Conjunction: the social context, the dentalium currency system, the Irish potato famine, the Elgin Marbles, and perspectives on the Industrial Conjunction.

THE SOCIAL CONTEXT

In the Industrial Conjunction, steam and fossil-fired mechanical advancements led to incredible increases in human economic productivity. However, such advances did not come without great social dislocations. The prevailing sociocultural context accepted change and new tool technologies, although sometimes reluctantly, which in the process also changed the social context.[134]

During a conjunction, a multitude of forces are at play. How these forces combine to create a social context is an interdependent process. Invention is not simply new technology but also a force that changes the relative balance between the entities in the social context. Lynn White, Jr., believes these entities include "culture, society, and ideology [which] have been portrayed as central to the development process."[135] The social context also determines the direction of the conjunction and therefore "economic performance and cultural values are linked."[136]

The Industrial Conjunction, which arose more quickly than the Tool or Agricultural Conjunctions, created tension between new and old historical periods, leading to civil and international conflicts. With industrialization, economic demand focused more specifically than before on single products, single environments, and single peoples.

> But despite all these effects, the Industrial Revolution in its first half-century only mechanized the production of goods that had been in existence all along. It tremendously increased output and tremendously decreased cost. It created both consumers and consumer products. But the products themselves had been around all along. And products made in the new factories differed from traditional products only in that they were uniform, with fewer defects than existed in products made by any but the top craftsmen of earlier periods.[137]

Historians generally recognize the Industrial Conjunction as a momentous period in human development. Eric Hobsbawm called the Industrial Conjunction "the most fundamental transformation of human life in the history of the world."[138] Others, however, do not see it as the seed for a new period of development, but as the fruits of an earlier seed. M. Fores believes the Industrial Conjunction is the logical outcome of the Agricultural Conjunction, which divided rural and urban life.[139]

Peter Mathias believes that "the term [Industrial Revolution] was first used by French commentators in the 1820s, seeing an economic transformation in England as deep-rooted, structural, and overwhelming in its impact as the political revolution of 1789 in France."[140] In fact, the idea of a "revolution" is misleading. "It is also a misnomer insofar as it implies a sudden transformation, a high speed change."[141] What made this period different was the almost imperceptible rate at which the world was changing day by day. These tiny advances eventually accumulated into a revolution that is clear only from an historical perspective. The *rate* of technical change is very difficult to quantify in any period, but it was probably quite high during this time.[142]

The focus of the Industrial Conjunction was on using technology and machinery to manipulate products, at first focusing on textiles made first from wool and then cotton. Textile production soon exceeded domestic cotton supply and this demand led to large-scale trade in cotton. "Raw cotton imports alone increased more than eightfold from 1780 and 1800."[143]

During the early eighteenth century, the textiles industry saw great progress through innovations such as new spinning techniques. James Hargreaves invented the spinning jenny and, coupled with water-powered machines, produced an extraordinary leap in textile output. Complicated spinning and weaving machines perhaps laid the seeds for the Electronic Conjunction. (Some believe that the variable weaving patterns in Jacquard looms were in fact primitive types of computers.) James Watt's invention of the steam engine pushed power sources beyond the simple use of animals.[144]

> James Watt's improved steam engine (first installed in 1776) was first applied, in 1785, to an industrial operation—the spinning of cotton. And the steam engine was to the first Industrial Revolution what the computer has been to the Information Revolution—its trigger, but above all its symbol. Almost everybody today believes that nothing in economic history has ever moved as fast as, or had a greater impact than the Information Revolution. But the Industrial Revolution moved at least as fast in the same time span, and had probably an equal impact if not a greater one. In short order it mechanized the great majority of manufacturing processes, beginning with the production of the most important industrial commodity of the eighteenth and early nineteenth centuries: textiles.[145]

European textile production required greater cotton imports, provided in large part by the United States. Southern cotton exports were a key reason behind British support for the Confederacy during the American Civil War. Change in trade patterns led to changes in environment. U.S. landholders cleared large swathes of forestland for growing cotton and introduced vast mono-crop systems that were susceptible to insect infestations (such as the boll weevil). Arnold Toynbee pointed to a series of inventions that changed the nature of cotton manufacture industries. These great inventions include:

> the spinning-jenny patented by Hargreaves in 1770; the water-frame, invented by Arkwright the year before; Crompton's mule introduced in 1789; and the self-acting mule, first invented by Kelly in 1792, but not brought into use until Roberts improved it in 1825.[146]

Toynbee held an overall optimistic view of the impact of the Industrial Conjunction on people, especially in terms of labor. He also saw substantial social costs in the globalization of the world's economy, especially its role in increasing poverty, but saw the rise of trade unions as a countervailing force.[147]

FIGURE 2.3 **Milestones in the Industrial Conjunction**

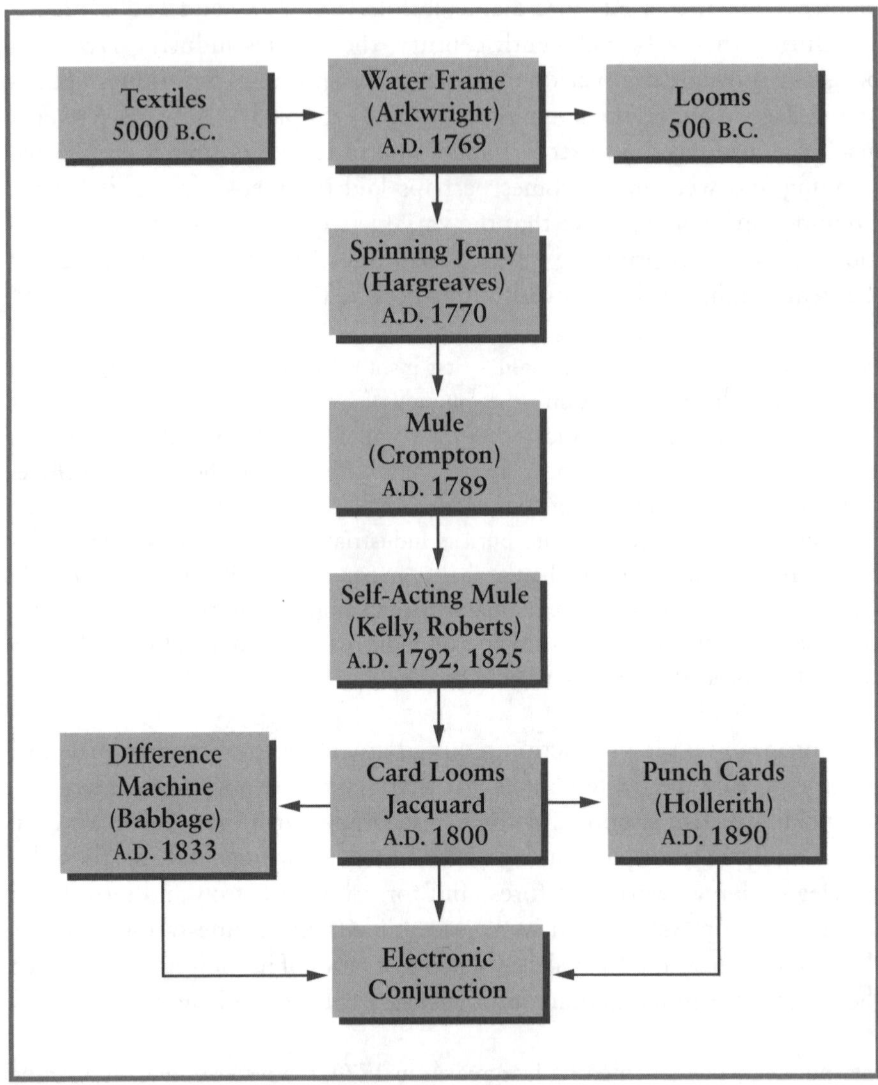

As he noted in 1884, "free trade, for instance, is a sound policy; and no doubt, for all nations at a certain stage of development, but it is open to anyone to say that free trade is only good under certain conditions."[148]

The Industrial Conjunction introduced an enormous series of advances in technological capacity and in the human ability to change the environment. For the first time, humans had the ability not only to eliminate species or change habitats in a specific land region, but also to substantially influence the species and habitats on the land, sea, and air.

The air became a new medium for concern. During this period, the buildup of greenhouse gases began and thus the beginnings of the problem of anthropogenic sources of global climate changes. Al Gore believes "the most significant change thus far in the earth's atmosphere is the one [climate change] that began with the industrial revolution early in the last century and has picked up speed ever since."[149]

Scientists recognized the climate change problem during the Industrial Revolution. John Tyndall wrote in 1861 about what we now call the "greenhouse" effect. Around the turn of the century, Swedish Nobel prizewinner Svante Arrhenius and an American geologist, T. C. Chamberlin, both offered possible theories on changing atmospheric conditions and temperatures.[150] Similar to the "overkill hypothesis," the "global warming" theory today is highly contested.

The Industrial Conjunction reveals the different manifestations of the relationship between trade, environment and culture in a completely different and more intensive pattern. Here, the disconnect becomes widespread and a normal consequence of progress. Figure 2.3 shows the lineage and the milestones in the Industrial Conjunction.

THE DENTALIUM CURRENCY SYSTEM

The horse died out in North America at the end of the last Ice Age, probably hastened by human beings. The Spanish reintroduced the horse to Western North America in the 1600s and it spread among tribes through trade. When trading, these peoples often used the sea mollusk shell called dentalium as currency. The term "wampum" is actually a Native American word for the dentalium shell.

Until about 1900, dentalium was a common currency for trade among many Native Americans. Dentalium shells populate the areas where the creatures live, but the specific shell used for currency is native to the area around Victoria Island off British Columbia.[151] The pre-Columbian use of dentalium as a currency extended over a large geographic area, stretching in a triangle between the modern cities of Chicago, San Diego, and Nome, Alaska. For several hundred years, dentalium provided a currency system based on a commodity, much as the global economic system once used the gold standard. The primary difference between the gold and dentalium standards was that gold was a finite commodity, leading to a constant quest for new sources of gold, whereas dentalium could reproduce and was thus theoretically infinite.

Humans also used dentalium as decoration, adding cultural value to its financial benefits. The Ogala Sioux made dentalium shell dresses (even though they were two thousand miles from the Pacific Ocean). "Members of the Nez Perce tribe wore [dentalium] shells through their noses, earning the name 'pierced nose' from early French traders."[152]

Dentalium as an infinite resource produced a unique regulatory system. The "bankers," who lived in the areas where the dentalium was found, needed to ensure a stable supply, since the currency's value was inversely proportional to its scarcity. When the bankers harvested too much dentalium, the economic result was probably an inflationary increase, similar to an increase in the (current) money supply. Dentalium extraction beyond a sustainable level lowered the supply in ensuing years, leading to deflationary conditions. Native Americans no doubt ran a series of surpluses and deficits around some optimal point in their currency and their dentalium stocks. Monetary and dentalium life cycles probably co-varied.

Dentalium use eventually came into conflict with European fur trade. Native Americans living near the Fraser River in modern day Canada hunted sea otter for food and clothing supplies. The Europeans changed Native American hunting patterns due to demands in fur-scarce Europe. Over time, furs began to replace dentalium as the favored trading currency between Native Americans and Europeans. Dentalium slowly fell out of use as a currency and rendered dentalium holdings worthless.

Fur harvesting (for the Europeans) was so successful that European traders soon found they had an enormous excess of furs and needed to develop new trading markets in China. Europeans then began exporting furs from North America to Asia in large quantities.[153] Changing European fashion trends raised and changed demand for furs. As fashions and outfits changed, this led to the hunting of various fur-bearing animals. Demand for otter shifted to beaver and then to mink. Local extinctions, to some extent, followed tastes in fashion.

Native Americans hunted sea otter unrestrained for almost a century for export to Europe. Predictably, these animals nearly became extinct. As otter populations became low, the North American fur industry moved further inland to take advantage of other fur-bearing species. There were so few sea otters left along the coast that it was not economically viable to hunt them. In the end, the Native Americans had no sea otters and the dentalium had become worthless. Partly for these reasons, Native American populations in the area plummeted and many tribes became extinct.

The dentalium case demonstrates the complex interaction between trade, environment, and culture that begins to emerge in the Industrial Conjunction. Subtle changes in one culture, transmitted through trade, now had the capacity to produce significant environmental impacts and changes in distant cultures. The new disconnect could prove lethal for species and peoples in far-off places.

THE IRISH POTATO FAMINE[154]

During the Potato Famine, from 1845 to 1847, more than one million Irish people immigrated or died of starvation.[155] In addition, over fifty thousand people died of diseases such as typhus, scurvy, and dysentery. Within a decade, the Irish population fell from over eight million to less than six million. In an attempt to flee the oppression, starvation, and disease that gripped Ireland, Irish citizens became the country's greatest export.

Although the potato blight infected crops in the United States, Southern Canada, and Western Europe in 1845–46, the Irish were most at risk. The English forced Irish subsistence farmers to export corn, wheat, barley, and oats to Britain, which left the potato as the sole dietary staple for the people and their animals. While other potato-producing regions were able to turn to alternative food sources, the Irish remained dependent on the potato. The results of the blight were disastrous. Despite widespread starvation, British-imposed Corn Laws virtually prevented imports of other foods to replace the potato.

The "white" potato, now known as the Irish potato, originated in the Andes Mountains of modern day Peru. In 1532, the Spanish arrived in north Peru and brought the potato to Europe in the second half of the sixteenth century. Since potatoes belong to the same botanical family as the poisonous nightshade, there was a belief that potatoes were poisonous and as a result, people did not eat them (similar to Europe's initial reaction to the tomato).

Potatoes became fashionable in the mid-eighteenth century when Marie Antoinette wore potato blossoms in her hair. During the eighteenth century, European monarchs also discovered the potato's nutritional value and ordered large-scale plantings and the potato literally took root in European cuisine. In Ireland, 90 percent of the population relied on the potato as their primary source of caloric intake. (Since the famine, the Irish have expanded their diets; however, the potato continues to be a dietary staple in 130 countries today, including Ireland.[156])

Up to the point of the Irish potato famine, economic and population pressures forced Irish families to sell grain crops to pay rent, while relying on stored potato stocks to feed themselves and the livestock, especially pigs, during the winter. As land holdings were subdivided into smaller plots to feed a growing population, they lost the old husbandry and agricultural techniques. Farmers began to specialize in potatoes, resulting in lower production of other staples such as milk. When the famine hit, the Irish people no longer possessed the agricultural skills or resources to save themselves or their families. At the same time, Ireland experienced rapid population growth, which left many peasants in subsistence living conditions.[157]

In the early 1800s, the British introduced a tenure system into Ireland that gave Protestant landlords control of 95 percent of the land. Every cottage contained a garden equal to an acre and a half and a farm plot equal to five acres. As the population grew, the size of the average farm became smaller and smaller. Because of overpopulation, people moved to less fertile areas where the potato was one of the few sources of food that could grow. Absentee landlords who wanted to maximize output with little or no investment in the population or local economy owned most of these lands.

The British instituted Penal Laws which forbade the Irish from speaking their language, practicing their faith, attending school, holding public office, taking certain jobs, owning land or "own[ing] a horse worth more than $10."[158] The British government justified its Penal Laws by claiming them necessary to retain the "tough" character of the Irish. The Penal Laws and the Potato Famine dealt a double-blow to the Irish and long-term changes in climate conditions made the situation worse.

The blight came and went on several occasions. According to one farmer, in late September of 1845, a "queer mist came over the Irish Sea . . . and the potato stalks turned black as soot." The next day, the potatoes were "a wide waste of putrefaction giving off an offensive odor that could be smelled for miles."[159] The potato blight (*photophthora infestans*), which caused the Great Famine of Ireland, results from a pathogen that spreads rapidly among crops during certain weather conditions. The disease attacks not only the crops in the field, but also the crops in storage during a mild and damp period.

In 1845, the potato blight destroyed 40 percent of the Irish potatoes and the following year almost all the crops were ruined. Successive crop failure led to "Black '47" with increases in famine, immigration, and disease. Although potato crops from 1847–51 were unaffected by the blight, famine conditions intensified due to lack of potato seeds for planting new crops—they had been eaten.

Approximately 500,000 Irish faced eviction during the Great Hunger (1845–47). Many died of starvation or disease and the lucky ones were consigned to mismanaged and inadequate "poor houses." The alternative to eviction and starvation was either living in "poor houses" or emigration, which rose to over two million from 1845 to 1855. In 1851, a quarter of a million people left for destinations overseas. Emigration continued through the 1850s and into the 1860s, with an average of about 125,000 people per year.[160] Emigrants tended to follow family routes, which brought them mostly to Great Britain, the United States, Canada, New Zealand, and Australia.

As the famine proceeded, the Irish were unable to import other starch substitutes under the Corn Laws. British interest was in maintaining a healthy balance-of-payments position. Prime Minister Sir Robert Peel repealed the Corn Laws, enabling the Irish to import grain from North America. For this humanitarian impulse, the less lenient Lord John Russell replaced Peel. Relief measures, such as corn importation, did arrive from North America; however, these shipments were mere tokens to the relief necessary to comfort the starving.

To lessen the plight of the Irish, Russell approved the purchase of corn and meal in November 1845. The problem was that by this time the Irish subsistence strategy had also become too narrow. The extensive dietary focus on potatoes and corn caused dysentery and scurvy, due to the lack of some nutrients in these crops, and resulted in additional deaths. The British still believed that it was in the best interests of the Irish to continue exporting agricultural goods from Ireland, so that they could pay their rents and loans.

To limit the number of people seeking relief, the British government instituted the Poor Law Extension Act of 1847 to deny aid to tenant farmers with over a quarter acre of land. This Act promoted emigration, increased land clearance, and disintegrated the structure of rural society—beneficial to British landowners, who sought profit and larger plots of land. According to the Poor Laws, landlords were bound to support peasants sent to the workhouse, a cost of twelve pounds a year. Instead, some landlords exported peasants to Canada on "coffin ships," which cost six pounds per person. Coffin ships were "wet, leaky holds" of timber ships returning to North America that were "crammed in with as many as 900 [people], with barely room to stand."[161] Perhaps one-half of them died during the voyage and the other half arrived in North America unable to disembark, without assistance, due to sickness and starvation. Mary Robinson, President of Ireland, described the famine as follows:

> An event which more than any others shaped us as a people. It defined our will to survive and our sense of human vulnerability. The nightmare images of the bailiff,

the workhouse and the coffin ship have equally terrible equivalents for other people at this very moment.[162]

One hundred and fifty years after the famine, the results are evident in the number of Irish descendants scattered around the globe, the treeless Irish landscape and the shells of Irish homes rendered uninhabitable after the landlords evicted their tenants. While the blight provided the catalyst for the famine, "the calamity was essentially manmade, a poison of blind politics, scientific ignorance, rural suppression, and enforced poverty."[163]

The blight that devastated a nation remains a pest of the potato plant worldwide. In the 1990s, Ireland once again has fallen victim to potato blight and has suffered poor potato crop output. A new aggressive blight, cousin to the blight of the 1840s, first reported in the early 1980s, spread from Florida to Maine in the United States. The fungus thrives in the wet weather that has beleaguered the states of Idaho and Oregon, as well as Maine and other parts of the United States. In 1994, New York's third largest cash crop, potatoes, lost 3 percent of its $50 million crop to the blight and in 1995 Maine lost $25 million.

Because the current blight can reproduce sexually, it possesses greater genetic variation, spreads faster, survives harsher weather, and resists more chemicals than the blight that caused the famine in the nineteenth century. In addition, the spores can last for months in the soil. Ireland has actually banned the original "lumper" potato, a poor quality potato that grew in abundance in Ireland before the famine, and heartier strains are now under cultivation. Scientists are researching potatoes that have proven to be more resistant to blights than others: Kennebec, Sebago, Sequoia, Merrimack, and Cherokee.

The potato famine occurred during the heart of the Industrial Conjunction. It shows how the environment can have an enormous influence on culture and can help shape it. The potato, originating from the other half of the world, became Ireland's entire subsistence strategy. This singular focus, similar to the focus on mammoths and buffalo, produced an enormous impact when the resource was no longer available. Here we find the exact opposite of the Tool Conjunction, a situation where the subsistence strategy is largely the result of the impact of foreign rather than local environments.

The potato has become a symbol of the sedentary lifestyle. People honor the potato for its food value but others lambaste it as a symbolic prison. Hunter-gatherer peoples regard the cultivation of plants as part of a plot to change them into farmers and in essence domesticate them. In the process of creating lifestyles built on domestication, these people lose some sovereign freedoms, a cost attributed to the price of "civilization."

The transition from a relatively free, diverse, gentle subsistence to suppressed peasantry yoked to a metropolis is a matter of record . . . Faced with forced farming, Chief Washakie of the Shoshone said, 'God damn a potato.'[164]

THE ELGIN MARBLES

Pericles had the Parthenon built following the Greek triumph over the Persians in 479 B.C. The Parthenon honored Athens' patron goddess Athena and the monument's decorative sculpture represented great scenes in Greece's history. The ninety-two metopes (friezes) showed the victories of Greek gods and heroes.[165]

The history of the Parthenon reflects Greek history. In 1690, the Turks captured Athens and erected a mosque inside the shell of the Parthenon. In 1800, Lord Elgin exploited Turkey's alliance with Britain to gain the Turkish Sultan's favor and amass a huge collection of antiquities from central Greece, the Aegean Islands, and Asia Minor, where Greek civilization had once flourished. He then turned his attention to the monuments of the Parthenon, located on the Acropolis. Lord Elgin was able to persuade the Turkish leaders in Constantinople and Athens to give him permission to draw, make casts, and excavate around the foundations, on the condition that he not destroy the monuments.[166] On his own accord, Elgin then proceeded to remove parts of the sculptured decorations and stripping of the Parthenon began in 1801. While the mutilation of the monuments was partially due to carelessness, it was also done intentionally for ease of shipping. Over a period of ten years, Elgin's men dismembered the Parthenon and removed sections of the buildings on the Acropolis.

When the Marbles from the Parthenon arrived in England, they were the subject of commercial bargaining between Lord Elgin and the British government. The British Parliament debated and then condemned Elgin for robbing antiquities and destroying monuments. The Parliament decided by eighty-two votes to thirty to purchase the Marbles from him for thirty-five thousand pounds and proceeded to give them to the British Museum.

Of the ninety-seven surviving blocks of the Parthenon frieze, fifty-six are in the British Museum and forty are in Athens (and the remainder elsewhere). Of the sixty-four surviving metopes, fifteen are in the British Museum while eighteen remain in Athens. In many cases, parts of the same sculpture reside in museums in Athens and London.

The government of Greece argues that the Marbles are an integral part of an existing cultural monument, the Parthenon, and to an architectural complex, the Acropolis, and that they occupy a central position in the cultural heritage of Greece. Since Elgin illegally took the Marbles while Greece was under foreign occupation, the Greeks assert that they are the rightful owners. The Elgin Marbles also fall under UNESCO's definition of cultural property, although the agreement significantly excludes the vast majority of foreign antiquities now held by the British Museum. In cooperation with UNESCO, the Greek government is sponsoring a construction and restoration program for the Acropolis, the building of an adjacent Acropolis Museum that will house the Marbles, and a program for environmental protection of the sculptures.[167]

The British response is that the removal of the Marbles was proper under the applicable international law that existed at the time of Lord Elgin's actions for three reasons. First, returning the Marbles to Greece would set a precedent for the universal removal of major acquisitions of the world's museums. Second, retaining the Marbles in the British Museum over the course of 150 years has protected them from the high levels of atmospheric pollution in Athens, which has noticeably damaged the Parthenon Marbles on the Acropolis. Finally, the Marbles have been in England for more than a century and in that time have become a part of the British cultural heritage. Like other works in the British Museum, they have entered British culture. In this way, the Marbles help define British identity while inspiring British arts.

At the heart of these arguments is the role that trade, whether considered legal or illegal, plays in a nation's cultural environment. This "environment" builds upon the relation between cultural property and cultural definition.[168] "For a full life and a secure identity people need exposure to their history, much of which is represented or illustrated by objects."[169] The perspective suggests first that nations are entitled to preserve their cultural "environment" through trade measures and second that there exists an economic value to culture. Tourism to Greece is important to the country's economy and part of the lure is in antiquities such as the Parthenon. In 1996, 9.8 million tourists visited Greece and spent $3.75 billion.

PERSPECTIVES ON THE INDUSTRIAL CONJUNCTION

Trade, environment, and culture in the Industrial Conjunction brought the global economy squarely and strongly into the lives of average people and made it a dominant part of their subsistence strategy. In the process of extending this system to the popular and global level, the environmental and cultural aspects of the product were often secondary to a particular economic utility. With this undeniable progress came a cost and further disconnect. The onset of the Industrial Conjunction was in fact a huge environmental disaster on many dimensions. Spiritual content in products disappeared in favor of generalized product appeal on utilitarian grounds.

What emerged in the products was the beginning of a subsistence strategy expressed in economic, environmental, and cultural terms, but where the disconnect between these factors had become widespread. The symptoms of the disconnect are easily seen in the three cases and in three differing ways. In the first case, the fashion industry in Europe and its changing fads had a disastrous impact on the lives of native peoples in North America and specific fur-bearing species that lived there. In the second case, Ireland's high trade dependence on an imported and adopted crop, the potato, left it vulnerable to disease which had a devastating impact on the Irish and their culture. In the third case, Greece sought the return of monuments taken and now on display in the British Museum. In each instance, the breaking of the social context and the three factors in it led to dispute.

The consequences of disconnecting trade, environment, and culture in earlier times now had become somewhat of a dominant lifestyle. Along with the great progress of the time are numerous stories that illustrate the contradictions in this progress. As we enter the Electronic Conjunction, it will be very difficult to prevent a deeper disconnect.

All three cases illustrate the complexities in the Industrial Conjunction and plant some seeds for the current disconnect. In all the cases, there is no clear evidence that modern institutions have done a better job of dealing with these problems compared to ancient ones. These problems show how the development of products and trading systems encourages the growth of trade, environmental, and cultural connections. The next chapter examines trade, environment, and culture in its modern context. Therefore, it focuses on species and habitats in the Electronic Conjunction.

TRADE, CULTURE, AND ENVIRONMENT IN THE ELECTRONIC CONJUNCTION

THE ELECTRONIC CONJUNCTION introduces a new technology, the computer, and a device that has little direct impact on culture or environment. This is not to say that the overall impact is small, in fact it is quite substantial, but that the influence of the computer is indirect on the social context. This chapter discusses the advent of the computer and the complex changes in the social context it causes. It also explores a series of case studies that highlight the relations in the social context in this period. The fact that these cases occur in the Electronic Conjunction does not mean they are necessarily electronic or computer-related. The computer, similar to the hoe in the Tool Conjunction, sets in motion a chain of events that produces indirect impacts of much greater consequence than the direct impacts that result from the introduction of a new tool.

The Electronic Conjunction is creating new types of multilateral regimes and new types of international sovereignty. These new institutional regimes and their disciplines are already emerging. Trade, cultural, and environmental issues are now agenda items for organizations such as NAFTA (North America Free Trade Agreement), the European Union, the World Bank, and the WTO. While environment and culture are creeping into the language and reality of trade discourse, they have done so on separate tracks. Today's trends will push people and policymakers to integrate these separate social interests into more unified policy measures.

There are at least three good reasons to argue that trade and environment and trade and culture should be treated along parallel or similar tracks in multilateral trade negotiations. First, protecting cultures and environments from obtrusive trade are considered non-tariff barriers, and therefore, belong to a similar genre of institutional measures in trade fora. Second, and perhaps more importantly, trade cases with environmental and cultural aspects are becoming more common on separate tracks. Such cases tend to invite "forum shopping," or a search for the legal venue with the highest chance of winning a case. Forum shopping will ultimately weaken WTO disciplines. Finally, the natural and historical linkage between culture and environment suggests treating them together is quite natural.

By the time of the Electronic Conjunction the disconnect is in full force and is evident in many parts of life and in many peoples and places. The scope of globalization makes the conflicts between trade, culture, and environment—signs of the disconnect—a rather common and everyday occurrence. The conquering and subjugation of nature is nearly total and, outside of some patches of the planet that remain in a natural state, the land area is either completely urban or an amalgam of human and natural influences. The tendency for mass production and macro-system approaches now is commonplace and many transnational companies have earnings that exceed the output of countries.

Cases in the Electronic Conjunction fall into two types: those that focus on species and those that focus on habitats. The types of problems in species versus habitat cases are quite different and reflect respective instances of more and less specificity in the disconnect problem. Indeed, these two types of cases invoke completely different circumstances, impacts, and possible solutions. Before discussing these cases, first it is necessary to describe the context of the Electronic Conjunction and its development.

THE SOCIAL CONTEXT

Many scholars agree on the uniqueness of today's Electronic Conjunction. Eric Hobsbawm compares the Electronic Conjunction to the profound changes in the Stone Age and the onset of the Tool Conjunction.[1] While it may seem that the computer has come suddenly upon people, it has actually taken an extremely long time to develop. Similar to the "gestation" period needed to give birth to the Tool Conjunction, the Electronic Conjunction has also had a long process of maturation.

> [The computer] was a new kind of tool, but one with ancient roots. In the past 250 years, human life and society has undergone a profound change, perhaps the greatest since the dawn of the Neolithic Age some ten thousand years ago.[2]

The culmination of the Electronic Conjunction is a new type of lifestyle and thus a new social context. Zbigniew Brzezinski sees events of today as the embodiment of the rise of a "technotronic" society that is "shaped culturally, psychologically, socially and economically by the impact of technology and electronics—particularly in the area of computers and communications."[3] Kenneth Boulding calls this era a "post-civilized" period, where knowledge rather than social or biological drives will lead to new creative systems and power structures.[4] Walter Anderson believes that "words like tool and machine are only barely adequate to describe what is happening now. We are indeed dealing with information tools and information machines, but we are also dealing with many new patterns of connection—connections between people and machines, yes, but also connections among people, among ecosystems, among all living things."[5]

The Electronic Conjunction will lead to large-scale changes in social structure. Daniel Bell believes that the Electronic Conjunction is creating a "post-industrial" society, but it is barely beginning. Today is, in fact, a transitional time spanning the Industrial and Electronic Conjunctions. Bell refers to this phenomenon as "living in interstitial time, something that occurs at the onset of every conjunction."[6] Amitai Etzioni calls today the "post-modern era."

> A central characteristic of the modern period has been continued increase in the efficacy of the technology of productions which poses a growing challenge to the primacy of values they are supposed to serve. The post-modern era, the onset of which can be set at 1945, will witness either a greater status of these values by the surging technologies or a reassertion of their normative priority.[7]

The Electronic Conjunction has roots in earlier conjunctions and, in many respects, the computer is an old invention. Its development traces back to earlier innovations such as the abacus, which was developed in the Agricultural Conjunction, and the Jacquard loom, which was invented in the Industrial Conjunction. The abacus and the loom were in fact primitive types of computers. "Like the Industrial Revolution two centuries ago, the Information Revolution so far—that is, since the first computers, in the mid-1940s—has only transformed processes that were here all along."[8]

For almost a quarter of a century, the computer was solely the domain of scientists and researchers, often using mainframe computers. By the 1980s, the computer had entered average and everyday lives in a profound way because "the *deux ex machina* [god from the machine] of today's world is the electronic digital computer in all of its forms."[9]

A tool is invented to make possible something that was formerly impossible—or extremely difficult. The evolution of the computer over the last 150 years has occurred to serve such a purpose . . . the computer was desperately needed as a tool to help people manage a rapidly increasing volume of information.[10]

The elements of the computer were actually devised during the Industrial Conjunction. In 1833, Charles Babbage proposed a steam-powered analytical engine called a "difference machine." In Babbage's system, calculations were the outputs of a complicated system of mechanical levers and gears that one had to physically manipulate (you needed to turn a gear) in order for it to work. This was an analog type of computer in that the computation powers were analogous to the physical manifestation of it. (Later, the discussion will focus on the modern computers which are "digital" in nature.) "What has proved so astonishing about Babbage's concepts is their resemblance to those of modern computers."[11] This innovation was only the beginning of a series of incremental innovations.

Babbage's invention became available to the public within two decades. Around 1850 W. T. Odhner began commercially selling the Thomas arithmometer, a simple calculating device containing a rack and pinion mechanical gear assembly.[12] Odhner, a Swede working in Russia, manufactured and developed a commercial model of the arithmometer that sold up until the Russian Revolution. During the Russian Revolution Odhner escaped to Sweden and the company he began continues to make computers today. The invention of these calculating machines abetted other scientific research. Charles Darwin, a friend of Babbage, used a difference machine for calculations to support his findings in the 1859 publication of *The Origin of the Species*.

Joseph Marie Jacquard contributed one of the real breakthroughs of the era in his design of a machine for mass-producing separate lines of textile products. This invention was responsible for fundamentally changing the textile industry in its use of programmable looms. These programmable looms were perhaps early types of computer programs. Jacquard may have been responsible for two conjunctions!

Joseph Marie Jacquard (1752–1834) was a French inventor working in the high-technology industry of the time: textile weaving. In order to weave a complex pattern into a brocade or carpet, the warp or machine-direction yarns must be separated in various sequences to permit the shuttle with the wool yarn to cross the machine . . . Around 1800 in Lyon, Jacquard developed a system using punch cards to determine the yarn picker as in an on or off position.[13]

The Jacquard technique for creating textile products drew on earlier inventions. One important step in the process was the development of the player piano, which used a string of punched paper as a programming medium for creating music. Herman Hollerith's idea of a punch card later combined the Thomas Arithmometer with the Jacquard punch card to develop a card reader based on a 16 by 12 matrix, or 192 possible holes on the card. The first use of the punch card system was for the census in the United States in the late nineteenth century, followed by Canada, Austria, and Russia in the early twentieth century. Punched paper remained a major computer programming medium well into the 1970s.

The vacuum tube, a key part of computer evolution, was the result of work by Thomas Edison in 1903 and John Fleming in 1904. Lee DeForest later refined Edison's invention over the next thirty years, while he worked for the Federal Telegraph Company in Palo Alto, California. World War I stimulated computer development and encouraged DeForest's efforts. The need to organize data for the personnel and ballistics requirements required extensive calculations that led to intensification of computational technology.

Thomas J. Watson was another driving force behind the development of the computer. He began by revolutionizing the use of calculators for sales analysis at a company called National Cash Register. In 1911, Watson was hired by a new firm called CTR, which included elements of a company that originally was formed by Harry Hollerith. In 1920, CTR incorporated in Canada as International Business Machines Company, Ltd., and in 1924 changed the entire company's name to a set of initials that became known as IBM. In 1935, IBM released a commercial version of an automated test-scoring machine called the IBM 805. This device was still something less than the modern computer. Alan Turing, a renowned mathematician, laid out the abstract basis for modern computers in 1936. During World War II Turing worked on the Enigma project to decipher German messages. In 1943, he used what is thought to have been the first programmable computer (Colossus I) to assist in the decoding process.

In the late 1930s, Howard Aiken, a graduate student at Harvard, proposed a new type of computer and went to IBM to meet Watson and discuss his idea. In 1938, Watson set up a team with Aiken to produce the "Automatic Sequence Controlled Calculator" or Mark 1. Weighing five tons, the machine came on-line in 1944 with a first task to calculate ballistic tables for the U.S. Navy. The first task program given the computer (the M-9 Gun Director) was to predict airplane flight paths in order to shoot them down. In the defense of Antwerp in 1944, "90-millimeter antiaircraft guns directed by M-9s engaged 4,883 German V-1 'buzz bombs' and shot down 4,617 of them—an amazing accuracy of 95.7 percent . . . 89 of 91 attacking German V-1s were destroyed."[14]

The development of the modern computer progressed along a different track from the M-9 gun director. In 1943, vacuum tubes replaced the electromechanical relays and the result was a much quicker machine. The U.S. Army Ordnance Corps, because of increasing ballistics requirements, decided to build a new class of computers. Called the Electronic Numerical Integrator and Calculator or ENIAC, the machine came on-line in 1946. ENIAC was the size of a small house, weighing thirty tons spread out over 1,500 square feet and containing seventeen thousand vacuum tubes. "It was capable of performing three hundred multiplications per second, in contrast to the best electromechanical computers, which could do one per second."[15]

Transistors greatly increased calculation power. In 1947, Bell Laboratories developed the first transistor based on a collection of metalloid or metal-like materials called semiconductors. Remington Rand commercially sold a new computer using transistors called the UNIVAC in 1954. In 1955, the integrated circuit (IC) was invented which united the power of many single transistors. This tremendously increased information storage capabilities. In 1957, IBM released an all-transistorized calculator, the IBM 608.

The Intel Corporation began producing higher quality ICs called Large System Integrators (LSIs) and in 1970 created dynamic Random Access Memory (RAM) followed by an advanced microprocessor in 1971. Starting in 1974, Intel installed 8008 microprocessors in computers produced by Digital Equipment Corporation. The 8080 was ten times faster than the 8008, its parent. IBM released System 360 (a mainframe computer) in 1964 and Wang Laboratories released the Wang 1200 word processor in 1971 and a business computer, the 2200, the following year.

Apple Computer, a company begun by Steve Jobs and Steve Wozniak, began selling personal computer kits and eventually full computers in 1976. Radio Shack released the TRS-80 in 1977. In 1981, IBM produced the 5150 Personal Computer (PC), in part based on the use of the Intel 8086 chip. By 1982, IBM PCs held 17 percent of the market and by 1983 their share rose to 23 percent, a year when the total market was substantially growing. By the end of the decade, IBM controlled the hardware computer market and most machines ran on IBM-compatible DOS platforms.

In the 1990s, major producers such as Compaq and Dell produced clones that cut into IBM's market share of computer hardware. Software development, however, quickly became the dominant part of the computer industry, led by Microsoft Corporation. The power of the computer resides in the chips in it and this part of the industry found the Intel Corporation preeminent. By this time, the impacts of the Electronic Conjunction were becoming evident and some of these impacts reflected old rather than new issues.

In the mid-1990s, the World Wide Web (or Internet) was a niche market of professionals who were at the forefront of using new technologies. By the late 1990s, the Web became a reality that is changing communication and business (and many more things). The technology is merging a variety of aspects of trade, environment, and culture and the overall social context. Computers linked through the Web connect people from all over the world. This process, like the development of the stone tools in the Tool Conjunction, is the result of incremental innovations.

In the Electronic Conjunction, incremental software innovations followed with the opening of the Web backbone infrastructure to the public at the end of the Cold War. Research institutions and universities were the first to use it. This knowledge "escaped" to the private sector and was the basis for a series of innovations (Web browers) that started with Gopher (a product of the University of Minnesota), and then included Netscape, and later Microsoft Explorer.

By the end of the twentieth century, E-Commerce (electronic commerce) had become a reality and was changing the structure of many industries and the lives of many people. Speculation by many scholars and policymakers pondered whether humanity had entered a period of sustained economic growth buoyed by the advent of the new technologies. Around the year 2000, the trade aspects of the Electronic Conjunction had started to formulate, but the relation to culture and environment had yet to solidify. By this time, perhaps 300 million people had access to the Web in a world of six billion people, thus a penetration rate of 5 percent. This is an astounding increase from virtually no use a decade earlier. There are over a billion Web pages and information on millions of subjects is available on the Web. The information can be found through search engines that began as rather mechanical devices (such as Yahoo!), and evolved into increasingly intelligent devices for knowledge gathering and knowledge management.

The Electronic Conjunction is not only a period of unique technological progress but also a link between various historic conjunctions. Computer technology provides the means for combining old technologies in new ways. The Tool Conjunction, for example, introduced the concept of developing applied technology and the Agricultural and Industrial Conjunctions carried these refinements further and focused them on agricultural and industrial products. With the computer, the Electronic Conjunction combines separate advances in the prior conjunctions into a more integrated and coherent system of progress. It is the computer's ability to focus technological progress that makes its impact so powerful. Ironically, the disconnect becomes stronger with this increase in focus.

The Electronic Conjunction is, of course, the product of many forces besides computational machinery. Advances in telecommunications, sometimes through networks built during the Industrial Conjunction, have made computing on the Internet a global communications system as well as a potent and widespread application of computer technology. Out of the Electronic Conjunction came the World Wide Web, designed as a communication network meant to survive World War III.

Widespread computer use and the general onset of the Electronic Conjunction began around 1970, twenty-five years after the development of the first "true" computer (dating back to about 1945). The growth in computer capacity over this time was phenomenal. By 1970, computers "were 100,000 times faster than earlier models,"[16] and today's are more than a million times faster. Over the next quarter century, these trends actually accelerated, but this should not have been a surprise from a historical standpoint because the same trends occurred in the Industrial Conjunction.

Moore's Law asserts that the price of the Information Revolution's basic element, the microchip, drops by 50 percent every eighteen months. The same was true of the products whose manufacture was mechanized by the first Industrial Revolution. The price of cotton textiles fell by 90 percent in the fifty years spanning the start of the eighteenth century. The production of cotton textiles increased at least 150-fold in Britain alone in the same period. And although textiles were the most visible product of its early years, the Industrial Revolution mechanized the production of practically all other major goods, such as paper, glass, leather, and bricks.[17]

Similar to most inventions, the Electronic Conjunction came about due to a favorable social context. The invention of the computer met a number of social needs especially to "anticipate the future in order to plan ahead."[18] Planning meant a differing type of invention. The prior inventions focused on improving lives in an immediate sense, to provide more food or more material possessions for survival. What was different about the Electronic Conjunction was that computer technology was built on the abstract idea of improved organization and efficiency. The machines of the Industrial Conjunction, for example, were technological achievements but were not built on abstract ideas but on principles of mechanics and physics. Those inventors did not focus on the abstract in developing their inventions. This abstract quality of innovation is much more evident in today's inventions, especially in the computer.

FIGURE 3.1 **The Electronic Conjunction**

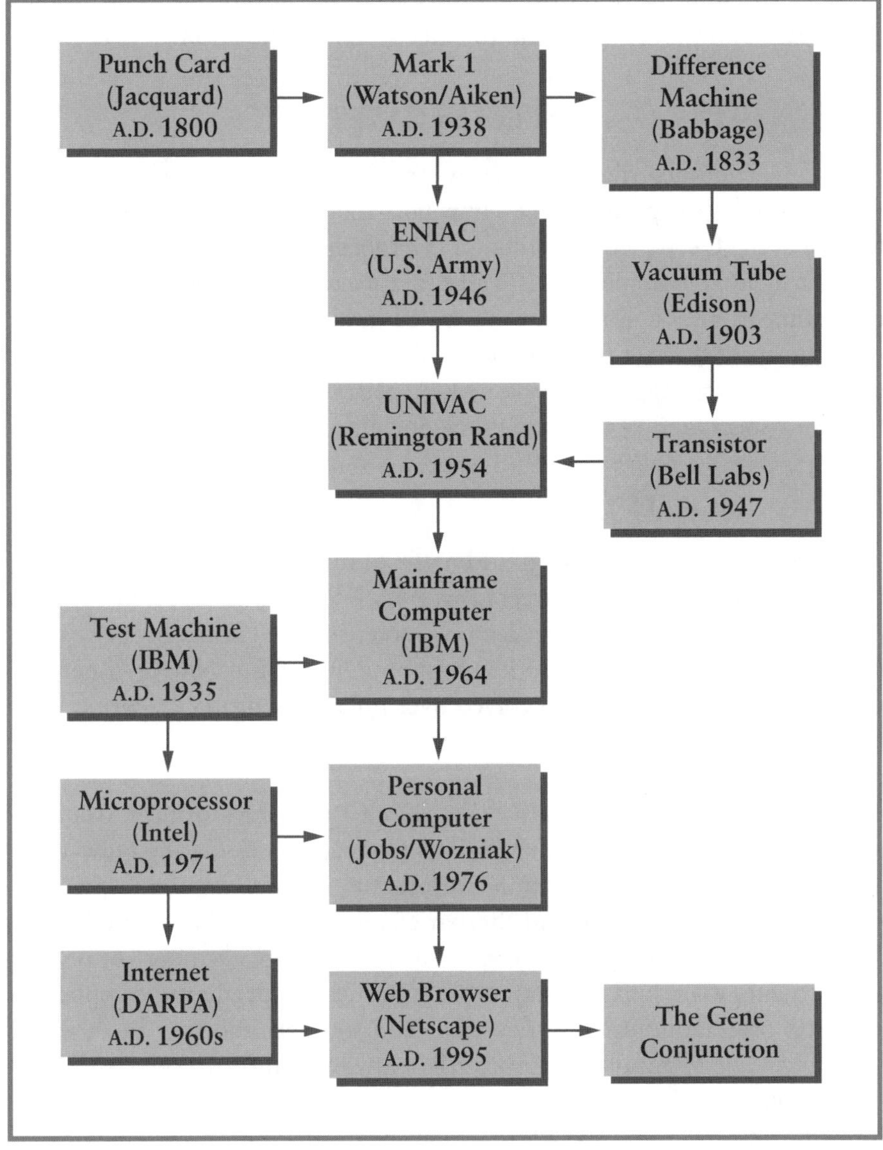

The Electronic Conjunction has the potential to produce great changes in lifestyles and therefore generate very differing kinds of interactions between trade, environment, and culture. The discussion of cases in the Electronic Conjunction is broken down by the types of impacts that occur and thus into their particular and general typologies. Thus, the first six cases focus on species cases and the second six on habitat cases. Figure 3.1 shows the lineage and the milestones in the Electronic Conjunction.

SPECIES CASES

This section describes six cases where the Electronic Conjunction provides examples of specific species impacts. The species focus reveals the influence of the Electronic Conjunction in exposing the dynamics of the social context today. These species cases all contain elements of trade, culture, and environment, although they are combined in different ways. The reporting of each case follows a four-part format that focuses on the social context and its elements: 1) the Environment Aspect, 2) the Trade Aspect, 3) the Culture Aspect, and 4) the Case in the Social Context.

FUR AND MORALS[19]

European countries banned the import of fur from animals caught in leg traps. The import ban is directed at North America, especially Native Americans in Canada, who use leg traps to ensnare a variety of fur-bearing mammals. These animals are key components of the Native American subsistence strategy that has evolved over millennia, probably dating back to the Tool Conjunction.

THE ENVIRONMENT ASPECT In March 1991, the European Community (EC) proposed a ban on fur imports from countries that had unacceptable humanitarian standards for harvesting fur. The move was a response to popular sentiment decrying the "barbaric" means for catching wild animals for their furs. The regulation prohibited the commercial import of beaver, otter, coyote, wolf, lynx, bobcat, sable, and raccoon products. It applied to products originating in countries where: 1) trappers continued to use the leghold trap or 2) trapping methods fell below humanitarian standards. The regulation covered both whole fur skins and products that included parts of fur skins. In June 1991, five more species were added to the original list.[20]

Environmental groups argued that animals caught in leg traps needlessly suffered and they found support from celebrities such as Brigitte Bardot. There were reports that before hunters came to check their traps, many animals starved to death or gnawed off their own limbs in order to escape. Numerous other animals were also snared in the traps and needlessly died. "Anti-fur" movements around the world have hurt sales in the fur industry. The boycott of products associated with baby seals (who are killed for their

TABLE 3.1 U.S. Fur Skin Exports, 1989–92 (Millions of U.S. Dollars)

	1989	1990	1991	1992
EC	25.4	16.9	24.0	21.5
EC (%)	20.7	18.1	25.9	24.9
All	122.7	93.4	92.5	86.3

Source: Data made available by the Office of the U.S. Trade Representative, Washington, D.C.

skins) illustrates the economic power of consumers. In 1984, several private groups organized a boycott of Canadian fish products (which seals eat) in American and British markets, inflicting millions of dollars in economic losses.

THE TRADE ASPECT The threat of an EC fur ban plan was continued in the creation of the European Union (EU), although the ban's implementation has been continuously delayed. The regulation applied to EU members, as well as importers, but there is virtually no leg trapping in Europe largely because so few suitable animals exist in the wild. EU-based pelt farm owners also supported the resolution, in part, because of recession and, in part, due to cheap imports from Russia (often made from contraband furs). In 1996, importers again received derogations from the ban (see Table 3.1)

An implemented ban could result in considerable trade impacts. The United States, for example, exported $86.3 million in fur skins in 1992, with about one-quarter ($21.5 million) going to Europe. The largest importers were Germany ($6.4 million), Greece ($5.9 million), Spain ($2.8 million), Italy ($2.3 million), and France ($1.7 million).[21] These data do not break out sales of trapped versus farmed fur products. Herein lies a significant administrative problem. For the ban to be successful, officials would need to create some kind of eco-label certification for humane trapping practices.

The sheer volume of furs traded each year is staggering. Most U.S. fur skin exports are put into a "basket" category and this alone accounted for 1.8 million pelts in 1992—one half million to Europe alone. Easily the largest single U.S. fur skin export on a volume basis was muskrats (915,000), followed by nutria (259,000), beaver (157,000), and mink (55,000).[22] The products involved in the case fall under the following categories of the Harmonized Tariff Schedule or HTS (see Figure 3.2).[23]

FIGURE 3.2

**Products Covered
by the Fur Ban Prohibition**

1. Section VIII (raw hides and skins, leather, fur skins, and articles thereof; saddlery and harness; travel goods, handbags, and similar containers; articles of animal, other than silkworm gut)
2. Chapter 43 (fur skins and artificial fur and manufactures thereof) including:

   (a) Heading 4301 of the chapter which covers raw fur skins, other than hides and skins;

   (b) Heading 4302 which includes tanned or dressed furs (assembled or unassembled);

   (c) Heading 4303 which encompasses articles of apparel, clothing accessories, and other articles of fur skin.

Source: Data from U.S. Harmonized Tariff System, Office of the U.S. Trade Representative, Washington, D.C.

THE CULTURE ASPECT Native Americans in Canada and Greenland argue that their trapping methods draw from cultural practices dating back thousands of years. Native Americans believe their values hold the animals in far greater spiritual reverence than the European environmentalists sponsoring the fur ban. The leg trap is well suited for use in remote parts of Canada, the United States, and particularly Greenland. (Since Denmark actually administers Greenland and is an EU nation, this presents a further complication in the regulation.)

Native Americans counter that the ban would conflict with their traditional values and customs and deprives them of the means for earning a living. "The consumptive use of wild animals is not only critical as a source of cash income but also integral to subsistence economies and cultures."[24] Native Americans from the Cree, Ojibway, and Chippewa nations "accused politicians of destroying their culture and traditions, which are based on hunting mink, beaver and fox."[25] In fact, only about 5 percent of trappers from the tribes use leg-hold traps. Most use conifer traps that quickly kill the animals. Some tribes depend on export sales to Europe for economic survival. Of the 623 Native American communities in Canada, three-quarters of the fur from their traps are sold in Europe.

Chief Mercredi of the Cree nation believes that "if the ban goes ahead the EU will be responsible for cultural genocide."[26] The loss of income would surely lead to further disintegration and disconnect. The suicide rate among Native Americans in Canada is four times that of the general population and 70 percent of the adult population is unemployed. The Chief said the EU directive violates a 1966 international agreement guaranteeing people's livelihoods and a nineteenth-century agreement with Queen Victoria that honored their way of life. As Chief Mercredi observed: "I am often asked how humane our methods of killing are, and it seems by humane killing you mean killing quickly. I ask you if you know how quickly the chickens you eat have been killed, the cows, the lambs?" [27]

Native Americans argue that the ban impinges upon traditional customs and that Europeans practiced leg trap methods for thousands of years before this new moral outlook. Some Native American communities have responded to the ban by promoting fur products as a way of showing pride in native cultures. Product labels often read "Authentic Native Design," with the intent of inspiring "consumer pride about supporting traditional native lifestyles."[28]

Native Americans are not alone in their complaints about the ban proposal. Wildlife specialists believe leg trapping is the only practical means for game control in remote areas such as the Yukon.[29] As a practical matter, determining how the animal died merely by examining the pelt (or a fur coat) is an impossible task for EU import administrators.

THE CASE IN CONTEXT The EU regulation tackles a difficult cultural, ethical, and moral issue. But the morality only goes so far. The measure prohibits the use of animals for their fur when a leg trap has killed them, but says nothing about the ethics of harvesting animals for their furs. Europeans assume that animals killed on a pelt farm—probably many millions—are humanely treated but those caught by leg traps, and subsequently killed, are not. At least those caught in leg traps lived a life in the wild instead of in cages. Thus, the expression of humanity towards animals is in how people kill them rather than in how they treat them when they are alive. Perhaps the bottom line is that fur is certainly not necessary for warmth; many substitute products have long been available. Possessing a fur coat is still a sign of wealth and status more than anything, as it was in the earlier conjunctions.

The case is an ethical quagmire. Europeans have ethically "progressed," and renounced a practice they once held and even exported abroad. For the animals, the new ethic is progress with respect to the means, since they are dead in either case, but not to their ends. Morality here is a clear barrier to trade, but is it ethically defensible?

A new conjunction often results in conflict between the systems institutionalized during the last conjunction. Agricultural and industrial interests, for example, clashed across Europe and North America in the mid-nineteenth century with the onset of the Industrial Conjunction. This case illuminates a clash between the ethics in the Electronic Conjunction with the ethics in an earlier one, the Tool Conjunction. Native American lifestyles in many ways reflect the Tool Conjunction era. The Tool Conjunction, however, occurred many millennia ago. The case clearly shows that several conjunction contexts can exist at the same point in time.

BEAR WINE[30]

In the 1980s, there was an increase in bear poaching in North America originating from sources (and demands) in East Asia. The United States and Canada enacted legislation to deter the taking of bear parts for export, although the shooting of bear for private use is legal in many states and provinces of the two countries. China, in response to bear export bans in the United States and Canada, established a series of domestic bear farms for creating highly desired bear products. China is now the leading exporter of bear bile product. Some countries, however, ban the import of bear bile product. The new bans focus not on how the animals are killed, but how they are kept when alive.

THE ENVIRONMENT ASPECT Many consumers prize bear gallbladders for their medicinal properties. In countries such as South Korea, Japan, Taiwan, and China, bear gallbladders sell for astronomical prices and, because of their alleged medicinal properties, are often considered more valuable than gold. Bear parts have such value in Asia and are a significant reason that Asian bear populations have fallen at an alarming rate. The problem is so severe that some wildlife officials fear that bear populations in Asia may be extinct within a couple of decades.

Asian merchants came to North America in the 1980s to procure North American black bear gallbladders and bear paws, from such places as the Shenandoah Valley in Virginia or the Berkshire Mountains in Massachusetts. The gallbladders contained bile and paws were used as ingredients in soups or potions. Authorities warned that the poaching of the North American bear could lead to local extinctions. This fear led to the legislation prohibiting bear poaching in both the United States and Canada.

Enforcing the regulation was difficult. International trade in American black bear parts was largely unrestricted because eight states—New York, Virginia, West Virginia, Idaho, Wyoming, New Hampshire, Vermont, and Maine—allowed the sale and export of parts. Thus, it was difficult to determine legal from illegal products. Because it is impossible to tell an American black bear's gallbladder from that of a protected species, traders could claim organs originate from legally hunted animals. Canada has a similar problem. British Columbia and Manitoba banned the sale and possession of bear parts; in Quebec and Nova Scotia, both sale and possession are legal.

The 1992 annual Convention on International Trade in Endangered Species (CITES) meeting added bears to Appendix II, a category that permits regulated trade.[31] The listing effectively outlawed trade in all Asian bear species except the brown bear. The U.S. Fish and Wildlife Service (USFWS) actually opposed the CITES provision on the grounds that U.S. black bear populations were generally healthy, despite occasional poaching in some locales. The USFWS claimed the legislation would be too costly and that American black bears would be better protected by better cooperation between the states of the United States rather than by international treaty.[32]

Due to these preventative measures, supplies of bear parts fell but demand did not. In response, bear farms were built in China through joint ventures between private entrepreneurs and the government. Most of these bears originally come from the Yunan province in China, with about eight thousand currently in captivity. While bears are bred in farms, many are still caught in the wild. The farms were a great commercial success. China became a major exporter of bile and bile products and tourists from many countries visit the farms and purchase products.

It was precisely this success that has led the World Wide Fund for Nature (WWFN) and the International Fund for Animal Welfare (IFAW) to launch campaigns against the trade in bear gall bladders, claws, and paws. While farming is permissible under Annex II of CITES, the groups protest the horrid conditions under which the animals are kept and the threat of extinction that the capture of wild bears for farming purposes holds.

An IFAW visit to the Zhuhai bear farm in 1993 (located near Hong Kong in China) sparked the international movement against the bear farms. The visit revealed that the bears have tubes inserted into their stomachs several times a day in order to extract bile. The lives of these bears are much shorter than they would be in the wild and furthermore they live in constant pain. The bears live in cages so small that they must put their arms and legs outside of the cages. One IFAW official noted that "many of the bears . . .

appear sick with their faces covered in scabs . . . several of the larger animals have one paw missing."

A restaurant just outside the Zhuhai farm sells paws and soup; customers tour the farm to select the parts for their meal. In June 1993, IFAW launched a campaign to stop the farming practice, encouraging its 1.3 million members to write letters to China's embassies protesting the practice.

All five of Asia's bear species are so rare that breeding of captive animals has begun as a future source for the valued parts and bile. (All but two of the world's eight bear species are in danger of extinction.) The desire to kill the animal, however, is the same motivation to save it. In fact, officials from the World Wildlife Fund claim that the demand for bear parts is as severe as the demand for elephant ivory.

THE TRADE ASPECT Bear farms are a booming industry in China, with over eighty farms housing over eight thousand bears. The bile is a key ingredient in certain Chinese medicines and part of over eighty types of prescriptions that people believe can cure everything from athlete's foot to cancer.[33] Few have any documented medical value. The bile is taken directly, served with wine, mixed with Chinese herbs, or rubbed directly on the skin. These prescriptions are often sought in lieu of proven medical treatments. "The bile, liquid or dried, from gallbladders (especially those of grizzlies) is valued as a cure for everything from heart problems to piles. The paws go into a soup supposed to boost sexual vigor."[34]

The measure would ban the export of American black bear viscera to foreign countries and require the Secretary of the Interior to prepare and provide Congress with regular reports. The reports would describe the tracking of trade of body parts from American black bears and how to monitor illegal trade. An additional measure would ban the import of bear bile. Other countries have enacted similar legislation. Even the Hong Kong Agricultural and Fisheries Department restricted the trade in bear gallbladders and bile, but not on bear bile products.

Bear poaching is a trade problem in Canada because of the enormous trade profits. A bear gallbladder can be bought from Canadian hunters for less than C$100 (about US$73) and can bring C$6,000 in East Asia. A bowl of bear paw soup costs C$1,500 in Taiwanese and Korean restaurants. Poaching in Canada probably exceeds legal bear taking (twenty-two thousand annually) by perhaps a two-to-one ratio. A recent instance of bear part trafficking led to a fine of only $C10,000 in British Columbia.[35] Laundering of bear parts occurs throughout Canada, where laws on bears are less strict.

Bear bile has a worth in weight greater than gold or cocaine. Some in Canada compare the bear parts trade to the drug trade, with fewer risks.

THE CULTURE ASPECT I was on a research tour across northern China in August 1994, with a guide from an official Chinese travel agency and researchers from the United States, Korea, and Japan. On the tour from Beijing towards Vladivostok, Russia, our guide became lost and we stopped at a government office compound located outside the city of Jiang Li, China, to get maps and directions. Inside the compound the government travel agency also doubled as a bear farm. I saw approximately fifty bears in a concrete-lined outdoor pit. The smell was a powerful, musky odor and piles of feces lined the pit.

Besides the bears kept in the open pit, perhaps another 50 lived inside a building in solitary cages. There, they underwent milking (for their bile) and breeding. Cubs were raised in a nursery in another building to provide the next generation of input products.

Most bear farms are private business-Communist party ventures and very profitable. High demand and rising incomes have created outrageous prices and profits for the bear farms. The bile sells for $540 a spoonful or $150 a gram. The owners of the bear farm at Zhuhai (near Hong Kong in the South) grossed $402,000 in 1993.

The compound included a store, and outside sat an Amur tiger tethered to a stake like a goat. I could have petted the tiger, but declined. Inside the store, bear products were for sale. I bought a bottle of bear wine: "BDS" or *Bak Doo Soon* (Bear Gall Wine), written in Korean. This part of China has a sizeable Korean population, many of them refugees from the Korean War (and now refugees from the drought in North Korea). The Chinese government has allegedly not permitted them to return home to retain some political advantage over the Pyongyang regime.

The bottle of bear wine comes in a black box with yellow lettering and a friendly-looking bear. Product information is available in English, Korean, and Chinese. The product description has an English translation entitled "Introduction to Bear Gallbladder Wine" (see Figure 3.3).

What is interesting is the intent of the product's message, especially with respect to "retarding senility." The obvious target market is older people as they are more likely to believe in the healing powers of the bile and are more likely to be senile, or think they are. The alcohol content is far higher than that of most other wines (perhaps that is the healing secret!). Bear bile may have medicinal properties:

FIGURE 3.3

Introduction to Bear Gallbladder Wine

The Bear Gallbladder Wine is made from the gallbladders of half moon bears living in the China White Head Mountains, which is the International Nature Protection Area. Meticulously made with the modern scientific method, it is the latest super nutritious health wine.

The product is rich in nutrients, amino acids, vitamins and trace elements. It has the function of relieving fatigue, recovering vital energy and retarding senility.

If any cotton-like fungus precipitation appears, it will neither indicate the deterioration nor affect its efficacy. It is to be shaken before administration.

Ingredients: Fine-quality Wine, Bear Gallbladder Powder, Lycium chinese, White Sugar, etc. Alcohol contents: 38% (V/V)

Note: This information appears on the box containing bear wine, purchased by James R. Lee in northeast China in 1994. The maker of the product is the China White Head Mountain Industry Company, Ltd., Yanji, China.

Unlike rhinoceros horn, which [to Chinese] has a mythical reputation as an aphrodisiac, bears' gallbladders have proven medical value. They produce a substance called ursodeoxycholic acid, which is widely used in traditional Chinese medicine to treat intestinal, liver and cardiac-related diseases.[36]

Others are skeptical of these medical claims. Some experts believe the bile salts that produce the chemical vary widely and that the bear is an uncertain source for this chemical.

Bear farm operators and users of bear products claim the campaign against them derives from a kind of cultural narrowness. The condition of the bears compared to most "farmed" animals is far better and their lifetimes are certainly longer in relation to farmed animals in Western countries. The accusation of cruelty is thus said to be culturally one-sided.

What is the basis for deciding the proper kind of treatment given to "farmed" animals such as bears or cattle? Should animals of a higher biological order receive more "humane" treatment than those of lower intelligence? If the basis is intelligence, the pig ranks about the same as the bear and is much more anatomically similar to humans. Pot-bellied pigs are loved pets. Yet, pig protection efforts are rare.

One alternative has sought to artificially reproduce the chemical properties that make the bear bile attractive. Synthetic products do exist that contain properties similar to bear bile. While "the bile may contain some hormones . . . you do not need to kill wild animals to get that, they can be bought from a chemist."[37]

THE CASE IN CONTEXT How differing peoples view their environment is apparent in the bear case. North American and European children often have toy bears while Smokey the Bear is a cultural icon in the United States. In China, people eat bears and various other animals on a regular basis, no doubt partly due to the large population size and the limited amount of protein available. Thus, what people eat may reflect the type of human-environment interaction in their world and the cultures that are integral parts of that interaction. Nevertheless, reasonable people can espouse differing viewpoints on culinary outlooks that are realist or idealist in orientation, meaning that they can be exclusive or inclusive.

One explanation of the role of culture suggests a mixture of realist and idealist positions, and thus a world of contingent sovereignty. Following this view, sovereignty includes compromises across borders that include both realist and idealist outlooks.[38] Such compromises further suggest that countries do have some say in the environmental policies of other countries, especially their neighbors and thus in the culture-environment interaction. If contingent sovereignty does exist, does that mean people should accept the idea of needs of globalization over the needs of the nation-state? The answer is in part yes and part no. The difficult task is determining how to meet halfway between the global and nation-state systems. Determining this point may serve as the greatest conflict that results from the globalization tendencies in the Electronic Conjunction.

IVORY WARS[39]

The decline of the world's elephant populations in the twentieth century mirrors the much earlier demise of the woolly mammoth in the Tool Conjunction. Then, the source reason was the demand for protein; now, it is the demand for ivory. Modern ivory demand has decimated most of the world's elephant populations, especially those in Africa. Elephant protection, however, has succeeded in some places and populations have recovered. This success has resulted in a resumption of elephant ivory trade and the legalized killing of elephants.

THE ENVIRONMENT ASPECT Humans have hunted elephants for centuries but the killing of elephants on a massive scale began in the 1970s. Organized gangs of poachers used automatic weapons, profited from government corruption, and laundered tons of elephant tusks for export through several African countries. Since 1989, the CITES agreement prohibits international trade in elephant parts and products.

Both Asian (*Elephant maximus*) and African (*Loxodonta africana*) elephants are listed in Appendix I of CITES, meaning that trade in the animal or its parts is illegal. Male Asian elephants have small tusks but females are tuskless. Small elephant herds live in Nepal, India, Sri Lanka, Thailand and Sumatra (in Indonesia) that number between 29,000 and 44,000.[40] Asian elephants are severely over-hunted, forcing hunters to seek ivory from African elephants.

Between 1979 and 1989, the African elephant population fell by about 50 percent, from 1.3 million to 750,000. By 1992, the population fell to 600,000, and at this rate the African elephant would be nearly extinct by 2025. The Central African rain forests contain 45 percent of remaining elephants, with 31 percent in Southern Africa, 21 percent in Eastern Africa, and only 3 percent in West Africa.

Elephants reproduce slowly. Although their potential life span is approximately sixty years, fewer than 20 percent now live to the age of thirty. The elephant gestation period is twenty-two months and they have a high sensitivity to habitat and climate changes. Poaching not only affects population densities, it also influences the social structure of herds and their demographic and genetic makeup. Since the elephants with the largest tusks, the oldest ones, are the first taken, poaching is particularly destructive to the elephant social system.

Elephant herds are matriarchal, with the males forming small groups or wandering as loners until females come into estrus, which only occurs at very specific times of the year. With the decline in the male population, breeding opportunities are often missed, further slowing reproductive rates. Female elephant fertility occurs between the ages of twenty-five and forty-five and male elephants over thirty years of age are preferred breeding candidates.

The habitat home of African elephants fell by 20 percent over the 1980s. The human population explosion in many African countries resulted in greater competition for food, water, and land with the elephants. In Rwanda, for example, a country equivalent in size to the U.S. state of Maryland, the elephant population is expected to decline over the next twenty years, while the human population of 7.5 million is estimated to more than double, even with the recent civil strife and genocide.

Due to growing human settlement, the loss of forest cover in Central and West Africa affects not only the elephant but also entire ecosystems. Similar to mammoths, elephants act as seed dispersers and as vehicles for clearing vegetation, thereby allowing smaller flora access to sunlight in the dense rain forests. This, in turn, influences faunal distributions. "The extermination of the African elephant will reduce biological diversity and increase extinction rates [of other species] over much of Africa. This has enormous implications economically, aesthetically, and symbolically, as well as ecologically."[41]

Even with protection under CITES, elephant ivory trade continued. One reason is that only sixteen of the thirty-five African parties complied with the ruling. Illegal ivory traders simply altered their trade routes in order to get around trade restrictions and used loopholes in the regulations for trade opportunities. For example, raw ivory was carved only enough to meet the minimum requirements for reclassification as "worked ivory," before being exported to the Far East.[42]

THE TRADE ASPECT Ivory trade exploded in the 1970s due to the availability of automatic weapons and widespread government corruption in many African exporting countries.[43] In the 1960s, raw ivory prices were relatively stable with prices fluctuating between $3 and $10 per pound. In 1975, this figure jumped to $50 per pound, in part, because ivory was perceived as a valuable hedge against rising inflation. By 1987, the ivory price jumped to $125 per pound.[44] New manufacturing techniques, which enabled the mass production of ivory carvings, were required to meet the rising ivory demands in East Asian countries driven by rapidly rising incomes.

Hong Kong was the largest consumer of raw ivory from 1979 to 1987, according to CITES data. Japan was the second largest consumer (whose market share dropped sharply during the period), followed by Taiwan (whose consumption rose). For both Hong Kong and Taiwan, there was probably significant trans-shipment of products to China. The EC was also a large consumer, but dropped to a 4 percent share shortly after the ban. At the same time, the United States market share rose from 1 to 6 percent. Before the 1989 CITES ban, illegal and legal ivory exports amounted to 770 metric tons, or 75,000 elephants per year (see Table 3.2).[45]

TABLE 3.2 **World Raw Ivory Consumption (percent)**

	1979	1981	1983	1985	1987
Hong Kong	37	48	40	22	36
Japan	28	32	20	24	22
EC	18	5	6	7	4
U.S.	1	1	2	4	6
Taiwan	2	2	3	4	20
Macao	0	0	2	15	2
China	1	1	2	1	10
India	2	2	2	4	na
Other	11	9	23	19	0
Total	100	100	100	100	100

Source: Data from the Ivory Trade Review Group (ITRG) and the Convention on the International Trade in Endangered Species (CITES). The CITES Secretariat is located at the International Environment House, 15, chemin des Anemones, CH-1219 Chatelaine-Geneva, Switzerland.
na = not available

By 1985, reports of rising elephant poaching led the CITES Conference Parties to establish the Ivory Trade Reporting Group (ITRG). The ITRG is responsible for establishing and ensuring enforcement of ivory trade quotas in exporting countries. According to the quota system, each tusk was to be marked and coded by country of origin and the information entered into an international database that monitored the trade, alerted authorities when discrepancies arose, and collected information on herd numbers.

The ivory quota system went into effect in January 1986. Immediately prior to its implementation, there was a general amnesty on illegal ivory stockpiles. The quota prompted a massive price rise, coincident with a large increase in supply as illegal stockpiles were released onto the market. (The amnesty idea was not repeated when the ban was imposed in 1989.)

Ivory trade grew rapidly up to the point of the ban, with demand far

TABLE 3.3 **World Ivory Trade, 1950–80 (tons)**

Year	Tons of Ivory	Percent Change
1950	204	—
1960	412	+102
1970	564	+ 37
1980	966	+ 71

Source: Data from the Ivory Trade Review Group (ITRG) and the Convention on the International Trade in Endangered Species (CITES). The CITES Secretariat is located at the International Environment House, 15, chemin des Anemones, CH-1219 Chatelaine-Geneva, Switzerland.

out-stripping supply. Over the past forty years, the magnitude of the ivory trade has increased by 400 percent, even as elephant populations were rapidly declining. Trade rose each decade: 204 tons in 1950; 412 tons in 1960; 564 tons in 1970; and 966 tons in 1980 (see Table 3.3).[46] In the ten years preceding the ivory trade ban, the estimated market value of Asian raw ivory imports was approximately $55 million per year.

The international trade of ivory was relatively stable between 1979 and 1989 and the size of the tusks decreased significantly. In 1979, the mean weight of traded tusks was 9.8 kilograms, but by 1987 the average tusk weight was only 4.7 kilograms. This meant that those animals with large tusks—the elders of the herds—were very rare and that poachers were killing younger animals as well as females with smaller tusks. Because tusk size is decreasing, it is likely that more elephants may be killed in the future in order to obtain the same amount of ivory as in the past.

The ITRG singled out Burundi and South Africa as the two countries most involved in the illegal ivory trade. In Burundi, between 1976 and 1986, tusks from an estimated 200,000 elephants were traded. Sanctions were not a deterrent to trade. In one example, the fine for a Burundi truck owner was only the equivalent of $3,000 for transporting two tons of illegal ivory. In 1988, only one live elephant survived in this country, yet Burundian traffickers exported approximately one-third of the world's annual total of raw ivory. After a 1987 coup d'état, the new Burundi government promised to halt illicit ivory trading but did not.

At the October 1989 CITES meeting in Lausanne, Switzerland, there was considerable debate on whether to place the African elephant onto Appendix I. Many argued that if trade in elephant products were not banned altogether, the animals would face extinction. In proposing the trade ban, Kenya, Gambia, and Somalia argued that upwards of 100,000 elephants in Africa died each year and Kenya and Uganda "lost 85 percent of their native elephant population between 1973 and 1987."[47] In the Sudan, there was a 30 percent annual decline in populations and in Tanzania, the decline was 16 percent per year. The Southern African countries of Zimbabwe, Botswana, and South Africa, however, upheld the need to maintain the legal trade in elephant products. Legal trade would enable countries with flourishing elephant populations to manage them sustainably and use funds from the sale of ivory and other products to pay for management.

Enforcement is a problem even in developed countries. While the Lacey Act and Endangered Species Act in the United States prohibited ivory imports, it is very difficult to determine the difference between legal and illegal wildlife trade. During "1984, the United States imported approximately 7.5 tons of raw ivory, three-quarters of which reportedly came from Zaire, at a time when all commercial ivory exports from that country were banned."[48] Over 90 percent of ivory seized by U.S. customs officials was, in fact, mammoth ivory, not elephant ivory (see Chapter 2 on ancient mammoth ivory trade).

The elephant ivory ban was re-evaluated at the 1992 CITES meeting in Kyoto, Japan. Again, several Southern African countries proposed a downgrading of the African elephant to Appendix 2 status that permits regulated trade. They supported the formation of a cartel, with a monopoly over the export and sale of ivory, with only one buyer: Japan. Supporters maintained that new scientific methods could trace the origins of ivory to determine country of origin. Other African countries, particularly those in East Africa, argued that tourism, rather than trade would bring in the necessary funds for conservation. Strong international opposition prompted the four Southern African nations to withdraw their proposal. At the Kyoto meeting of CITES in March 1992, one attendee added this ironic note:

> As the ivory debate raged in Kyoto, 27 smuggled elephant tusks were discovered in a container of furniture at Kobe, less than 80 kilometers away. The container, from South Africa, provided ample evidence that the illicit trade in ivory continues in order to fuel the demands of ivory carvers in Japan and elsewhere.[49]

With the implementation of the ban, the ivory market collapsed, although some trading continued from stockpiles. In March 1993, the black market price for ivory stood at only $5 per pound. Ivory products continue to pour into China and Taiwan. In 1995, the United States imposed and, in the next year, lifted sanctions ($25.1 million per year) on Taiwan for continued trade in tiger and rhinoceros products—a unique action at the time. (Taiwan also trades in elephant ivory.)

THE CULTURE ASPECT Many Africans argue that the conservation methods of today descend from measures imposed on African communities by their colonial rulers who took no notice of the negative impact on local communities and environments. Through dislocation and exploitation, local communities had, in fact, greater incentive (and need) to poach the animals than to protect them under this system. With a loss of ownership of traditional lands, as renters, people had less reason to save species and habitats.

Perhaps the answer lies in the past. Mammoth tusks are found today in large quantities. This ivory is *not* fossilized. Rather, it is buried tusk that remains in a roughly intact form. Mammoth ivory is on average about five times as large per tusk as that of the modern elephant. Mammoth "remains survive in sufficient quantity in certain regions for their tusks to have become an article of commerce."[50] Trade in mammoth ivory today dwarfs trade in elephant ivory by a factor of ten to one.

Trade in mammoth ivory peaked in the eighteenth century, especially exports from Russia to Europe and China.[51] In some periods, this trade was considerable and continued until 1913, with the sale of 57,600 pounds of Siberian ivory at Yakutsk. Thus, ivory was not only the first traded product, but, since it is still an item of commerce, is also the longest traded product in human history.[52]

Some experts suggest that the mammoth ivory can be part of a solution to protecting today's elephant. The idea is that ivory demand, the reason for elephant killing, can be met by tapping into the existing but unfound mammoth ivory. "There may be 10 million mammoth carcasses lying in the deep freeze of the Siberian permafrost."[53] On the other hand, this also leads to a substitution problem. It is possible to distinguish between the two. Mammoth ivory is not as white as elephant ivory and somewhat coarser. Japanese craftsmen, who made ivory keys and personal stamps from ivory, complain about the poorer mammoth ivory quality.

In some aspects the elephant case resembles the bear case. It shows how a culture's reliance on one animal product can lead to the depletion and ultimate endangering of a species. In both cases, the animals' legend compels a cultural demand for it. It is true that a major demand for bear and elephant products is for use as an aphrodisiac. This element adds a strange twist, especially since the large majority of these particular consumers are men. Ironically, a patriarchical human society threatens the matriarchal society of the elephant.

THE CASE IN CONTEXT Due to the breakup of the Soviet Union and harsher economic conditions, mammoth tusks are once again being exported in large quantities. Some promote this trade, which is legal, to protect elephant populations. In 1990, U.S. customs inspectors seized several thousand ivory objects with about 95 percent determined to be mammoth ivory.[54] Detecting mammoth from elephant ivory is now a matter of concern. One researcher reports that a condition called vivianite discoloration occurs in mammoth but not elephant ivory (it is found in blemishes). The discoloration shows up under ultra-violet light, perhaps providing a cost effective means for ivory discrimination.

At the 1997 CITES meeting in Zimbabwe, the sale of ivory was once again permitted after having been banned for a decade. Three South African countries (Zimbabwe, Botswana, and Namibia) now can legally sell ivory abroad, with Japan as the sole buyer. With the recovery of elephant populations in these countries, a more market-based approach has been sought.

The move signals the transition from one period to another within a conjunction. Perhaps, to use an earlier term, this may generally demarcate a mini-conjunction. The initial approach to environmental solutions began with command-and-control mechanisms. Now, however, these solutions are, more frequently, taking on market-based formulations, evident in, for example, trading air pollution credits. In earlier periods, the market ruled first, and sometimes regulations were later applied. Markets have, in the past, often been a threat to the environment; perhaps they can also serve as a solution.

TURTLES AND TRADITION[55]

The Hawksbill turtle case highlights how trade can harm the environment through the transmission of cultural demands from one part of the world to another. With a global system capable of high technologies, these demands can have extraordinary and far-reaching consequences. A global system will tend to magnify these demands and focus impacts.

THE ENVIRONMENT ASPECT The Hawksbill turtle is in danger of extinction. In April 1990, five environmental groups sued the U.S. government because it failed to enforce the Pelly Amendment. The Pelly Amendment protects many marine species, including the sea turtle. Japanese imports of Hawksbill turtle shell posed a threat to the animal's existence. "Much of the Hawksbill hunting [was] the direct result of merchants seeking shells in poor countries for shipment to Japan."[56] At today's rate of decline the Hawksbill turtle would be extinct in the early twenty-first century.

Six species of turtle are in danger of extinction: Kemp's Ridley, Loggerhead, Green Turtle, Hawksbill, Leatherneck, and Olive Ridley. The most important human-induced source of mortality is incidental capture in shrimp trawls. About 5,000 to 50,000 loggerheads and 500 to 5,000 Kemp's Ridleys die because of shrimping each year.[57] There are also substantial turtle deaths due to dredging and collisions with boats, which claim an estimated 50 to 500 loggerheads and 5 to 50 Kemp's Ridleys each year.

The demand for eggs, and their powers, also threaten the sea turtle. In Mexico, where turtle eggs are believed to have general and specific health benefits, poachers recently stole thousands of eggs. The military guardians of the eggs left their beach posts to fight insurgents in the Mexican state of Guerrero. The absence of the military allowed opportunistic and catastrophic poaching of turtle eggs. The poachers were caught but the eggs were ruined.

THE TRADE ASPECT Of the 110 signatories to the 1973 CITES treaty, 107 protect the Hawksbill turtle.[58] CITES allows countries to claim exemptions to the ban, as Japan did when it signed in 1981 regarding sea turtles. Between 1981 and 1990, Japan imported over 234,000 Hawksbill shells from more than twenty countries.[59] This amounts to an average of thirty metric tons per year and "Japan has been importing about twenty tons a year of such [Hawksbill] turtles in order to convert their shells into jewelry, combs and eyeglass frames."[60]

Legislative action to counter these trends was a long process. The 1978 Pelly Amendment to the 1967 Fishermen's Protective Act allows the President to use trade sanctions against countries trading in endangered species or when they are undermining the effectiveness of any international program to protect those species. The amendment requires the Departments of Commerce and Interior to monitor and investigate the activities of foreign nationals who violate international agreements.[61]

By January 1991, the U.S. Interior and Commerce Departments found that Japanese shell imports were endangering the survival of the Hawksbill turtle. The United States threatened to impose sanctions on imports of Japan's wildlife products, such as pearls and ornamental carp (using import bans or increased tariffs), a $200 million dollar a year market.[62] On March 20, 1991, the two Departments "certified" the allegations giving the President sixty days to determine whether or not to impose trade sanctions. The United States threatened sanctions on Japanese fish imports and other wildlife products unless Japan stopped importing turtle shells. Under intense U.S. pressure Japan complied.

On May 17, 1991, Japan agreed to phase out turtle trade over a three-year period.[63] This satisfied U.S. government requirements sufficiently to remove the trade sanction threat, but most of the environmental groups, as well as the U.S. government, wanted the trade stopped by the end of 1992.[64] On June 19, 1991, Japan announced that it would ban imports of sea turtle shells by the end of 1992 and would import no more than 7.5 metric tons of shells between August 1, 1991, and December 31, 1992. After that date, Japan prohibited imports of the Hawksbill turtle and the Olive Ridley turtle, another endangered sea turtle.

THE CULTURE ASPECT Sea turtles were widely used by humans in ancient times for food, ornaments, and leather and they continue to be used for these purposes in many modern societies. The scale of demand now threatens the sea turtle. In response to their decline, the United States prohibited the intentional harvesting of sea turtles in U.S. waters. Harvest of sea turtles and their eggs continues to occur throughout the Caribbean region, including Puerto Rico. People in the Persian Gulf area, especially in Qatar, believe that eating the turtle egg enhances health and fertility.

The *bekko* industry, largely based in Nagasaki, is a unique craft industry that is historically tied to Japanese culture. The industry uses sea turtle shells to make eyeglass frames, ornamental combs, and jewelry. These artifacts are not only a part of dress, but also serve as cultural symbols for Japanese who wear them. Workers in the industry generally followed traditions passed down from generation to generation. Over 2,000 people, including 660 craftsmen, worked in the industry in the 1980s with output worth approximately $125 million dollars per year. However, the *bekko* industry workforce was old and the number of workers required for production declining. The *bekko* culture is dying and environmental protection is hastening its demise.

The *bekko* industry now largely uses plastic products that closely resemble the shell of the Hawksbill and the last traditional generation of craftsmen has largely vanished. However, some customers still insist on combs and other items made from the real shell of the turtle and a black market persists.

The Hawksbill turtle case is fundamentally a disagreement over whether

Japan can continue to use an endangered species in the production of a traditional craft. The majority of sea turtles used for this craft are caught in the Pacific and Indian Oceans, the Persian Gulf, and the Caribbean Sea. Most Japanese imports were reportedly coming from Cuba and illegal smuggling probably entered through Hong Kong. Cuba proposed to downgrade populations of Hawksbill turtles from Appendix I to Appendix II at the 1997 CITES meeting in Harare, Zimbabwe. The proposal was rejected.

THE CASE IN CONTEXT The case illustrates the persistence of culture in creating demand for a far-off product. Here, a traditional industry is in conflict with the mores of a modern society. As with the fur case, popular perception held the need to acquire the "real thing," which meant that substitutes were not always adequate, leading to a black market.

The case poses a variety of legal problems. Cuban fishermen catch the turtles in international waters of the Caribbean Sea and export them to Japan. The United States government objects to this practice, even though it has no diplomatic relations with Cuba and does not export turtle shells. It is apparent that the problem cannot be solved at one single place in the world, but in many places at once and in tandem. Solving the problem means altering trade, environmental, and cultural practices in many parts of the world in some harmonious manner. Japanese, Cubans, and Americans all need education on the issue, but each requires differing types of education.

This case shows the powerful impact of culture. A single cultural artifact of minor value to Japanese was, in part, responsible for the near-extinction of the Hawksbill sea turtle. The case pitted jobs against culture against environment. The demand was culturally driven, but the supply was forced by economic gain through trade. These shells had little value in Cuba, but great value in Japan. This disparity in perceived economic value led to catastrophe for the Hawksbill turtle.

The turtle has crept into trade dispute settlements in a number of venues. The United States imposed import bans on shrimp caught from ships that lacked turtle-excluder devices. This measure was first aimed at the Western Hemisphere, especially Mexico. In 1997, the Unites States extended these rules to the Eastern Hemisphere and three Asian countries challenged the regulations in the WTO. The United States lost the case and the appeal. The dispute settlement panel ruled that environmental protection was legitimate but that the law applied in a discriminatory manner. This was the first instance where a CITES-protected creature was part of a WTO dispute.

SHARKFIN SOUP[65]

Eating shark is fulfilling because sharks eat people. Shark's fin soup has long been a prized Chinese delicacy because it contains "energizing" properties, although there is little scientific evidence to support this claim. The current demand and desire for sharkfin soup is enormous. The taking of sharks for soup has produced at least two environmental problems.

First, because of the harvesting of so many sharks there are now significantly depleted shark populations in many parts of the world. North America remains one of the few places left with abundant sharks, in part, because these peoples generally do not eat shark (although shark meat eating is now becoming more common there). The U.S. government actually promoted the fishing of shark because of its under-utilization.

Boats from many nations fish the Caribbean and the Pacific Ocean for shark and many fins are exported to Asia. Most shark fin exports go to Taiwan, Japan, China, Singapore, and Korea. Some sharks caught off North America are brought back to Hong Kong, prepared in canned soup, and exported from Asia back to the west coast of the United States and Canada, where sizeable Asian populations reside.

The second problem is the manner in which shark fins are taken. Ordinarily, the top and two side fins are removed and the shark is dumped overboard. Left powerless to move through the water, the shark sinks to the ocean floor and suffocates, because it needs water passing through its gills to breathe. Not only is this practice, of course, inhumane, there have also been rumors that finned sharks have floated to the shore and attacked swimmers. Such attacks or rumors of attacks do reduce tourism, a kind of "Jaws" effect, and thus do have some economic weight.

During the 400 million years that sharks have inhabited the world's oceans they have evolved into apex predators—residing at the top of the food chain among marine life. However, they are not able to withstand predation by humans. Because of demand for shark meat and for fins used in sharkfin soup, sharks have come under heavy pressure from harvesters in North American waters. In response, the U.S. National Marine Fisheries Service (NMFS) has instituted quotas on shark taking in the U.S. Exclusive Economic Zone (EEZ).

Shark meat can be expensive, but the fins have the greatest economic value. The fins contain noodle-like cartilaginous tissues used by Chinese chefs to thicken and flavor soup. Long strands are prized and unusually large fins can be worth more than the average $10 per pound.[66] Demand for shark fins has risen dramatically in the People's Republic of China (PRC). Economic liberalization in the PRC, which lifted restrictions against eating sharkfin soup, combined with increasing wealth, fueled the increasing demand for sharks.[67] Hong Kong alone consumes an estimated three million kilograms of shark fins in a year.[68]

The sandbar, bull, hammerhead, blacktip, porbeagle, mako, thresher, and blue sharks are sought after for soup. Only the lower caudal lobe from mako and thresher sharks is considered acceptable for use in soups. Around 100 to 200 million sharks per year die worldwide in the fishing/finning process, earning $240 million per year for suppliers. While the NMFS admits that no one truly knows how many sharks there are, estimates from test sample areas and mathematical models suggest that the following species are already near extinction: mako, elephant fish, lemon sharks, hammerheads, and great whites.

Increased shark fishing is of particular concern due to their slow rate of reproduction. As with the elephant, shark reproductive strategy is long-term in nature and produces few adults and most sharks need twelve to fifteen years to reach sexual maturity. Gestation periods can be as long as twenty-two months. The result is that, with the depletion of the shark population, it will take decades to regenerate the population.

In addition to their culinary appeal, sharks have both medical and ecological benefits to humans. For example, there is transplanting of shark corneas into human eyes (Costa Rica has become a center for this), shark cartilage is used to create artificial skin for burn victims, and shark-liver oil is used in hemorrhoidal medications. Sharks rarely develop cancer and perhaps the animal contains a possible cure for the disease.

Sharks help balance out the ecology in oceans by removing sick and diseased animals. Without sharks, some prey—for example, stingrays favored by hammerheads—would boom. In Australia, ecologists believe that increased shark fishing may have caused the spiny lobster industry in some areas to collapse since small octopi, whose numbers are no longer kept down by sharks, are preying on the lobsters.

THE TRADE ASPECT Since 1986, demand for shark products has grown as the result of a number of factors. One reason is that tuna and swordfish supplies fell, so fishermen turned increasingly to sharks and other alternative fish. For example, in Florida the shark catch doubled between 1986 and 1987. Demand for shark meat soon became popular and increasing demand drove up prices.

The United States outlawed live fining and protected thirty-nine species of shark in 1989. The NMFS produced a fisheries management plan for Atlantic and Gulf waters to protect the shark population. The plan reduced the commercial and recreational fishing through licensing requirements or quotas and banned shark finning and dumping.

When NMFS first produced a draft of its fisheries management plan in 1989, the fishing industry was outraged, complaining that in the mid-1980s the NMFS encouraged fishermen to enter the shark fishing business by conducting seminars on sharks (to offset declines in other fish). The government called sharks an "underutilized resource" and even gave them names of Chinese business people who bought fins. Since then, shark stocks have become endangered.

In addition to the efforts of the United States, international cooperation on shark preservation is emerging. A 1992 shark preservation conference held in Sydney recommended a ban on finning and established quotas and fishery management plans. Australia banned trade in great white shark parts and restricted fishing for several other shark species. South Africa declared the great white shark a protected species and imposed a ban on fishing and selling its jaws and other parts.

THE CULTURE ASPECT Many cultures regard sharks as a symbol of power. In China, they appear in soups and in the United States they appear as monsters in movies. The power of culture in this case combines with the power of economics to produce a deadly threat to shark survival. The Chinese cultural view of the shark has remained relatively the same over time: eat a powerful animal and you become one. To the American, the economics is another matter entirely: the decline of other fish has made the shark more preferable (and profitable).

THE CASE IN CONTEXT Trade serves to satisfy both the cultural and economic demands for shark. But trade sometimes originates in nonsovereign areas because sharks are often caught in international waters. Thus, shark taking is often regulated by collective rather than sovereign controls. In these instances, protection is the result of group recognition rather than on a single country's recognition of shark value. Such collective decisions however often result in choosing the "least common denominator," or practices that remain exploitative until they are near collapse.

Sharks have been supreme predators for perhaps sixty-three million years. Human beings have been supreme predators for at most fifty thousand years, since the dawn of the Tool Conjunction. This change in the predator order on the planet is a threat to sharks. The rapid ascension of humans on the predation scale rapidly tipped the evolutionary scale. The killing of sharks has been a problem only within the last decade of those sixty-three million years. The surfacing of sharks as a commodity has been a disaster for them.

BATS: THE TURKEY OF GUAM

Bats are one of the most feared animals on the planet. They are not great predators such as sharks, but the thought of their purported means of sustenance—blood sucking—causes a visceral reaction in most people. The people of Guam, however, do not fear bats. In fact, they honor bats and love to eat them. Human desire to eat bats has become an environmental problem because the demand has led to a decline in bat populations and a rise in the insects they eat.[69]

THE ENVIRONMENT ASPECT Guam sits at the south end of the Marianas archipelago, which was acquired by the United States at the end of World War II. Guam's habitat varies from swordgrass in the south to a "typhoon forest" in the north. In 1990, there were 133,000 people on the island with approximately 45 percent Chamorros, 25 percent Caucasian, 20 percent Filipino, and 10 percent "other." The Chamorros migrated to Guam around 3000 B.C. and built a subsistence strategy based on agriculture and fishing. The Chamorros consider bat a delicacy, which is eaten on special occasions such as weddings or festivals. Though the bat is now scarce, and legally protected, it is still a popular food in Guam.[70] The Marianas Fruit Bats are endemic to Guam.

Because of Guam's isolated location the bat serves a number of purposes in the island's environment that elsewhere are held by other species, especially birds and bees. The bats are insect predators, pollinators, and seed spreaders, key ingredients in Guam's eco-system. Bats themselves are vulnerable because of their slow rate of reproduction (only one pup per year), similar to the elephant and the shark.[71]

Human migrations can spread specific demands beyond the geographic confines of Guam. Many Chamorros live in the United States, and often relatives send them a reminder of home, such as bat treats. Demand has significantly reduced Guam's bat population and now Guam imports large quantities of bats from other countries in the western Pacific region. Cooks boil whole bats (even the fur) and sell them in markets or on roadside stands at the cost of $40 to $50.[72] Some Guamanians consider the bat a sort of national symbol for the island, though it is more comparable to the turkey than the bald eagle in the United States.

THE TRADE ASPECT Hunting and trapping has reduced Guam's bat numbers to only about five hundred. In fact, Guam now imports bats to meet consumer demand. From 1975 through 1988, Guam imported over 200,000 bats.[73] The year 1989 was the peak, with 17,000 bat imports that mostly came from the Philippines.[74] From 1980 to 1986, up to 18,000 bats were shipped to Guam from Western Samoa.

The plight of the bat, and other wildlife on Guam, is also under threat from the brown tree snake, brought to the island before and during World War II. The snake, which grows to around six feet in length, preys on bats and birds, animals that never before knew the snake. There are plans to introduce a predator (such as the mongoose) to reduce the snake presence but this obviously carries its own danger in producing a cascading series of ecological disasters.

Protection of bats on Guam is difficult in part because of lax enforcement. In 1989, two of the species of bats on Guam were added to the CITES protected list. However, Palau, a neighboring island under U.S. jurisdiction, is now the biggest source of Guam's imported bats (the trade in bats with Palau between 1975 and 1988 reached more than 99,000).[75] The United States Department of the Interior, since Guam is a U.S. territory, considers trade between the two islands to be a domestic matter since it also administers Palau. CITES does not apply to domestic trade, but such commerce could fall under U.S. legislation known as the Lacey Act (which also protects sea turtles).

To protect the bats, and some birds, the U.S. Fish and Wildlife Service annexed land on Guam to create wildlife preserves on the north and south sides of the island. This move met with resistance from the island government, as well as investors who own part of the land and want to develop a private refuge. Moreover, the redesignation of this land could affect military plans to use Guam as an alternative to bases in Okinawa and the Philippines.[76] The U.S. Fish and Wildlife Service would like to place a ranger on the island for enforcement purposes but funding prevents it.

THE CULTURE ASPECT Cultural forces drive the consumption of the bats. A survey of Chamorros on Guam found that 82 percent felt the fruit bat had unspecified "cultural" value.[77] There appears to be a strong relationship between the act of eating the fruit bat and the cultural significance of the bat. In the survey, three quarters of those who claimed that the bat had cultural value also said that they eat the animals. Thus, the act of eating a fruit bat provides cultural identity. Paradoxically, many Chamorros, whether or not they eat fruit bat, believe the fruit bat has a culturally symbolic value.

The survey also found that there is a significant relationship between age and both the practice of eating bats and the claim that the bats have cultural value. Over three-quarters of the respondents above forty-five years of age said that fruit bats provided cultural identity, versus less than half of those under forty-five. This could indicate that the practice of eating the fruit bats is declining in the population and that a generational gap in the relationship exists. Cultural orientation of indigenous peoples, kinship groups, and small communities may be an obstacle to that enforcement.

THE CASE IN CONTEXT Most people fear bats more than any other animal, even sharks. The desire of one small population, who does not fear bats, has caused catastrophe for bat populations in many countries. This case illustrates how very local, small demands in the Electronic Conjunction can have enormous impacts in many other parts of the world. The juxtaposition again reveals the varied disconnects that will occur in the Electronic Conjunction. Recall that Harris contrasts the outlook about the pig between Muslims and the Tsembengi of New Guinea, trying to determine the source of their divergent views. The outlook on bats in Guam and Carpathia are equally as divergent. The materialist view that sees environment as a determining factor in producing culture is strong in this case. Similar to the pig, the material reality produces very different outcomes for people and bats.

HABITATS

The first set of cases in the Electronic Conjunction focused on the species impact. These actions usually show a set of discrete and direct impacts. The following cases look at how the Conjunction is affecting habitats. The discussion thus moves from the specific to the general. This shift in perspective represents not only a change from a single direction of discussion to one much more complicated, and thus one more susceptible to suffer from the disconnect.

ELECTRICITY AND CREE

Unlikely forms of trade arise in the Electronic Conjunction that will over time become ordinary; trade will take on new forms. Most view trade as goods, but trade covers a variety of transaction types. One traded item is electricity. Electricity exports to the United States pose a threat to the culture of Cree Native Americans in Canada.[78]

THE ENVIRONMENT ASPECT In 1971, Quebec Premier Robert Bourassa announced that Hydro-Quebec, a province-run electric company, would begin a hydroelectric project that would dam several rivers in Northern Quebec and create tens of thousands of jobs. The dam would also provide surplus electric power for export and entice investment in Quebec by offering subsidized electricity to attract extractive industry.[79] Two months later, before completing a feasibility study, work began with the construction of roads into the James Bay area. Bourassa believed the project would create needed jobs, increase the economic autonomy of Quebec from English-speaking Canada and be the primary engine of economic growth for this part of Quebec. Inuit and Cree Native Americans argued that the dam project violated their right to self-determination.

Debate over environmental risks is central to this controversy. Flooding the area to create artificial lakes would alter an already fragile ecosystem. Environmental concerns, in part, led to a breakdown in contractual discussion between U.S. utility companies and Hydro-Quebec. James II, the second phase of the project, was delayed due to domestic and foreign pressures calling for a joint federal-provincial environmental impact assessment.

The sheer magnitude of the project represents the greatest threat to the environment. The Great Whale project (Phase I) would flood five thousand square kilometers of Quebec in an area where twelve thousand Cree and five thousand Inuit live.[80] Both Cree and environmentalists point out that these areas are the home of many native animals such as caribou, snow geese, marten, beaver, black and polar bears, and elk, among other animals.[81]

Decomposition of trees because of flooding creates a highly toxic form of mercury, methyl-mercury, which is passed down the food chain.[82] As fish are poisoned, so too are people and some other endangered species, notably the Beluga whale and the fresh water seal that live on fish native to the area. The environment may also suffer through aluminum mining and processing that extensive enterprises produce. In subsidies, the project will cost the utility and Canadian taxpayers between $1.5 and $10 billion.

THE TRADE ASPECT Northeastern Canada has more fresh flowing water than almost anywhere else on the globe. Hydro-Quebec, government owned since 1963, began to transform the natural waterways into a system of dams and reservoirs to generate electric power for Canada and New England. The first phase of the project (James I, or the La Grande Project) produced three power stations capable of generating 10,282 megawatts of energy at a cost of $13.8 billion. The next major stage in Hydro-Quebec's plans was to build a complex at another location on the Great Whale River called the James II project.

The Canadian National Energy Board, in 1990, granted Hydro-Quebec a license to export electricity to New York and Vermont if the production of electricity did not conflict with relevant environmental standards and that an environmental assessment was performed by the national government. Quebec appealed the decision because they argued that the James Bay Project was a provincial rather than a federal matter and eventually won the case. The Cree tribe appealed the case to the Canadian Supreme Court who ruled that a federal review of Hydro-Quebec dams was required if they intended to obtain export contracts. Although a legal victory for the Cree, they could not convince the Court to revoke the export licenses.[83] Moreover, the Court gave Hydro-Quebec permission to begin construction of yet another dam (Ste. Marguerite).

Hydro-Quebec intended to use the extra electrical capacity from the project to export power to the United States. It would overcharge U.S. customers for electricity and thereby use them to subsidize Canadian customers, especially in Quebec.[84] By the year 2006, the power company hoped to increase power exports to the United States from 1.5 in 1991 to 9.5 percent of total company sales.

Export earnings are only about 7 percent of Hydro-Quebec's total revenues. In 1992, the New York Power Authority canceled a $12.6 billion contract for a year-round supply of one thousand megawatts of power and put off a twenty-year, $5 billion contract to buy electricity from Quebec fearing possible environmental damage in Canada and because of the drop in demand and electricity prices in New York.[85] Demand for Hydro-Quebec power is growing only about 3.8 percent per year, less than the expected 5.7 percent. Originally planned for operation by 1996, the Grand Whale Project has been postponed until 2003. Finally, the New York Power Authority now states that any new contract "will not provide a market directly or indirectly for the construction of the Great Whale project."[86]

THE CULTURE ASPECT The dam threatens the Cree and Inuit cultures because they are nomadic hunters in an environment with scarce resources, and require large spaces of land to survive. The project effectively reduces their economic area to the point where hunter-gatherer subsistence strategies are no longer viable. The dam will result in the domestication of the Cree perhaps in a way the potato did for the Shoshone. The difference is that, in this instance, the very past of the Cree will be erased by the water. Their campsites, trapping lands, and burial sites have been, or will be, submerged, and with them important cultural symbols. Most Cree see the dam as the beginning of the end for them. As development proceeds and more Canadians inhabit Northern Quebec, Native American culture will continue to erode. Similar to the plight of Native Americans in the United States, drug and alcohol abuse, crime, and sexually transmitted diseases, as well as disease stemming from poor diets, are prevalent in the Cree and the Inuit societies (see the earlier EU fur import ban case). They are unskilled, unemployed, and uneducated for a modern society, and suffer from a loss of identity and self-worth. Skills in lobbying, law, economics, and public relations are now crucial to the Cree and the Inuit but hunting skills are not.

When the La Grand project broke ground, none of the approximately 5,000 Cree Indians and 3,500 Inuit were even aware of the project but learned of it from a newspaper. To this hunting culture, the flooding of ancestral burial grounds and traditional hunting areas was a specter of devastation.[87] Daniel Coon Come, Grand Chief of the Cree, said that "our land is our memory."[88] The International Water Tribunal recommended that Hydro-Quebec stop the James Bay Project in order to preserve the rights and culture of the native people.[89]

A primarily French-speaking province, Quebec is culturally different from the rest of Canada and seeks its own independence. The need to remain autonomous was one reason behind the Hydro-Quebec project. In pursuit of their own cultural and economic autonomy, Quebec is denying autonomy to the indigenous peoples of the province. Indigenous peoples living in Quebec fear that without federal protection, an independent Quebec would ignore their rights. The Cree and Inuit claim that they will secede from Quebec if Quebec separates from Canada.[90]

THE CASE IN CONTEXT This case highlights the new ways that trade can harm both environment and culture. Trade in electricity was unknown in the other conjunctions because electricity itself was unknown. Now this form of trade is also a major environmental and cultural problem.

The irony of the case is that this new form of trade, and this new technology, is in conflict with a society whose subsistence strategy evokes images of the Tool Conjunction. The point is that old conjunctions do not disappear; new layers appear on top of them. The Cree have survived the intrusion of European culture and power, but may not survive the flooding of their lands. This action does what weapons have not: force the Cree from their lands.

The case shows how new technologies and new types of trade will become important in the Electronic Conjunction; it also shows how single products can be crucial to a society. In a way, one can become as dependent on electricity in one's subsistence strategy as one can become dependent on mammoth or buffalo. Electricity is not only a new product but also one in great demand.

BIRD'S NEST SOUP

The reverence for bird's nest soup is due to alleged health and psychological reasons and thus has become a trade as well as an environmental problem.[91] The case demonstrates how species and habitat relate and that it is not easy to separate the behavior of one from the behavior of another. By the same token, it is difficult to separate the product from the process of creating it. This has relevance to modern trade disciplines. In recent times GATT, and now the WTO, has taken the position that its disciplines cover trade products but not the process that creates them. Thus, a country could ban tuna that caused food poisoning but could not ban tuna whose catching killed dolphins. This case provides insight into the subtle distinction between process and product.

THE ENVIRONMENT ASPECT Trade of swiftlet nests began in China during the T'ang Dynasty more than one thousand years ago (A.D. 618–907). China has long been the prime consumer of bird's nest soup, which they consider the "caviar of the East." Austerity policies in the 1960s and 1970s in China, and especially the Cultural Revolution, discouraged extravagance such as eating this prized soup.[92] Policy liberalization in the 1980s led to a surge in demand for bird's nest soup. To meet demand, China is now a large importer of bird nest by-products from countries such as Malaysia and Indonesia. This trade now threatens the swift populations in these countries and elsewhere.

Chinese have been eating the nest of the swiftlet, a bird about the size of a sparrow found in Southeast Asia and the Indian Subcontinent, for over one thousand years. The edible-nest (East Asian and Indian) and Black-nest Swiftlets weave a nest from strands of saliva. There are three types of swiftlet nests: 1) Edible Nests (*aerodramus fuciphagus*) or white-nest, 2) Swiftlet, including Indian (*aerodramus unicolor*), and 3) East Asian *(aerodramus maximus)*.

The secret of the taste of the soup lies in the swift's reproductive cycle. In building a nest, the male regurgitates a thin, long gelatinous strand from salivary glands under its tongue. The bird winds the strand into a half-cup nest which bonds like quick-drying cement and attaches to the inside of a cave wall.[93] The nests are relatively tasteless, usually served in soup or jelly, and mixed with chicken, spices, sauce, or sweets. For centuries, the nests were regarded as nourishing, tasty, a booster of health for the sick and aging, and an aphrodisiac.

The farming of swiftlets has grown enormously with demand and perhaps one-third of swiftlet products now come from domesticated birds. This farming sometimes impacts wild species, especially if domestic birds escape to the wild, which they do, and mate with the wild species. The problem has become serious enough that synthetic substitutes for swift nest are becoming available. However, even with farmed birds there still exists a demand for the actual product.

The harvesting of swiftlet nests is a potentially hazardous occupation. The nests are gathered from high, dark caves hundreds of feet high by special collectors who climb up and balance on bamboo poles attached to steep cliffs, in scenes reminiscent of *National Geographic* specials. This is a traditional occupation and the nest collection skills pass down from father to son, as are skills in the *bekko* industry in Japan.

Biochemist Kong Yun-Cheng analyzed the swiftlet nest and found that it contained a water-soluble glyco-protein that promotes cell division and a healthy immune system in humans. However, the nutrients are destroyed during the cleaning process. Therefore, the soup is actually of low nutritive value precisely because of the process by which it is prepared.

THE TRADE ASPECT Swiftlet nest prices have more than doubled in recent years. China was traditionally the biggest importer of birds' nests until the Communist revolution when the soup was discouraged as a bourgeois extravagance. Hong Kong is the biggest official importer of birds' nests, at about one hundred tons (grossing about $25 million) annually. In Hong Kong, fifty-five pounds of top quality white nests (the most prized) can be worth $50,000.

Not all nests are created equal. Black nests are the lowest grade of swiftlet nest since they must be cleaned to remove feathers. They are considerably less expensive than white nests. The nests are so valued that shipments are kept secret for fear that they may be stolen if recognized. A key group of brokers in Kowloon (the peninsula across Victoria Harbor from the island of Hong Kong) controls much of the international trade of swiftlet nests.[94]

The rising price and demand for nests led to an accelerated decline in the swiftlet population. Poachers and deforestation of swiftlet habitats contribute to the decline. Indonesia is the biggest supplier of swiftlet nests with Thailand ranking second, followed by Vietnam, Singapore (via trans-shipments),

Burma, Malaysia, southern India, and Sri Lanka. In most nest-producing countries swiftlet colonies are dwindling. Kong Yun-Cheng argues that if harvesting continues at its current rate local swift species may die out in five to ten years. The current economic problems in Indonesia and Thailand may put more pressure on the wild colonies through poaching and more aggressive harvesting.

Nest harvesters in Indonesia have begun "farming" swifts. Farming has led to crossbreeding for better saliva production. Colonies of Mossy-nest Swiftlets are cross-fostered with eggs of white-nest swiftlets by placing them in nest colonies. Once mature, the white-nest swiftlets return to the house and establish a colony. Indonesian nest traders claim that one-third of exports come from farms, but researchers of the World Wildlife Fund believe the farms produce far less.

THE CULTURE ASPECT Bird's nest soup is a revered concoction in East Asia, said to contain cures for a variety of ailments, ranging from rheumatism to lethargy. The soup is made from the nests of the swift; specifically the strands of the bird's saliva used to hold the nest together. The saliva is the essence of the soup and containers of it claim it is "capable of restoring equilibrium to the human body."[95]

While the Edible-nest and Black-nest Swiftlet are not yet on the endangered species lists of either CITES or the IUCN, measures to protect them are underway. Some supplier countries have domestic legislation to regulate importing/exporting, hunting, poaching, and selling of swiftlet nests. For example, since 1934 there has been an ordinance in Sarawak, Malaysia that permits harvesting of nests only once every seventy-five days. Sabah now allows only two harvests per year of white-nest swiftlets. Despite policies to protect the bird, numbers continue to decline, probably a result of illegal trade that constitutes a substantial percentage of harvested nests. Some propose placing the swiftlet species on CITES' Appendix II listing of endangered species where regulated trade is permitted.[96] This listing would protect not only the bird but it would also include the bird's nest as well. This linkage, some fear, would open the door to thinly veiled economic protection that would safeguard species by focusing on their habitats. If it is possible to protect swifts by protecting their nests then it is possible to protect elephants by protecting their habitats. Yet, the simple incongruity of a legal argument that separates a bird from its nest leaves a rather stark conclusion that this policy is not tenable.

Several environmental groups are now pushing to add the swift's nest to the list of endangered species under the CITES agreement. The reason:

demand for the swift's nest has grown so high that China, in part driven by rapidly rising incomes, is now a huge net importer of bird's nest products, especially from Indonesia, Malaysia, and Vietnam. The demand for the nest is so great that hunters no longer wait for the swift to vacate the nest before taking it. The chicks or eggs in the nest are simply tossed out. Swifts, which travel across many national borders in Southeast Asia, are now in widespread peril.

THE CASE IN CONTEXT The case shows the blurring of species and habitats under the manifold and overwhelming impacts of the Electronic Conjunction. The bird's nest soup case is a kind of kaleidoscope of trade, environment, and culture issues. The WTO has resisted process issues from entering into their disciplines but this resistance is slowly eroding. The WTO ruled against a U.S. ban on shrimp imports from Asia from ships lacking devices (turtle-excluder devices) that minimize the deaths of sea turtles. (As noted, it was the first WTO environmental case that involved a CITES-listed creature.) The U.S. lost due to discriminatory implementation of the measure, not because it had used a trade measure to achieve an environmental goal.

Free traders might find the swiftlet case a Trojan horse for process issues within the WTO, if it can attain CITES standing. If the swift receives protection, the protection of the nest must follow. The "nest" of an animal can be an extremely broad concept. If we can protect the nest of the bird then, as in the spotted owl case, it is necessary to protect an entire habitat as a sort of "super-nest." By the same logic, would it then be permissible to protect the burrow of the groundhog, the hole of the snake or the cave of the bear? What is a nest? Is it simply the place of warming the egg and feeding the chicks or is it more than that? In this way, the swift is more frightening to the free trader than the bat.

SUGAR: DEVELOPED ADDICTION[97]

The large-scale introduction of sugar into the human diet is one of the great changes in the human subsistence strategy in the last fifty thousand years (as discussed earlier). Sugar has changed the human diet and, in the process, the global landscape. Sugar trade led to enormous changes in peoples, cultures, and environments. This case looks at sugar's history and its relation to modern events.

THE ENVIRONMENT ASPECT Refined sugar comes from sucrose, a chemical substance present in all green plants. The most important sources of refined sugar are beet and sugar cane; the latter a perennial giant grass that belongs to the same plant group as maize and sorghum. The domestication of sugar originated in either the Pacific Islands or the western Bengal area. Sugar cane is grown in the damp heat of tropical or semi-tropical climates, as it needs strong sunlight and abundant water. Typically, these climates are found in many developing countries.

Sugar beet, a root crop, can only be grown in temperate zones. The vast majority of the sugar beet is grown in developed countries. This makes sugar one of the few major agricultural commodities where developed and developing countries are in direct competition with one another.[98]

The role of sugar in the overall human diet, especially as an energy source, has drastically changed over time (as noted earlier). The enormous rise of cultivated sugar as a human energy source (20 percent of the requirements for people in industrial societies) translates into the complete transformation of habitats to grow sugar-producing crops (especially canes and beets). Providing sugar for the consumer has created enormous trade networks worldwide. In this process, landscapes and species change, as do basic living standards that can result in war and human degradation.

THE TRADE ASPECT Arab traders brought sugar to Europe in the sixteenth century and it soon became a staple in European diets, especially in sweets, cakes, pastries, and the like. Demand for sugar grew and was met by large-scale cultivations in European colonies. The British brought sugar cane to Jamaica, the Portuguese to Brazil, and the French to Louisiana in 1751.

When sugar was introduced into England, it was classified as a spice, but used mostly for "medicinal" purposes. By the sixteenth century, it was also a preservative in some recipes and for decoration on cakes and cookies. The introduction of tea, coffee and chocolate into Europe boosted demand for sugar and greatly encouraged the expansion of the Caribbean sugar industry. In the 1800s, sugar became a common food in England for at least two reasons: 1) the rise of the temperance movement which advocated sugared tea as an alternative to alcohol and 2) the inclusion of dessert as an accepted part of the mid-day or evening meal. Sugar rapidly became the quickest, cheapest, most palatable source of energy available and was the single most important addition to the British diet during the nineteenth century.

Planting sugar produces a variety of environmental side effects, which are not so sweet. The introduction of sugar to Java (in Indonesia) reduced rice production, in part due to incompatibilities between the seasonal cultivation of the two. One major reason for the decline in Javan rice production, and the rise in rice imports, was most likely the appropriation of land and outright seizure of it for sugar production purposes.

Sugar production in Brazil led to a variety of environmental and social changes. Some areas were completely deforested and converted wholesale into sugar plantations. Native Americans were extinguished or enslaved and West African slaves brought in to work the land. To feed them, land was cleared to grow manioc and only manioc. This resulted in especially poor dietary conditions; one cannot subsist solely on manioc.[99]

The history of sugar trade is inextricably mixed with that of colonialism and slavery. European settlers who planted cane and built sugar mills in the Eastern Caribbean depended on the slave trade. Between 1450 and 1900, 11.7 million West Africans were captured and imported to the Caribbean. Sugar played a role in that holocaust.

The sugar industry was highly dependent on slavery. In 1838, one-quarter of the world's sugar came from the British Caribbean colonies. However, the decline of the sugar cane industry in the second half of the nineteenth century was as much due to the increased production of European sugar beet as to the abolition of slavery.

Satisfying the European and North American sweet tooth meant the creation of a massive mono-industry throughout many tropical and subtropical regions. When independence came to many developing countries in the twentieth century, their position as a supplier of sugar in the world economic system was already entrenched. Many countries remain dependent on sugar as a source of foreign exchange because of decisions made long ago by colonial rulers.

One striking case is the Philippines, where sugar was grown as a subsistence crop long before it was grown for export. Since the mid-nineteenth century sugar has been the Philippines' leading export crop and most Philippine sugar are exports to the United States. The U.S. government limits those exports under a quota system established in 1934 by the Jones-Costigan Act: a law passed in the middle of the Great Depression. With increased U.S. domestic sugar production and the switch from sugar to high fructose corn syrup in many U.S. manufactured foods, the overall size of the quota has been dramatically reduced over time.

The International Sugar Agreements (ISA) meant to control the world market prices, but its efforts have been largely ineffective. The world price sank from about 60 US cents per pound in 1974 to about 40 cents in 1980 and then to less than 3 cents in 1985. This drop caused the Philippines to suffer from a "sugar crisis" in late 1985.

Sugar production causes deforestation, soil erosion, and loss of biodiversity. Deforestation, in turn, results in widespread soil erosion and devastates forest ecology; in the Philippines it led to the extinction of one third of the known snail and bird species.

Deforestation, in part due to sugar cultivation, led to the "Ormoc deluge" (a major rain event) in the Philippines and caused over five thousand deaths in November 1992. In the 1950s, the watershed area around Ormoc was planted with sugar cane, which does not absorb flood waters as well as mature jungle habitats. Only 10 percent of the mountain range still had forests at the time of the floods.[100] Floods at Nueve Ecija, in a northern province of the Philippines in July 1992, were allegedly the result of massive deforestation. Only 11.7 percent of the fourteen thousand hectares in the area remains covered with forest; much of the watershed has been converted into sugar plantations.

The collapse of the sugar industry, in the 1980s, was also the result of falling commodity prices. The decline only exacerbated social and environmental problems. On Negros Island, which produces 60 percent of Philippine sugar, a 1985 survey conducted by the National Secretariat of Social Action showed that 40 percent of children under the age of fourteen were malnourished. One year later this total rose to 73 percent. As migration and upland cultivation continued, forested areas declined. Both human and environmental health declined as sugar output grew.

Many sugar cane workers live under conditions of extensive poverty. In response, ISA treaties contain clauses stating that country members must ensure a decent standard of living for sugar workers. However, fair labor standards remain ineffective due to the lack of systems to monitor labor standards and mechanisms to punish countries that abuse worker's rights. Similar to issues of environment and culture, labor issues have thus far been excluded from WTO disciplines.

THE CULTURE ASPECT Sugar has been a part of human lifestyles for millennia, but has been a significant part of the human diet for only a few hundred years. In this time, sugar has gone from a diet rarity to a common commodity. Sugar is part of important cultural festivities in Christian, Jewish, and Muslim societies (and more). What has happened is that this commodity, once limited to a few special occasions, has become available, integral, and affordable throughout the year. Yet, the entire chain of events set in motion actions that had devastating worldwide impacts on people and their environment. The only difference today is that now such changes will occur much more rapidly.

The irony of sugar is the excess it breeds. It is generally believed that people in consuming countries with high sugar diets actually hurt their health through over-consumption. Describing the reason for this over-consumption is difficult. Some regard over-consumption of sugar as a type of addiction that leads to a condition of compulsive usage.

THE CASE IN CONTEXT The prevailing view of trade disciplines distinguishes between product and process and thus implicitly between species and habitat. Can this distinction apply to other areas? Is it possible to separate culture between specific customs and general rituals? In other words, can we isolate and treat differently cultural particulars and generals without touching the very foundations of religion and belief? No. This question is important as institutions attempt to make rules on cultural and trade matters. Sugar is used by custom within a ritual, much as a species is part of a habitat.

Trade might provide another basis for analogy. Traded products can be final demand or input products. In trade, the trend has been toward a growing proportion of input products. These inputs could be services. Could country development sectors purposely promote products of a cultural nature? Can the commodification of culture create a set of new input products? The answer lies in ownership. A country could demand licenses for the use of its culture in a variety of entertainment venues and support the development of cultural products through infrastructure investments.

The continued commodification of culture into products has the capacity to transform culture into base products that will be treated no different from automobiles in terms of key trade concepts such as transparency, discrimination, subsidy, and the like. The key will be to prove that cases are more about culture than money. Sugar is so infused in culture that such separation is unlikely, but it illustrates how difficult it is to show that cultural products are fundamentally different from other traded products.

PISCO

Trade may expose the differences in the Electronic Conjunction between different cultures and the environments they live in. Pisco, a South American brandy, is the focus of a debate between Peru and Chile about who owns a cultural and environmental idea.[101] Again, the case blurs the issues of product and process and species and habitat. The idea of ownership exposes a completely new dimension of issues.

THE ENVIRONMENT ASPECT The cultivation of grapes for pisco began centuries ago by the adept engineering of the Incas. The region, along Peru's southwestern coast, is naturally a dry, infertile desert region. Inca emperor Pachacutec, however, channeled Andean melt waters into the desert. The irrigation project had mythic origins.

> When the Inca emperor Pachacutec offered his hand in marriage to a fair maiden from the Peruvian hinterland and was turned down in favor of her plebeian boyfriend, he might have been forgiven for being miffed . . . he gave in gracefully. In fact, just to show how sporting of a chap he was, he offered to grant the lady her dearest wish. She, evidently not a material girl, said that her dream was that the waters of the River Inca be brought to her hometown in the desert. Fifteen days later, forty thousand laborers wiped their collective brow, dropped their shovels and sat down beside the 30-mile canal they had just dug. The heart-smitten Supreme Panjandrum dubbed this waterway the "Achirana."[102]

In 1547, the Achirana provided European immigrants with a sufficient water source to plant vineyards with the Negra Corriente grape. The vineyards were so prosperous that within ten years Peru had thriving wine exports to Argentina, Chile, and Spain. Over 100,000 acres of grape were planted in Peru alone. Peru's success led to similar attempts in neighboring countries. The widely grown Criolla grape of Argentina and the Pais grape of Chile are no doubt descendants of the Negra Corriente grape originally imported by the Spanish. The Europeans, however, craved their native brandies and continued to experiment. "Through trial and error they found a grape called the Quebranta that produced a pure, highly potent, aromatic brandy which eventually became known by the port from which it was exported to grateful drinkers abroad: pisco."[103]

By the nineteenth century, a scourge of *phylloxera* (plant lice) eradicated many Peruvian vineyards and the lands were replanted with cotton and other fruit crops. The Argentine and Chilean mountains and deserts were natural barriers against the spread of the pest, not so in Peru. Political and economic upheavals took their toll on Peruvian vineyards in the twentieth century.

THE TRADE ASPECT The quality of the grape depends on a supply of clean water. Water pollution is an enormous problem in all parts of Peru. A new national environmental agency is being created with the help of a

$2 million donation by the Inter-American Development Agency. "It is expected that a significant improvement in legal mechanisms will be enforced by 1995."[104] Peru's abysmal water conditions in the Inca region are a result of domestic and industrial waste, including mining and pollution. The Peruvian cholera epidemic of 1991 quickly spread due to poor sanitary conditions.

There is a growing trade dispute between Peru and Chile over the right to use the name pisco. "Peruvians hold a deep-seated national pride in pisco, which they make from the cream of the grape harvest and have been drinking at parties and rowdy peasant festivals for more than 400 years."[105] Chilean pisco has already found small export markets in the United States and Europe. To Peruvians, their culture is constrained by their economic policy. Peruvian exporters suffer from problems caused by hyperinflation and an unfavorable exchange rate.

Pisco itself is being globalized. The United Kingdom imports grapes and Taiwan imports Tacma wine grown in the Inca region to make their versions of pisco. "Peru is planning action under international patent agreements—the same ones that guard copyrights over everything from computers to pharmaceuticals—to keep the pisco name exclusively for Peru."[106] Chile has lost a WTO dispute settlement case (and its appeal) brought by Peru and other countries over lower and thus discriminatory taxes on pisco than other imported spirits.

THE CULTURE ASPECT Godofredo Gonzalez del Valle, whose family has been making pisco for four generations, says making pisco is all in the stomp. "To make real pisco, you have to take your shoes off, crush the grapes and let it ferment in clay bottles. In Chile they make something called pisco, but it doesn't taste as it should . . . Only Peru has the soil, the climate, and the tradition in making pisco that give[s] our drink a special taste, and which allow[s] us to call it pisco."[107]

Pisco has been part of Peruvian culture for over four hundred years and is part of a traditional Peruvian meal. Pisco production has been passed from generation to generation and is a ritual in many families. The government promotes pisco as being Peruvian, using the slogan "*Pisco es peruana*" (Pisco is Peruvian).

The Incas also had a drink called chicha, made from fermented corn and water.[108] Chicha was a ceremonial drink for the Incas and made only by women, the so-called "Chosen Women." One of the chief occupations of the Chosen Women was making chicha for the Incan nobles and priests, which required the crushing of the sprouted corn after it had been boiled. At

Incan feasts and ceremonies the liquor of corn was as sacred as the kernel they named "life giver." No ceremony began without the Inca lord or priest's pouring chicha on the ground to honor the corn goddess, Mama Sara.

THE CASE IN CONTEXT This case highlights cultural intellectual property and how it is closely tied to the environment. The Peruvians argue that pisco is a unique product of an environment and a culture. Environment and culture have a long-standing relation in human history. Trade has disrupted this nascent relationship, but it may also act to preserve unique cultures and environments. Convincing the public about the uniqueness of pisco may be the key. If the public believes that the authenticity of pisco derives from a place and a people, these preferences will reflect in the markets and the value of the product. In a way, the consumer may determine the future of pisco as much as lawyers will. Who wants pisco from Taiwan?

The inclusion of new trade disciplines such as intellectual property has been commercial in orientation. Environmental and cultural groups argue that if these new rules apply to business and economic innovation, then it should apply to environmental and cultural innovations as well. In adding more and more dimensions of issues to trade, environment, and culture factors, the more likely a disconnect will occur.

CORAL: DEFORESTATION IN THE OCEAN[109]

Deforestation is a problem on the land and in the sea. The forests of the sea—coral—are disappearing at an alarming rate from a variety of sources. Aquarium collecting may be one reason for the decline of coral, but tourism, global warming, and fishing practices are also leading causes.

THE ENVIRONMENT ASPECT Coral reefs are "among the most threatened ecosystems on the planet."[110] Coral, a very sensitive organism, establishes itself in clear warm waters lacking sufficient nutrients to sustain other marine life. The coral animal "harnesses" microscopic algae, which provide the coral with food and oxygen, while the coral gives the algae carbon dioxide and other necessary life-producing materials. As a coral reef develops it provides a home for a variety of organisms, all dependent on each other for life. The coral itself is very sensitive to water purity and temperature changes; therefore, if the coral is subjected to drastic changes, the reef may die.

Coral also protects coastlines from storms and erosion and is an important resource for many countries. Coral is exploited in products such as filler for concrete, gift shop souvenirs, and decorations for aquariums. These rather low-level economic benefits are in juxtaposition to its substantial environmental benefits. "Among the most biologically diverse ecosystems on Earth," the coral reefs of ninety-three countries have been damaged or destroyed by human beings. Although covering only 0.17 percent of the ocean floor, coral provides a home for one-quarter of all marine species. Known as the "tropical rain forests of the ocean," coral reefs serve as the home for "one-tenth of all fish caught for human consumption."[111]

Coral reefs also contribute to science and medicine. Certain reef organisms produce kainic acid, which can be used "as a diagnostic chemical to investigate Huntington's chorea," a nervous system disease. Other chemicals produced by reef species are vital parts of cancer and AIDS research.[112] "Corals themselves produce a natural sunscreen" and "their porous limestone skeletons are promising for bone grafts in humans."[113]

THE TRADE ASPECT Humans have already destroyed between 5 and 10 percent of the world's coral reefs. Between 40 and 60 percent of coral reefs are at risk in the next sixty years. This loss comes from a variety of sources, including:

1. Dense coastal populations which increase sewage and waste production that affects water purity
2. Heavy coastal development, logging, farming, mining and dredging which increases the silt in the water, thus blocking out light necessary for algae photosynthesis and potentially smothering the coral
3. Over-exploitation of fish and decimation of the reef community
4. Harvesting coral for use in home aquariums

Coral reefs are vulnerable to macro-trends such as global warming and the increasing intensity of the sun's ultraviolet rays due to ozone depletion. Tourism is one micro-trend that threatens coral. Although tourism relies on the coral reefs to attract customers, it also contributes to reef destruction due to the construction of tourist resorts and the carelessness of the tourists themselves. People attempting to capture the beauty of the coral reefs walk on them, stir up sediments or break off pieces of them for souvenirs (this is a problem at the Great Barrier Reef). Cruise-liners and tourist boats often drop anchor over the reefs causing tremendous amounts of damage that takes years to repair.[114]

Two types of coral degradation are intentional: 1) mining the reefs for building materials and 2) catching fish around coral reefs in order to satisfy the growing demand for decorative products and salt-water home aquariums. Sri Lanka, India, the Philippines, and Indonesia mine coral to produce cement. This practice has resulted in the complete destruction of certain reef systems. There are over 1.5 million kilograms of coral harvested worldwide each year, and the United States "accounts for more than a third of the world demand for [coral and tropical fish]."[115] The coral industry is a big business; for example, "871 species [of living coral] were imported to the United States in 1984, about 250,000 in 1991."[116]

One chemical used to capture certain fish species that live in and around coral reefs is sodium cyanide. The chemical not only sickens other fish, it also kills the coral. For the past twenty years, more than one million kilograms (1,100 tons) of sodium cyanide have been used in the reefs. This amount is sufficient to kill five and one-half billion people.

CITES added stony corals to Appendix II in 1985 and protection of coral has expanded since then. "Seven reefs are now protected as World Heritage Sites" and the "World Bank plans to put 15–20% of its $3-billion bio-diversity budget into marine and coastal habitats."[117] One suggestion is to map the world's reefs using satellite and aerial surveillance equipment to better monitor them. These numbers stand in comparison to several million spent on coral products.

Worldwide expenditures on aquarium products equal over $4 billion per year. The United States imported $1.6 billion in aquarium products per year. The leading coral exporters are the Philippines, Sri Lanka, Caribbean nations, nations in the Red Sea area, East Africa, Indonesia, the South Pacific, and Singapore.

Perhaps the most famous coral reef is the Great Barrier in Australia. Australia created the Great Barrier Reef Park in 1975 to regulate and monitor the use of the reef so that it remains healthy. The reef was divided into different sections: one for scientific research, one for tourists, and one for commercial fishing and harvesting. These sections enabled Australia's government to monitor how different activities affect the reef.[118]

Coral receives protection in many countries. The Sudan has banned export of marine ornamentals and in 1991 Sri Lanka banned trade in coral (but not in tropical fish). Kenya, New Caledonia, and the Maldives have licensing and regulatory systems, and the Philippines and Indonesia have some restrictions (but that are often not obeyed). China partially banned the collection and damaging of coral by declaring a National Coral Reef Reserve in Hainan Island. On the import side, Germany prohibits the sale of certain corals.

The United States declared several coral reef sanctuaries and bans oil and gas activities permanently from these areas.[119] A U.S. House of Representatives bill claims that $50 million in Florida's tourist business relates to coral reefs. In 1989, Florida shut down its coral industry to protect its reefs and has taken protective measures including: "licens[ing] collectors . . . in some cases set[ting] limits on catches,"[120] and ticketing tourists who abuse sanctuary corals including "anchoring in coral, spear fishing, and hanging on to coral while scuba diving.[121]

In June of 1990, U.S. President George Bush declared a ten-year ban on offshore drilling near the Florida Keys, in part to protect the reefs. In addition, in 1990, Hawaii "banned the taking and selling of stony coral and in 1991, of any 'rock with marine life attached.'" Guam outlawed "the import and collection of all stony coral, living or dead," and Puerto Rico "classes live rock as protected earth crust."[122] Although the United States banned the import of coral from the Philippines, where export is legal, it continues to import coral from Indonesia, Singapore, and other places.

THE CULTURE ASPECT The aquarium trade is a big business within the United States, which is "the world's largest consumer of tropical fish."[123] Over ten million aquarium hobbyists in the United States have between two and three billion fish. Aquarium enthusiasts now prefer the home mini-reef, which takes between fifteen and several hundred gallons of water. The foundation of such a mini-reef is "live rock," chunks of dead coral and non-coral limestone that serve as the balance of the captive ecosystem. Marine aquariums such as this constitute 15 percent of American aquarium sales and North Americans (mostly Americans) spend $240 million every year solely on equipment and animals.

The idea that aquariums lead to mental stability is not new. Many Chinese believe that fish lead to good health. Why do North Americans and Europeans have aquariums? To most, it is a hobby. Others focus on the fish and grow attached to them as pets and companions. Some have aquariums because they are said to provide a calming effect, reminiscent of sitting by an ocean. The aquarium, sometimes with a recording of the ocean playing, is said to be enormously therapeutic.

Perhaps aquarium owning is the result of lonely, detached lives in urban societies and symptoms of social anomie. The creation of a mini-environment in one's home with aquariums is a symptom of urbanization, where dwellers in high-rise apartments seek some relation to nature in an unnatural world. The phenomenon may be the result of the large population that lives in the middle part of the North American continent, sometimes nearly a thousand miles from any ocean or sea.

Coral is an apt analogy for the relationship between environment and culture. Anthropologist Kroeber in fact described culture as similar to coral in that it grows on preceding generations.

> A simile that may further help the realization of what culture is and how it works is that of a coral reef. Such a reef may be miles long and inhabited by billions of tiny polyp animals. The firm, solid part consists of calcium carbonate produced by the secretions of these animals over thousands of years—a product at once cumulative and communal and therefore social. Without these ancestors, there would have been no reef. [124]

THE CASE IN CONTEXT Deforestation was extensive during both the Agricultural and Industrial Conjunctions, but limited to land areas. In the Electronic Conjunction, it is now possible to deforest the ocean. Coral is the forest of the ocean. The damage to coral in the last twenty years alone equals the deforestation rates of forests now and in earlier Conjunctions. This progression of trade issues into new territorial areas is clearly one that marks the Electronic Conjunction. Where trade, environment, and culture were earlier exclusively land issues, today's issues extend to the oceans, the polar areas, space, and non-terrestrial bodies. Thus, issues today not only extend to new types of products (such as electricity) but new environments as well.

Coral has also crept into multilateral trade disciplines. The first case presented to the NAFTA Commission for Environmental Cooperation concerned a cruise ship pier that was to be built near Cozumel, Mexico. The pier construction and the cruise ships allegedly posed a danger to an offshore reef. This pier controversy has pitted the diving part of the tourist industry against the cruise part of the industry.[125] Countries have also banded together in the International Coral Reef Initiative (ICRI) in an attempt to integrate coral protection and tourism policy.

MOM, APPLE PIE, AND HAMBURGER[126]

Sugar cultivation caused enormous changes in the earth's land usage, but probably no product has led to more changes than the hamburger. How did the simple hamburger not only become the symbol of America but a worldwide icon? The answer lies in a shifting subsistence strategy induced by greater affluence but also in national history and cultural myths. The hamburger is also the culmination of a long-standing subsistence strategy.

THE ENVIRONMENT ASPECT To gauge authenticity in the United States some items or ideas are said to be as "American as apple pie." Yet, for every slice of apple pie consumed by the average American, perhaps ten or more hamburgers are eaten. Clearly, one reason is price. The actual price to income ratio for hamburger (beef) in the United States is among the lowest in the world. Meat was not so long ago rather expensive but now is cheap. Economics has, in part, driven the increased popularity of the hamburger.

Part of the hamburger lore is enshrined in American myth. America is still a country with a strong rural roots symbolized by the "cook out." In suburbia, the "cook out" is a regular, ritualized event celebrating the wildness of the country. The event harkens back to the days of the settlement of the country, when the first migrants probably lived more like hunter-gathers rather than sedentary agriculturalists.

Some argue that there is a biological cause for the love of hamburger and that a genetic taste for beef exists.[127] The great ethnic and racial diversity of Americans who love hamburgers probably weakens this idea and whether they are hamburgers, kabobs, or other names for roasted, ground meat, this food type is clearly part of many cultures.

In the 1970s, the United States accounted for 6 percent of world human population and 9 percent of world cattle, but consumed 28 percent of the world's beef and accounted for one third of world beef imports. The United States imports about 10 percent of world beef production. The total land area in the world devoted to raising beef equals the size of many countries. (In this regard, hamburgers mirror U.S. oil consumption patterns.)

Not only does American beef consumption have an impact due to size, U.S. meat consumption trends drive beef demand patterns worldwide. In the cattle industry, there is a nine- to twelve-year cattle cycle with the steer-corn price ratio acting as a key predictor of market trends. The huge role of the United States in the global beef market has internationalized this cycle: the global cycle resonates the American cycle.

Meat eating is not universal and scholars believe that our pre-human ancestors were largely vegetarians aside from occasional scavenging. Taboos on eating beef differ from culture to culture. The Kalapalo, a tribe from the Upper Xingu delta around the Orinoco River delta in South America, refuse to eat the meat of virtually any land animal.[128] Perhaps their meat aversion is because there are so few meat animals where they live, outside of tapirs, monkeys, and oversized rats. This explanation suggests that the American love of hamburger has changed as environments have become terraformed into cattle production areas. By this explanation, American's love of hamburger is the culmination of thousands of years of cultural materialism.

> The cultural materialist view regards dietary behaviors and values within a comparative, ecological-historical frame, with differences in dietary practices resulting from recurrent, rather than idiosyncratic, causal processes and co-evolving with the human ecological systems in which they occur.[129]

What is different about today is that the link between diet and ecology is disconnected if the ecology impacted by the American love of hamburger is actually in Brazil. In this way, materialism has become separate from the ecological cultural influence in expressions such as diets. As much as hamburger is being exported from Brazil to the United States, so too is the environment of a treeless and grassy plain exported from the United States to Brazil.

THE TRADE ASPECT Pork is more associated with developing countries and beef with developed ones. This preference is in part because of differences in capital investment and land availability, but also due to the types of production and operating requirements for these two animals. Pigs can forage for themselves all year, but cattle cannot. Some basic investments are often required for cattle production (barn, fences, and so forth). In ancient Europe, pigs were the dominant animal and from the "Roman era through the twelfth century, extensive woodlands favored swine as the principal domesticated animal."[130] From the years 1200 to 1400, during the Middle Ages, the price of pork rose enormously. This was in part due to large increases in the price of salt, which was used in processing pork. When economies began to recover in the sixteenth century, abandoned farm lands were reclaimed after the Middle Ages hiatus. However, cattle, rather than pigs, were the major source of meat during this time.

Fernand Braudel believes that in this period the price of cereals kept the price of beef high. As a result, farm production focused on cheese (the poor man's meat or liquid meat) that was a much cheaper source of protein.[131] Beef prices also competed with horsemeat prices, which were much cheaper. Horsemeat had been a working class solution to the fate of aged work animals for centuries.

Large-scale trade in beef began during the Industrial Conjunction. In the 1800s, British and Scottish investors poured millions into the United States and Canada, and later Uruguay and Argentina, to develop beef export industries. These investments were to meet demands from a growing British middle class who could afford to buy meat on a regular basis. In North America, these demands pushed U.S. westward expansion and the establishment of the transcontinental railroad. The breakthrough in transportation led to great changes in the livestock industry. In Uruguay and Argentina, not only did the railroads contribute through transportation, but also brought in British blooded animals that were bigger and meatier (a kind of early bio-engineering).[132]

Americans were not always part of a beef culture. In fact, "the first generations of European settlers in most of the colonies in America and Australia ate pork more than any other flesh."[133] In the United States, the westward growth of the country included a discernible pork culture: in fact, Cincinnati was first called Porkopolis because of its enormous concentration of pork processing and shipping facilities. Chicago later replaced Cincinnati with respect to the leading meat processor and beef replaced pork as the subsistence meat of choice. The move westward to open grazing land deepened the beef culture. As it spread west, the building of railroads, again through English and Scottish investment, accelerated the process.

The beef industry's development in the United States faced one considerable competitor: the buffalo. By 1870, despite the reduction of their traditional grazing lands by over one-half, there were still six million buffalo left on the Great Plains. In the ensuing years, buffalo were slaughtered for both economic and political reasons. The economic motives were first driven by quick profit.

> Between 1872 and 1874 alone, over 12 million pounds of buffalo meat and over 32 million pounds of bone, for manufacture of bone china, were shipped out of Dodge City; and, largely as a result of the English demand for leather during the Crimean war, 1.3 million buffalo hides left there during the same period.[134]

The political means for the wanton destruction of the buffalo is well known: the act meant to deprive the Native Americans access to a valued resource. To wipe out the Native Americans and open new lands for farmers and ranchers, the U.S. Army began a slaughter campaign. Millions of buffalo were shot, killed and left to rot in the sun solely to prevent Native Americans from using the resource. The Native Americans relied on the buffalo, as noted earlier, for food, clothing and a variety of other reasons.

> Of the 3,700,000 buffalos destroyed from 1872 through 1874, only 150,000 were killed by Indians. When a group of concerned Texans asked General Sheridan if something should not be done to stop the white hunters' wholesale slaughter, he replied: "Let them kill, skin, and sell until the buffalo is gone and allow civilization to advance."[135]

The slaughter of the buffalo also removed a great competitor to establishing the cattle industry. First, cattle contract a variety of diseases from buffalo, such as brucellosis. Second, and more importantly, buffalo is a substitute for beef. How could a viable commercial cattle industry develop when there was free buffalo meat readily available? The buffalo had to be destroyed.

The cattle industry also produced derivative products with value. In the late nineteenth century, "American cattle yielded 13–14 million cowhides annually."[136] As a result, the United States became the largest footwear exporter in the world, alone equaling the combined exports of all the major competitors. Over time, the demands of the U.S. footwear industry outstripped domestic production. Even with its own huge cowhide production, the United States imported 75 percent of its hides by 1914. The United States today remains the leading exporter of cattle hides. About 3.6 million hides were produced in 1995 and 56 percent were exported.[137]

The growth of the beef industry also led to changes in wild species beyond North America. Feral cattle populations exploded on the pampas in Uruguay and Argentina. In fact, the cattle in the Americas were largely feral from the sixteenth to nineteenth century.[138] Most Australian cattle first came from South Africa, but they turned out to be too wild. Later, English cattle were brought to Australia in large numbers.

The United States was historically a net exporter of beef but it is now an enormous importer. Latin American countries that have cut down large areas of forestland in order to raise cattle for export have met a good portion of U.S. demand. One clear example is Costa Rica, where the country exported its rain forest to the United States.

The debt crisis left many countries in the developing world economically devastated, including Costa Rica. During the 1970s, it borrowed heavily from commercial banks, especially in short-term maturities and market-determined variable interest rates. The economy was especially vulnerable to external shocks and the oil price increases in 1973 and 1979 and the global recession in the early 1980s were especially harmful.

The recession of the early 1980s was critical to the development of the beef industry in Costa Rica for two reasons. The first reason was decreased demand for primary products from Costa Rica and other countries. Second, the United States instituted an aggressive monetary policy that weakened the Costa Rican currency. Costa Rica had to export more volume to receive the same value.

Many Latin American nations, such as Costa Rica, turned to cattle ranching to obtain crucial foreign exchange. The demand for beef in the

United States was extraordinarily high and these dollar-hungry nations chose clearcutting and deforestation for cattle ranches as one formula to earn dollars. In particular, Costa Rica deforested much of its tropical rain forests and Latin America as a whole lost 11 percent of its rain forests to cattle ranching. The Costa Rican government established specialized exchange rates and credit instruments in order to encourage cattle ranchers to expand beef exports or to attract new investors into cattle ranching. Beef exports from Costa Rica increased nearly 500 percent from the 1960s to the mid-1980s. Cattle pasture land increased from 27 percent to 54 percent of total land area.

Deforestation due to the expansion of cattle ranching also led to soil erosion. Tropical rain forests have delicate ecosystems that protect soils from substantial amounts of erosion. With the loss of forests, Costa Rica now has a problem of topsoil erosion, consequently depleting the land of its nutrients and ability to regenerate. The long-term effects of this depletion have been the overall reduction of the land's productive life.

Costa Rica today receives greater earnings from the preservation of its rain forests (through tourism) than it did from its destruction for beef exports. Ecotourism represents an economically and ecologically viable alternative to deforestation in that it too provides foreign exchange and saves the forest. However, part of this source of long-term revenue has been lost for short-term income.

THE CULTURE ASPECT American demand for beef is slowing, especially as the health risks of meat over-consumption become increasingly publicized. Because of lower demand and high trade barriers, the Costa Rican government removed the credit instruments and subsidies that promoted cattle ranching. In this way, the government is shifting policy to more sustainable forms of earning foreign exchange.

The demand for beef in the United States represents a culture identification embodied in representative institutions such as McDonald's, Wendy's, Burger King, and others. The hamburger is not only an American symbol, but also now a global icon. The Earth may be, however, simply unable to sustain the meat eating habits of "billions and billions" of hamburger eating people, especially as "McDonaldization" occurs throughout the world.

McDonald's is of course more than hamburgers—it is a culture unto itself. As McDonald's and other fast food franchises that specialize in hamburgers expand worldwide, the menu is altered to fit specific national diets. In India, McDonald's serves no beef and in Japan it emphasizes fish in the menu items. Thus, the culture of the product is more important than the product itself. Perhaps the hamburger is really an agent of a more popular culture attraction: service.

M. Sahlins argues that the American predilection towards beef is neither cultural nor genetic, but the result of eroticism: "a sexual code of food which must go back to the Indo-European identification of cattle . . . with virility and is tied to international trade and international political economy." Sahlins believes that eating beef is part of elite social status. Perhaps this conceptualization goes too far in emphasizing Freudian interpretations for beef eating, but it does cause some introspection. After all, if some Chinese men believe they achieve greater sexual potency by ingesting elephant tusk products, then it is fair to ask if American men may believe the same by eating hamburgers.

The hamburger is part of a ritual in culture, a habitat in the environment and a process-related trade issue. Early American settlers, especially in the West (at least in mythology) ate an end-of-the-day meal (often venison) around an open campfire, usually roasted game that had been shot. At this time, the hamburger had not been "invented," nor an industry created to support it. Over time, beef replaced the wild game, especially as deer were wiped out in many areas. The meal was an important event in sharing the wealth of the land but also in providing social cohesion to the group (similar to the mammoth and buffalo hunts).

THE CASE IN CONTEXT The ratio of meat in the human diet has changed over the history of conjunctions. In fact, today's reliance on meat consumption is much higher than any time since the Tool Conjunction. The difference is that this extra demand was met in the Tool Conjunction by expansion to new areas. In the Electronic Conjunction, the extra demand for meat will be met through intensification of agricultural practices in a world lacking new areas for expansion. Countries cannot avoid the pressure to adjust agricultural subsidy policies in a way that promotes a better environment. This implies a de-emphasis on meat in policy. What are the implications of national policies that overtly discourage the eating of meat? Would this be a barrier to trade?

There will continue to be a plethora of cases dealing with health and fair trade. The European Union has already lost WTO cases to the United States and Canada over bovine hormone use. This case links the new advances in gene technology with old ways of doing things. These hormones make cattle grow quicker, which seems to be good for the environment—given a certain production level—since the cattle will spend less time on pasture and thus more time set aside for regeneration. But this trend will put some small farmers out of business and encourage the growth of big farmers, which is bad for the environment. Thus, the case puts health and environmental issues on opposite sides of a trade issue from a number of perspectives.

The hamburger case is the latest chapter of the environment, people, and cultural practices in North America over the last thirty thousand years. The shift from the mammoth to the buffalo took thousands of years and was somewhat the result of natural causes while the shift from the buffalo to the cow took less than a century and was completely the result of human decisions.

PERSPECTIVES ON THE ELECTRONIC CONJUNCTION

The cases in the Electronic Conjunction start from a rather specific focus and spread out to a general impact. At either level, the cases show a clear intensification in the disconnect and a deterioration in the relationship between the economic viability of people and the culture and environment they live in. The events in Seattle were exclamation points and clear expressions of the distance that has grown between the factors in the social context during this newest Conjunction.

The disconnect between the reality of situations where trade, environment, and culture come together and the institutional approach to the three factors is palpable. The disconnect has risen from an item of intellectual interest in a historic perspective to an overriding issue for the people of the world.

Some short-term measures are necessary to allay the public fears of globalization. In the long term, institutional changes are vital to correct the direction of trends of today and the divisive historical trends of the past. Simply put: there need to be new approaches to how factors of trade, environment, and culture relate to civil society (a group that acts according to the prevailing "social context") and in institutional fora. This means a different approach to the Electronic Conjunction.

CHAPTER 4

BEYOND THE ELECTRONIC CONJUNCTION

THE FUTURE OFFERS a variety of new technologies, new social configurations, and new institutional challenges, but the real issues of the twenty-first century are likely to resemble those of long ago. This chapter provides four differing perspectives from which to view these long-standing issues. *Part one* contrasts the Electronic Conjunction with the Tool Conjunction in terms of major trends and themes. *Part two* examines different perspectives on the Electronic Conjunction, specifically on approaches to regulating environmental and cultural issues. *Part three* discusses environment and culture issues in the next efforts at trade liberalization. *Part four* examines two key ideas that will characterize the Electronic Conjunction and its impact in the twenty-first century: cultural feedback and the endless debate. *Part five* looks forward to the Gene Conjunction.

THE ELECTRONIC CONJUNCTION IN CONTEXT

This section compares the Electronic Conjunction with the Tool Conjunction. The purpose in comparing distinctly different periods is to clarify similarities and differences that emerge from extreme chronological perspectives. Most examinations of historical changes look at continuous patterns of comparison and contrast. There is good reason to believe that historical patterns are not necessarily linear or progressive with respect to the human condition or the state of the environment.

COMPARING THE TOOL AND ELECTRONIC CONJUNCTIONS

The technological changes in the Tool Conjunction produced new realities in trade, culture, and environment. Trade at this time served quite a different purpose than today. Then, trade was largely limited to the transfer of information and new technologies due to limited bulk transportation capacities. Over time, trade played a greater role in subsistence strategies as bulk transportation capacities grew. This reality stands in stark contrast to the Electronic Conjunction where trade can be completed entirely in digital information, possessing (virtually) no bulk whatsoever!

There are of course great differences between these two periods beyond differences in technology. Trade in the Tool Conjunction was carried out on a point-to-point basis, passing from a single buyer to a single seller. Sometimes the trade of a product between two points might take several years, passing from village to village along a transportation route. The sole producer of the good, the person who made the bows, knives, or chipping tools, often sold the product. Products were the outputs of *individuals*.

In the Electronic Conjunction, however, trade passes through a system comprised of *groups* of buyers and sellers. There is much more separation today between the creator of a product and its consumer. The vast number of social and material interactions that now take place with respect to creating, producing, and selling a modern product is entirely different from a Tool Conjunction product. As the modern product is honed for the market, through focus groups, surveys and the like, it becomes more and more a social rather than an individual invention. This is quite different from the more utilitarian nature of ancient tools and the focus on individuals. The point is that just as trade acts to drive a wedge between culture and environment, so too does the conjunction increase the distance between consumer and producer and thereby enlarge the disconnect on another dimension.

The following section compares the Tool and Electronic Conjunctions on the basis of four attributes:

1. the rate of incremental change
2. the degree of trade diffusion
3. the cultural direction of the period
4. the environmental impact

Both the Tool and Electronic Conjunctions exhibit a high *rate of incremental change* in technology that culminates in extraordinary long-term changes in lifestyles. Recall that stone, and later bone tools, underwent slow but steady progress in the Tool Conjunction over the course of thousands of years. There was a gradual refinement that led to an almost imperceptible improvement in the effectiveness and efficiency of the tools in the period. This incrementalism is also evident today in gradual but seemingly never-ending changes in communication and computer technology. Surfing and data-mining techniques in the Electronic Conjunction show a similar pattern of piecemeal technological advancement as in the development of chipping and flaking techniques in the Tool Conjunction. Before, these techniques were intended for use in the "hunt" for game. Now, these techniques are used in the "hunt" for information, sometimes using "killer" applications.

For many who live in the Electronic Conjunction today, the pace of change has become too quick, just as it may have been in the Tool Conjunction. Then, technological change may have occurred over the course of a generation. Now, it may occur frequently over the course of a year. The pace of change is thus a relative concept.

The computer, the energizing tool of the current conjunction, is not a single invention but a combination of many. Consider the pace of technological change in the last two decades. The personal computer emerged in the mid-1970s and one of the first was the Radio Shack TRS-80. The TRS-80 was one piece in the evolution of the personal computer. Another technological step was the development of the IBM "286" computer that was followed by the mostly non-IBM "386," the "486," and the Pentium. On the software side, "DOS" gave way to "Windows," while users of Word Perfect who started with Version 1.0 encountered incremental upgrades that led to Version 8.0 (at last count).

What do computer users of today have to do with the hunters of forty thousand years ago? Both no doubt felt a shock due to the high rate of change that weakened the relationships in the social context. Surely, people who lived in the Tool Conjunction felt somewhat similar when stone flaking technologies gradually gave way to the use of tools that are more sophisticated and a variety of differing materials. The shift from stone to bone may have been equally as confusing as the shift from DOS 3.1 to Windows 95.

Societies and social contexts constantly undergo changes in their economic and social systems. The difference in the pace of incremental change can be significant for social structures. Rigid social structures come under considerable pressure in periods of high social change. In the Tool Conjunction, incremental changes occurred but were no doubt spread out over several years (at least) and provided considerable generational stability.

The pace of change then and now is very different. Incremental changes are now occurring almost every year and, subsequently, there now exist very few periods of technological stability. Thus, one essential part of the disconnect is the pace of change versus the capacity of people to absorb change. The objective of policy today should be to welcome the new technology but also to assure social stability during such periods of high technological change. As the rate of technology change increases, the need for humans to adapt more quickly to these changes also increases. Is there an adaptive limit in our capacity for change? The answer is yes, although that limit may differ according to individual cultures. Highly structured societies may be more vulnerable to change than those less structured.

There are also varying forces propelling incremental changes in the two periods. In the Tool Conjunction, new hardware or product tools drove change. New software or process tools now significantly drive technologies. Today, the logic of tool use is more important than the material bases on which tools are built. This focus on process is an inevitable condition given the type of tool that the computer is. The Electronic Conjunction is based on a series of "bytes," the building blocks or "atoms" of the digital world. In the Tool Conjunction, stones were pared down and put back together in differing configurations to create new tools. Now, programmers combine bytes into commands that follow logical structures and the result is computer software.

A second area for comparison is that of *trade diffusion*. Through trade, a product spreads and is built upon by the many peoples who encounter it. Thus, incremental changes occur in many places and a conjunction is built on many different pieces of a puzzle that contribute to an overall change in the human condition. Because of this diffusion of change, the gradual incremental steps in the conjunction slowly create a new social context that enables more change. The conjunction process latently introduces almost imperceptible adjustments to society and provides the basis for more changes.

In both the Tool and Electronic Conjunctions, the scope of the change was widespread in a geographic sense although the spread of these new technologies was not uniform. New technologies in the Tool Conjunction spread from modern day Madrid to Moscow over the span of many years, perhaps millennia. New tools in the Electronic Conjunction spread from Moscow to Madrid to Minneapolis to Montevideo to Mombassa in the course of days. The scope and speed of change is clearly much more widespread today. Trade today diffuses and extends the course of technological change throughout the globe much more broadly than it did forty thousand years ago.

TABLE 4.1 **Comparing the Tool and Electronic Conjunctions**

Indicator	Tool Conjunction	Electronic Conjunction
Rate of Change	High	High
Rate of Diffusion	Slow	Fast
Cultural Content	High	High
Environment Impact	Species	Habitat

A third area for comparison between the two periods is that of *cultural content*, especially when it involves new technologies spread through trade diffusion. The impact of trade and technology is a powerful force that can change cultures. Trade tends to expose cultures to new ideas from the outside, thus creating general (or macro) cultures at the expense of specific ones. Trade in culture, which can include exports of music, movies, and other types of art, has long been a common cause of transaction and conflict between countries. The commodification of culture is now rampant in today's Conjunction, but this phenomenon has always been present in history. Trade in "Venus" statues during the Tool Conjunction was in part culturally motivated. The conclusion is that culture has always been an important part of trade but never before has it been so commercially pervasive.

A final area for comparison is the *environmental impact* of trade during a conjunction. The environment invariably tends to suffer during these periods of extraordinary change. Technologies produce new ways of channeling environmental resources and often result in habitat and species loss. New technologies often arise out of the need or desire to reap greater outputs from the environment. The Tool Conjunction greatly impacted species, but the scope and scale of possible impacts in the Electronic Conjunction are much broader and deeper. The overkill hypothesis, explaining the disappearance of certain mega-fauna forty thousand years ago, is an apt simile for today's assault of the world's bio-diversity. Moreover, the aggregation and breadth of pollution problems today did not exist during the Tool Conjunction. Table 4.1 compares the conjunctions based on several system attributes.

THEMES IN THE ELECTRONIC CONJUNCTION

The cases that have already occurred in the Electronic Conjunction, discussed in the prior chapter, reveal the breadth of environmental and cultural implications that result from modern trade intensification and globalization. Out of the prior cases, it is possible to glean six key trends to characterize the Electronic Conjunction.

First, the number of trade conflicts that center on culture and environment will increase. Different cultures hold varying moral views with respect to the environment and, as trade brings cultures together, cultural differences will inevitably lead to dispute. The bear case directly illustrates such a difference in cultural beliefs. One reason the case attracted so much attention is the way in which the bears ultimately met their death; they are boiled alive. The bears cry out in pain as they are dumped into the huge vats before their deaths—cries that cannot be tolerated by many people.[1] However, many of these same people have eaten fresh lobster—lobster that met its death in the same fashion as the bear. These two examples illustrate the depth or intensity of cultural variations between groups that engage in trade.

Second, the types of disputes in the Electronic Conjunction will expand as trade interactions spread to include more product types and more cultures. It is clear that cultures view and value environmental resources differently. For example, the demand for Hawksbill turtles in Japan posed a threat to their survival on the other side of the planet. The turtle shell was highly valued in Japan but of low value in Cuba, therefore creating a strong impetus to trade. Despite its perceived low value in Cuba, traders continued to reap huge economic benefits due to the high demand for the turtle shell in Japan. Both Japan, as the importer, and Cuba, as the exporter, found economic benefit in trade, but at the expense of the turtle. This case suggests an instance of "discovered" economic value arising due to differences in cultural customs. This discovery of value only pertains to commercial matters, not to recognition of any inherent or intrinsic value to the sea turtle itself.

The Guam bat case focuses on the cultural-environmental nexus in the social context. Guam's people regard bats as having a high economic value but most other people in the world assign them a negative economic value and view them as something whose exploitation is a virtue. This creates a "lose-lose" situation for the bat, where not only do people want to get rid of the creature for reasons of taste but also due to unfounded myths and fears.

Third, culture will continue to pose a substantial threat to the environment in the Electronic Conjunction. Demand for cultural products remains so strong today that, in many cases, black markets have arisen to supply products even when synthetics or like-product substitutes are readily available. Illegal trade appears in cases involving bears, elephants, turtles, and other species. There remains strong demand for cultural products, even as incomes grow. These products are often traditional, which makes them a symbol of a way of life. The higher incomes seem not to lower the cultural value of a species but, rather simply, make it more affordable.

This elevated income and steady demand has in part led to the decline of wild animal stocks, used in many traditional products, and the rise of new types of farming operations. Farms have arisen that specialize in bears, snakes, monkeys, and other animals. The very concept of a farm is undergoing massive changes in the types of species under domestication. The concept of domestication is being applied to more and more species, almost like a second Agricultural Conjunction. There is considerable evidence to support the idea that the trends of today are echoes of past trends, put together again in differing combinations. One change is the extending of the agricultural advances of the past that occurred on land to include ocean innovations. "Within the next fifty years fish farming may change us from hunters and gatherers on the seas into 'marine pastoralists'—just as a similar innovation some 10,000 years ago changed our ancestors from hunters and gatherers on the land into agriculturists and pastoralists."[2]

Fourth, the impact of culture on the environment through trade will reach new issue areas and new types of economic transactions. These are again old issues at heart. The Cree, Native Americans living in Canada, are one people especially vulnerable to the new impacts. Not only are the Cree prevented from exporting fur skins to Europe (an old problem with a new twist), their lands are being flooded in part to export electricity (a new problem with a new twist). The coral case, likewise, illustrates areas where a relatively new type of demand threatens the environment. Keeping coral in aquariums does not meet a basic human need, but provides a sense of well being for the hobbyist. Some environmentalists argue that this "hobby" is a greater threat to coral than even global warming.

Fifth, growing global cultural demands will increase the rate and scale of global land-use changes. The hamburger and sugar cases illustrate the enormous changes that these two products alone have brought to cultures and environments. A conjunction leads to an overall increase in wealth or income. Rising incomes in many countries now permit people to buy hamburger and sugar (and other products) in greater amounts than ever before. Some of the greater demand for such products was due to population growth, but some are also due to changes in lifestyles and cultures. This is evident in a country such as China, where personal caloric consumption is rising faster than the population.

FIGURE 4.1

Six Key Themes in the Electronic Conjunction

1. There will be more trade conflicts.
2. There will be more types of trade disputes.
3. Culture will threaten species.
4. New trade will influence culture and environment.
5. Culture will threaten habitats.
6. Culture will react to trade/environmental changes.

Sixth, cultures will be at risk as trade patterns change and produce new types of direct and indirect impacts. Japan was directly impacted and substantially changed its *bekko* tradition after the turtle import ban, while the Cree were forced to adopt alternative industries because of the European fur import ban. Some impacts, however, will be quite indirect. Peru argues that the unique tradition of pisco is at risk by imitators from other countries. The ownership of certain names is one area of curious overlap between claims of earlier, current, and future conjunctions. Besides being an important part of the World Wide Web, domain names are also an issue in the context of ownership and labeling. The EU, especially, is pushing for specific protection of products emanating from European cultures and environments. Thus, the policies regarding Internet domain names also apply to real, historical products such as Scotch Whisky, Camembert Cheese, Champagne champagne, and Irish gin. Figure 4.1 summarizes the main ideas in the six trends.

APPROACHES TO CONJUNCTIONS

This section takes a philosophical look at the confluence of trade, environment, and culture with respect to its larger impact on social development in the next century. The twenty-first century will mark the full intrusion of the Electronic Conjunction on global society. This intrusion will require the creation of new rules, as the following four parts describe. The first area for discussion is how the rules might result from or impact actual conduct in societies. Second, how does trade, environment and, above all, culture relate to the process of development? Third, if culture were part of trade rules and policy, what mechanisms would it include? Fourth, rather than treating culture as a liability to reform, perhaps there are ways to harness unique cultural attributes to solve environmental problems.

Trade often breaks the traditional culture-environment link, leading to a disconnect, as one set of cultural imperatives causes changes in far-off environments or as new technologies are imported. However, any attempt to regulate trade to avoid this problem may produce an even worse outcome. Just because there is a problem does not mean it should or can be solved by rules or institutions.

MAKING CULTURAL LAW IS LIKE MAKING SAUSAGE

There is an American belief, passed down by German immigrants, that polite people should never observe two sights: the making of sausage and the process of making law.

Sausage is a cylindrical tube of meat that blends leftover animal parts—mostly pig and cow offal including lips, nostrils, and other meat scraps—and mixes them with fat and spices. The sausage is packed in individual parcels made of the guts or intestines of the animal. The reason for avoiding the viewing of sausage making is obvious: if people knew what was in the sausage and the process for making it they would never eat it. The second forbidden observation is the real process for creating legislation and ultimately law. For the optimistic and often naive American, the realization of how democracy actually works would certainly shatter their belief in the American system.[3] Enacting laws about culture in a global context will certainly invite the worst of both of these sights.

When culture and trade come together, culture is a powerful and potentially lethal force capable of destroying both species and habitat. Unbridled cultural demands are acceptable only as long as resources are available in abundance. As a result of population growth this luxury of abundance no longer exists. With increased global interdependence, the survival needs of a people are inexorably tied to the survival needs of other peoples. At the same time, more people will compete for a dwindling base of resources that will be, in part, defined by their cultural outlooks.

A necessary step to making global cultural rules, with respect to trade, would be in designing precise limits between acceptable and unacceptable behavior. Is it possible to create some absolute markers of cultural behavior?

In fact, the shifting ground of cultural beliefs in trade fora presents a major challenge to a more static rules-based system. How much of a country's broadcast television time is necessary to maintain a domestic culture? Do the French really need 50 percent of their television and film broadcasts to be in French in order to maintain the survival of the language? Can a country withhold import rights based on cultural beliefs? Do Israel's kosher meat import rules act as technical barriers to trade? Issues such as these underscore a more general question. What is cultural excess?

Cultural excess describes behavior outside the realm of the majority of accepted beliefs of most cultures around the world. While there should be some exceptions that allow derogations from trade rules as part of a cultural belief, there must also be a way to declare some of them too extreme if they are causing substantial economic or environmental losses. Vincent Cable believes that some rules on cultural excess already exist, citing the existing "GATT exemption for culturally offensive material (Article 20)."[4] The WTO thus recognizes that countries are free to choose their own definitions of what is a "culturally offensive material." The definition will clearly differ in government offices in Riyadh, Saudi Arabia, or Copenhagen, Denmark. There is a natural tendency to be country-specific in this regard and this peculiarity can be the cause of later disagreement. The writings of Salman Rushdie are treated quite differently under British and Iranian law.

Trade systems already do include the residue of moral decisions. "Trade preference systems—in the EU and the United States—are also increasingly being used to reward or to penalize behavior on ethical grounds."[5] Both the Generalized System of Preferences (GSP) and the Lome Convention contain exceptions based on moral principles related to labor and human rights conditions. These principles may provide the basis for more general moral and cultural codes of conduct related to culture in the WTO.

Cable sees globalization and global integration as forces that, in two instances, may sharpen cultural differences rather than blend them. First, as "globalization" deepens, latent differences in cultural preferences will rise through exposure to other goods, services, and ideas. Second, global integration is now embracing a range of participants—the big Asian countries, the former Soviet Union—where the contrasts of cultural values are particularly vivid.

Cable also sees conflict between conjunctions, as entrenched historical interests battle newer ones. The slowing of impeding change in cultures and environments is said to defend tradition. The fervent French defense of farming interests at the end of the Uruguay Round was expressed in terms of defending traditional French values and protecting the environment and lifestyles rather than more traditional arguments based on issues of national security, equity, or regional balance.

One objection to culturally based rules is that they are sometimes counter-productive. For example, most citizens of developed countries and their governments oppose child labor and there is serious discussion of creating rules on the trade of products created with the work of child labor. However, rules against child labor may remove key breadwinners from developing country families. Similar to defining what is offensive, there could be differing definitions of what is a child and what is child labor.

> The other reasons why ethical values and trade measures mix badly is that there are often hidden motives involved. This is especially true for two potentially very divisive and important issues on the new trade agenda: trade and labour standards; and trade and environment.[6]

Culture and environment issues will arise in the WTO and other multilateral fora. With the likelihood that both culture and environment issues will grow in number and diversity with respect to trade, the probability of a jurisdictional overlap between competing multilateral fora does not seem preposterous. Organizations need to begin thinking about how these issues may overlap. Initial discussion might focus on certain sectors or sets of them.

CULTURE, POLICY, AND DEVELOPMENT

How culture fits into these institutions regulating economic exchange will tend to fragment until there is an over-arching theory and policy about how culture, environment, and trade figure into the general process of development. As humans do develop, this theory and policy will need to undergo constant refinement and revision.

The general role of culture in the development process, which naturally impacts environments and trade, is well recognized but not well understood. Wole Soyinka, Nobel Laureate for Literature, sees a dynamic relationship between culture and development. He quotes Amilcar Cabral, with a clearly deterministic viewpoint, in declaring that:

> Culture . . . is an essential element of the history of a people. Culture is perhaps, the resultant of history, just as the flower is the resultant of the plant. Like history, or because it is history, culture has a material reality in the environment in which it develops, and it reflects the organic nature of the society, which may be more or less influenced by external factors.[7]

The idea of cultural adjustment is now part of many development policies. In some instances, development is actually constrained to allow culture to keep pace and, in other instances, it is used as a means to speed development. This attempt to include culture as a factor in the development process is a double-edged sword because it also opens the door for large-scale social engineering. Manipulating cultures to achieve developmental goals may well mean warping the culture and destroying it in the long term. The danger is that as culture is used to promote development, desires to slow progress to maintain cultural coherence may be either ignored or shunned. Development may favor certain cultural practices but ignore others. Since trade is part of mainstream development strategies, there may be a tendency to opt for cultural attributes favorable to competing in global markets.

Ismail Serageldin of the World Bank believes "accelerated change brings discontinuities and does not allow for the evolution of perceptions to cope with and internalize change."[8] The World Bank, through its policies, would prefer to keep cultural identity intact and to promote empowerment (both of people within governments and developing country governments vis-à-vis developed ones). In practice, empowerment may be contrary to the existing cultural identity in development projects where rigid, top-down political systems exist. Thus, the policy may carry the untoward consequence of also promoting discord. Serageldin recognizes this tendency to produce internal conflict in a country. Other multilateral statements echo this view. The 1982 UNESCO (United Nations Educational, Scientific, and Cultural Organization) World Conference on Cultural Policies in Mexico City concluded that development is more than just economic progress.

> Balanced development can only be ensured by making cultural factors an integral part of the strategies designed to achieve it; consequently, these strategies should always be devised in the light of the historical, social and cultural context of each society.[9]

Serageldin sees four ways in which cultural norms are the natural outgrowth of a healthy civil society that can survive the transition from a traditional to a modern society. First, there should be no dichotomy between modernity and tradition. The modern themes of art, writing, and ideas resonate the art, writing, and ideas of long ago. Second, spirituality and modernism are not natural enemies. Societies are a mix of both, old and new, and always have been. Third, there is not a vast gulf between the societies possessing high and low technology. Both technologies are inevitably part of any society, with the newer grafted onto the old. The key is in how the

FIGURE 4.2

UNESCO Legal Instruments to Protect Culture

1. Convention for the Protection of Cultural Property in the Event of Armed Conflict, 1954 (in force in 90 states)
2. Convention Against Illicit Traffic of Cultural Property, 1970 (in force in 88 states)
3. World Heritage Convention, 172 (in force in 152 states)
4. World Heritage List (552 sites in 112 countries: 418 cultural, 114 natural, and 20 mixed)
5. Convention for Underwater Cultural Heritage (in preparation)

Source: Data from Ismail Serageldin, *Culture and Development at the Millennium: The Challenge and the Response* (Washington, D.C.: World Bank, 1998), p. 27. Speech distributed in pamphlet form.

technology fits into the social context and the type of disconnect that results. Finally, cultures are not exclusive to a particular people.[10] The problem is not in an inherent weakness in culture, but rather in the difficulty of establishing identity and from it culture in a period of rapid change.

> The world is in the grip of profound transformation, as globalization makes the planet an ever smaller place. Revolutions in telecommunications and capital flows have created bonds across continents, and the ubiquity of consumer items are calling into question the very sense of place and social identity.[11]

Some precedents on cultural law and practice do exist but it is not possible to definitively say whether these efforts have led to success or failure. The World Heritage List consists of 552 sites around the world and the World Bank is financing cultural operations in twenty to thirty countries. Figure 4.2 shows the legal instruments available to UNESCO to protect culture, including: protection of cultural artifact trade, protection during conflict, and protection of specific sites, most of which are man-made, and others that are natural or mixed. There are plans to add protection to underwater cultural sites.

Perhaps another way to assess the role of culture is to think of it in explicitly economic terms. Robert Klitgaard discusses the notion of "cultural capital" and the apparent lack of cultural preconditions that are requirements for development. Cultures may lack the capacity for absorbing rapid or far-reaching changes. Accumulating capital is an intrinsic part of the development process and part of this process is the accumulation of cultural capital. These two goals may in fact be at odds with one another.

> Policies and economic systems adapt to culture and cultures to them, policies can change cultures, cultures have their own dynamic of change, and valuations of development ends and means are themselves shaped by culture. Development itself is a culturally loaded term.[12]

How to balance culture and development in policy requires some elaboration of the benefits of culture so that one can measure them against the benefits of development. As a result, measuring cultural assets is both important and difficult.

> Current work drawing from environmental economics is trying to get a more refined appreciation of the costs and benefits of managing cultural assets. The costs of the loss of irreplaceable heritage and the benefits of preserving it, beyond the utilitarian commercial benefits, of say tourist revenues, are not easy to determine. Adapting a range of techniques—from hedonic pricing and travel cost methods to contingent valuation—to estimate the intangible benefits of cultural assets is one step in that direction.[13]

Perhaps the time issue needs addressing when considering culture in a completely opposite development context: that is, in slowing development rather than accelerating it. Conjunctions have focused on speeding development, but perhaps the time has come to consider slowing development to preserve environments and cultures. In the end, such an approach might lead to fewer social disruptions, fewer disconnects, and more sustained progress.

Perhaps the outlook should not view changes in culture as the products of the conjunction, but rather as the causes for it. Ali Mazrui believes that both ideology and technology are rooted in culture.[14] Mazrui opts for slowing development, so that the transition for some is slower and less dependent on Western influences. Mazrui embraces the idea of a cultural audit and that there should be measures "of cultural biases to inform us about the moral constraints (and support) for development."[15] Daniel Etounga-Manguelle believes that Africa needs a program of cultural as well as structural adjustment assistance.[16]

The idea of integrating culture into development has been around for a long time but so far has produced rather limited results. Franz Boas in the 1920s called for the use of applied anthropology and planned cultural change in development strategies. Margaret Meade, in 1952, led a team of anthropologists intent on applying culture to development; their efforts only brought the problem of cultural relativism into open dispute. Klitgaard argues that such cultural polices should be pro-active but efforts to this point have been misguided for four reasons:

1. Cultural differences across disciplines
2. Oversimplification of culture
3. Scientific problems
4. Misuse of policy analysis[17]

CAN CULTURAL EXCESSES BE DEFINED?

Cultural excess exists when economic and environmental impacts exceed a reasonable level of sustainability. This definition, however, is so relative it borders on being tautological. Sustainability, the use of a resource only within a certain rate of generation, or the polluting of the environment only within a certain rate of absorption, is itself defined from a particular cultural perspective and a given point in environmental time. Culture thus plays an extraordinary role in creating conditions for sustainability, but also in defining it. Sustainability is not only a reflection on environment and development issues, but political and cultural ones as well.

In an institutional framework, rules on culture will be absolute, but cultural excess is relative and can differ by both time and place. Cultural excess may force a change in the morality of people's economic demands *over time* and thus a change in environmental values. Beliefs about powerful animals are a good example. Many cultures have long prized certain large or powerful animals such as bears, sharks, whales, lions, and elephants. In earlier times, these animals were killed for a number of reasons, one of which was clearly prestige for the hunter and another the removal of human predators. The perspectives on large felines such as lions and tigers are good examples of how these moral outlooks have changed with time and development.

The current protection of lions and tigers (notably) are because there are so few left. Tourists pay enormous amounts to see these animals and shooting today is mostly carried out with a camera. It is also now recognized that these animals are essential parts of a healthy eco-system. This recognition prompted the re-introduction of another predator, the wolf, into some parts of the northern United States, in part to keep down exploding deer populations that were causing extensive crop damage. It is not the lion that had changed, but the level of human technological progress and the conditions and perceptions that arise from it. Technological progress lessens the need to eliminate food competitors such as large felines. Prestige is also found in other ways today, such as in owning a fast car.

A clear example of changing perceptions relates to the cedar tree (see Chapter 2). When cedar was in ample supply in the Middle East, it was an object of great desire and even became cause for war. As cedars became limited they also became venerated, precisely because there were so few. In Lebanon, tourists continue to visit the remaining cedar forests, as if to continue the veneration and rue prior behavior. The cedars, or rather the lack of them, show the visitors that development is not necessarily an upward progression with respect to the environment. The record, in fact, often seems to suggest an inverse relationship.

Cultural excess can also have a relative meaning because *of place*. The prior examples looked at how culture can change over time. Cultural excess may also differ across geography, meaning that the availability of the resources, and values attached to them, may depend on relative local endowments. Relative resource availability may influence relative cultural morality.

The fur case provides a good example of the link between availability and morality. Fur-bearing animals are largely absent in Europe (in the wild) and thus morality is drawn from animal treatment in captive situations. North Americans, who have abundant fur-bearing animals, have no need for pelt farms. This is not to endorse Marvin Harris's materialistic orientation to explaining culture, but rather to say that the culture and environment dynamics between differing peoples in differing places can produce distinct outcomes and worldviews. In this view, the environment does not merely determine the culture, but is a critical factor among others that help mold culture.

Differences in environmental endowments can assist in determining cultural values and thus cultural excesses. For example, a person coming from an environment with ten tigers will look on the act of killing ten tigers differently than a person from a country with ten million tigers. To a Norwegian, a forest will mean something different than to an Egyptian. Naturally, as environments differ so do cultures.

There are also differing approaches to development and these differences can shape particular strategies. Some societies may want to shun development. There are people today, such as the Batek, who live more like people from the Tool Conjunction than the Electronic Conjunction. Should these peoples be expected to live under the accepted cultural values of the Electronic Conjunction? Is it reasonable to force people, such as the Cree and other indigenous peoples, to join a new conjunction? The idealistic answer is no. The realistic answer is that they cannot resist such powerful global forces.

The Cree case involving building dams and exporting electricity points to a relatively unexplored perspective of culture, environment, and the role of indigenous peoples. This area is a key point of disconnect in the Electronic Conjunction. Alan Durning lays out the following policy elements to protect indigenous peoples and their cultural and environmental rights. These include 1) respect for basic human rights, 2) identifying native lands, 3) providing legal assistance, 4) passage of the U.N. declaration on indigenous peoples, and 5) new policies for development agencies such as the World Bank that also intend to protect cultures.[18]

Just as cultural excess occurs, so too do trade and environmental excesses. Defining cultural excess depends on the (relative) interpretation of trade and environment norms. Defining trade or environmental excesses is also relative to cultural views. Defining a cultural norm or excess in any one of these entities is thus contingent on the definitions in the other two. As the world has become more multidisciplinary, so too should the institutions that people create become broader and with more inter-linkages in the issues they deal with.

Some existing trade concepts and disciplines may be transferable to the new areas of environment and culture. For example, one might call the dumping of a trade product as a kind of excess. Thus, there are already trade remedy mechanisms that might apply to a cultural dumping case. The trouble would be in measuring the cultural impacts in an economic context in order to calculate a fair level of countervailing duties.

In reality such cases already do exist. Canada accuses the United States of dumping cultural product (sports information) and the United States accuses Canada of dumping environmental product (softwood lumber).[19] Thus, acceptance of cultural and environmental issues in the WTO may mean accepting the idea that subsidies and dumping practices may apply to them as well. New thinking may include the recognition that there exists a nascent trade-off between cultural and environmental issues in trade fora and these two entities can be pitted against one another.

Policy reflects the norms and values of a country. As norms are institutionalized and made into policy, they become more narrow and rigid in their application. An inevitable collision occurs when a civil system of norms, based on contingent and relative beliefs, meets a legal system based on absolutes. If policies tilt toward the emphasis on law, there is danger of overregulation. If policies tilt toward a looser civil approach, this may provide loopholes that will weaken the system. This "soft" nature of cultural and environmental issues seems to pose the most difficulties for the "hard" rules of the WTO.

The problems of substantial environmental and cultural change during a conjunction are not new. During a conjunction the balance between trade, environment, and culture is thrown awry because of the differential impact of technology. Excesses are expected in a conjunction and thus perspectives on culture, environment, and trade can quickly change. These changing perspectives, coupled with new tools, provide a basis for excesses to occur. Here again, reasonable people can ask for some degree of objective truth that will not be simple to provide. The conjunction itself is the result of excess—of adopting differing ways of living and differing lifestyles.

Perhaps the last thing that the forces of change in the Electronic Conjunction need is regulation. It would be ironic if the end result of the regulation of environment and culture, through recognition in trade disciplines, produced the very unwanted result of choking off progress and killing the Electronic Conjunction.

CULTURAL APPROPRIATENESS

This section departs from the discussion of cultural excess as a problem to a theme focusing more on culture as a solution. Under this model, no excess exists; rather, a culture is neither excessive nor deficient but molded to fit a particular environment. This molding may well provide the outline for environmental restoration because a healthy culture can improve an unhealthy environment. This section first discusses the idea of restoration ecology. Second, it examines the role of cultural appropriateness in restoration ecology.

The idea of cultural excess is based on a global perspective where there exists a general set of agreed-upon norms across countries. Cultural excess is one symptom of a top-down cultural outlook. This view is absolute and heavily infused with a Western orientation and bias. A bottom-up approach might focus on cultural appropriateness in providing both trade opportunity and environmental protection at a local level. The idea is to use culture to focus efforts on trade and environmental improvement. Some grant-making foundations, such as the Rockefeller Brothers Fund, support sustainable resource policies that are suited for a particular region and culture.[20] This focus on cultural appropriateness is part of a newly emerging research and policy area called "restoration ecology."

The restoration ecology approach focuses on solving specific environmental problems. This approach to cultural and environmental sustainability is not only one of preserving existing pristine environments, but also of improving already degraded environments. The idea is to create conditions for sustainability from areas that lack it. Restoration ecology thus places the relative human experience within an environmental landscape and within a particular cultural context. Trade results from the utilization of resources that a sustainable environment and economy provides.

> Ecological restoration is a fast-growing and relatively new art and science. Restorationists build "natural" ecosystems—marshes, forests, deserts, and waterways more or less as they were at some period of time before human activities damaged them."[21]

Restoration ecology is perhaps most appropriate in areas such as East Asia where environmental conditions are quite unique and undergoing rapid change. There is also a need for remedies to old problems. In China, there remain few pristine environments in most parts of the country (as noted, most of the forests in China were gone by the seventeenth century). In Vietnam, the environment has been severely disrupted by nearly a half-century of war. Environmental degradation in these two countries is clearly not the result of culture, but factors of poverty and war. Just as harming the environment is not new, neither is the idea of protecting the environment.

> Indigenous peoples created the world's first protected areas centuries ago. Their sacred places—sacred forests and mountains, sacred springs, rivers, lakes, caves and countless other hallowed sites and areas—were regions removed from everyday access and resource use, the abodes of nature spirits and powers with which people communed but did not interfere.[22]

The idea of protecting diversity can be applied equally to environment and culture. Similar to the fate of many species, many cultures are disappearing. Yet, they are still a substantial part of the world's population and eco-systems.

> The 5,000 to 8,000 . . . indigenous peoples in the world account for as much as 90 to 95 percent of the world's cultural diversity. According to a recent report by the

indigenous rights organization, Cultural Survival, there are more than 5,000 such peoples, with a total population of more than 600 million, 10 to 15 percent of the world's population. They today inhabit, and claim as traditional homelands, at least 20 percent of the earth's surface and perhaps as much as 30 percent, four to six times more territory than is encompassed within the entire global protected area system.[23]

The problem remains the disconnect between the day-to-day lives of people and the relation to the environment and the cultural context in which they exist. How do we put the relationship of trade, environment, and culture back together after a period of divergence of at least two thousand years? The first step is to recognize the dissonance between natural ways of life and the rigidity of global rules.

Indigenous peoples ways of life are grounded in place. Their subsistence practices rely on the use of local resources and ecosystems to a great degree. Many economies have economics based on the subsistence use of natural resources, and live by agriculture, agropastoralism, or nomadic pastoralism, often supplementing these with hunting, fishing, and collecting wild plant resources . . . Many indigenous peoples, over time, have also developed indigenous social and cultural mechanisms that regulate land use to sustainable levels, or at least moderate its impact on the environment.[24]

The cultural appropriateness approach differs from the cultural excess approach in that rather than "weeding" out cultural practices that do not fit a general norm, it actively embraces the wisdom in different cultures and uses them to create sustainable environments. Rather than trying to seek a single acceptable norm across cultures, trade regimes, and environments, it embraces the diversity of cultures and environments as solutions.

The cultural appropriateness approach disdains global perspectives and brings the focus of environmental and economic protection efforts down to the local level. But this is only a temporary solution. This local approach will inevitably conflict with the global forces that are an inherent part of any period of high change, including the Electronic Conjunction. Perhaps a middle ground might incorporate both the ideas of cultural appropriateness and cultural excess.

The natural diversity of cultures and environments in the world translate into diversity in trade products. There may be variety in the types of products flowing from a particular area, but not diversity in the norms that underlie multilateral trade disciplines. Some fear growing diversity in trade norms, and the non-tariff barriers to trade that often accompany them.

TRADE, ENVIRONMENT, AND CULTURE IN THE NEXT TRADE ROUND

The next phase of trade liberalization may be an important step for determining the extent and direction of globalization in the early part of the twenty-first century. The phase, whether it is the form of a WTO round or other venues, will be significant in setting an economic agenda and addressing non-economic issues, especially environment and culture. Many would prefer to leave behind such nagging, but unresolved, issues and move on to new liberalizations in emerging products and markets. It is most likely not possible for the WTO to move too far ahead without finalizing these old yet unresolved issues.

There are varieties of viewpoints on the including of cultural and environmental issues within a trade institution such as the WTO. These viewpoints include: 1) the WTO should incorporate environment and culture issues within its strictures, 2) parallel global environmental and cultural institutions, similar to the function the WTO performs with respect to trade, should arise, and 3) the WTO should stay out of the areas of culture and environment altogether. This latter group includes many who believe the WTO has already gone too far.

THE NEXT WTO ROUND

Called the "Millennium Round," since the onset of the talks would roughly coincide with the year 2000, these negotiations meant to point to a hopeful future in the third millennium. Early on, there were signs that culture and environment issues would be contentious areas for negotiation. Surprisingly, some of the greatest proponents of national cultural rights (such as France) oppose including culture in the Millennium Round for fear of losing national sovereignty on the issue.

The shaping of the next round of trade talks has been underway for at least two years, or shortly after the finalizing of the Uruguay Round negotiations and agreement. In May 1998, the EU gave its chief negotiator, Sir Leon Brittain, permission to seek the beginning of talks on a new trade round. The United States endorsed the idea but vacillated between endorsing an ambitious "big round," similar to the broad scope of the Uruguay Round, and a "small round," which might focus on a few limited sectors, especially unfinished business in agriculture and services. The United States and other governments seem to have little desire for open-ended trade talks such as the Tokyo and Uruguay rounds. Some developing countries, such as Malaysia, oppose a new round altogether. Others analysts believe that further economic problems (such as the Asian financial crisis) around the world may make a "big" round less likely. The events in Seattle made this "big" round idea quite remote.

Culture remains a volatile issue. Disagreement over trade policy in audio-visual services almost prevented the completion of the Uruguay Round. French broadcast rules limit foreign television broadcast times to no more than 50 percent of the total airtime. The United States contended that the quotas violated member states' obligations under the GATT. Despite the rules, Europeans are voting with their eyes: eighteen million viewers from the five largest European countries tune in each week to see American programs. In the late 1990s the most popular television show in the world was "Baywatch," a show about California beach lifeguards. American films represent 82 percent of the films shown in Europe and this dominance is bolstered by the fact that American media groups own some 60 percent of European distribution networks.[25]

The outlook on the Millennium Round evokes differing views from the perspectives of developing and developed countries. Developing countries accuse the developed of hypocrisy in pushing for more rules relating to non-economic issues, while they themselves tend to ignore the rulings. Developing countries point to the example of the United States and a 1998 WTO case concerning imports of shrimp to reduce related sea turtle deaths. The United States may well refuse to honor the decision and simply accept the penalties and pay for it—because they can afford to.

Trade will be an important factor in determining environmental and cultural diversity, a recognized problem. Cultural diversity is also declining, partly because of the decline in environmental diversity. Cultural decline has often been associated with deforestation or other types of large-scale land use change that has forced the relocation of traditional peoples.

Individual cultures are becoming extinct at a rate comparable to that of the environments and the species within them. Of the world's six thousand languages "half will likely disappear within a century as speakers are driven off their territories and assimilated into dominant societies."[26] Indigenous peoples also claim homes in areas where there is the greatest amount of biological diversity, especially in tropical areas. In fact, one-quarter of all prescription drugs in the United States are derivatives of plants found in developing countries. As these cultures are lost so too is a knowledge of many species and their uses in an ecological setting, and more importantly how these species can be sustainably used in an economy.

There is a growing consensus that trade should not grow at the direct expense of the environment or culture. There are some basic ideas elucidated in the Rio Declaration and in the WTO's Trade and Environment Committee (and elsewhere) that lay out some basic guidelines for trade and environment regulation. However, firm principles with respect to culture are still elusive.

The concept of environmental protection as a reasonable justification for altering trade patterns is already present in multilateral trade disciplines. Therefore, the suggestion of introducing and broaching the issue of culture is not so fantastic. It is already apparent that what constitutes free trade, and fair trade, is itself culturally bound.[27] John Jackson puts this contradiction nicely:

> If a nation can avoid the importation of goods from a poor third world country where the method of production is moderately dangerous to humans, why would a nation also be able to prohibit the importation of goods produced in an environment that differs in many social and cultural attributes from its own society? Other countries may have a somewhat different view of the trade-offs between economic and welfare values of production, and human life or health.[28]

The next two parts discuss the possible environment and culture issues for discussion in the next trade round. As in earlier cases, they include both old and new problems.

UNRESOLVED ENVIRONMENTAL ISSUES

The bundling of differing social concerns in products, including culture and environment, will grow in the future. This bundling can occur in a variety of contexts. The leap in electronic technology will make it easier to create virtual worlds, and in fact it is these virtual electronic worlds in which trade in the future will often occur. The virtual nature of trade will make it easier to introduce environment and culture into the essence of the product, but also make it more difficult to disentangle components. Trade will combine the practical aspects of the product—how well it performs a task for so much money—with discretionary choices based on social goals of environment and culture.

The growing numbers and types of products appearing on the market indicate the degree of cultural and environmental diversity in the world market. In earlier conjunctions there was less differentiation in products because the value added in cultural and environmental terms was less. For example, oats and other grains were one of the first plants domesticated by humans and have been a traded product since the Agricultural Conjunction. While there has been trade in oats for more than three thousand years, it was not until the Industrial Conjunction that Quaker Oats cereal or oatmeal was mass-produced. Likewise, while people have been sending messages for millennia, it is only in current times that messages, or information, can be mass-produced in the form of junk mail.

This is not to say that there were not differentiated trade products before now. Rather, it is to say that these products were often the work of a single artisan (as noted earlier) and not a mass production process. This singularity in purpose had an enormous impact on the product context and meaning. When mass production took over, the product became the output of a large community of people and not the vision of an individual.

Second, where the trends for thousands of years had been the adding of more middle layers of services between buyers and sellers, the Electronic Conjunction will reduce the intervening layers closer to its original conception: the producer trading directly with the consumer. New trade products will not only be international but also interpersonal in nature. In the process, what is being sold and what is being bought will be more than a product, but a combination of complex social demands.

Here is one case of this growing amalgam of culture, environment, and trade interests in a single product. I needed some shampoo and thought I would try something a little bold. I usually just buy "basic shampoo," but sometimes I will buy "basic shampoo that controls dandruff." I had no idea about the diversity and sheer magnitude of products now available. I discovered that one no longer merely "washes" their hair, but "treats" it to a Mayan blend of fruits and berries that are the products of the rain forest. Buying the product not only is part hair treatment, but also protects the forest eco-system. The shampoo resonates Mayan lifestyles and cultures; washing one's hair with natural potions not only relays this experience but also helps save it for others to experience and savor. If I wash my hair with this shampoo, a concoction of environmental elements arranged in a cultural pattern, then perhaps I will experience some of the Mayan culture, past and present. Not only is shampooing a "recall" experience, no animal products were used in creating or developing the product.

The product message is sublime but clear: the natural products are good for one's hair and also provide social goods that fall into cultural and environmental domains. The problem is that the fair labeling of products to the extent that they fulfill social obligations of culture and environment are not the type of product attributes that are easy to regulate or validate. What one party believes to be sustainable business practices with respect to culture and environment may be diametrically different from those of another group. The differing beliefs may mirror differing histories, identities, geographies, and numerous other factors.

Today's products are more than simple representatives of technologies that increase efficiencies. They are now embodiments of efficiency within the context of biological and social awareness. Not only does a new refrigerator keep food cold, admittedly its primary purpose, but also it saves energy, thus reducing climate change, and does not emit CFCs, thereby protecting the outer ozone layer around the planet.

There are three key trade issues regarding environment that need resolution in the next trade negotiation round.

1. *There needs to be an agreed-upon definition of the relationship between multilateral environmental agreements and trade disciplines.*

The standing of measures in multilateral environmental agreements (MEAs) and the trade disciplines in the WTO is unclear. This is especially the case with respect to dispute settlement issues, the export of domestically prohibited goods and intellectual property principles related to conservation.[29] Many WTO members believe there is sufficient room in existing WTO rules to recognize some MEA rules. There are a variety of proposals on how to begin the task of matching trade and environment agreements. Argentina proposes determining which of the MEA regulations are clearly not WTO-consistent as a means of deciding which are. Canada proposes five "principles and criteria" the MEA would need to meet for approval:

1. The MEA is open to all countries.
2. The MEA reflects broad-based international support.
3. The provisions are drafted as precisely as possible.
4. Non-party trade is permitted with countries possessing equivalent environmental standards.
5. The trade measures in the MEA follow WTO criteria.

Canada proposes that the MEA measures meet three other standards as well: economic efficiency, effectiveness, and non-discrimination. Korea and New Zealand promote a "differentiated approach," or a set of environmental areas where removal of some trade concessions would be legitimate. Developing countries such as "Korea, Egypt, Turkey, Argentina and others said that a balanced package of measures, including technology and financial transfer and capacity building, was necessary to achieve MEA objectives."[30]

In these efforts, there is the clear sense that environment and trade disciplines need better reconciliation and coordination.

2. *Trade disciplines and trade measures do not address the role of process.*

If an environmental problem is related to a particular *end* product that is traded, then WTO disciplines permit the legitimate use of a trade measure. The product emphasis in international trade law is especially suited for creating rules, policies, and regimes that have an economic objective in mind. The product emphasis is not suited for solving many environmental problems because these products are not easily captured within the attributes of a product. There are three approaches to process issues and the product's impact on the environment: by the dominant plant, the specific species, and the use of the habitat.[31]

First, environments are often tremendously dependent on a single dominant plant type: fir trees in cold temperate climates, deciduous forests in more moderate climates, and tropical hardwoods in tropical rain forests. One important link with trade is its effect on these dominant plant types. The link may include a large number of end products that rely on a specific plant or type of plant as a product input. Solving a problem related to a dominant floral type, and its implementation, may require cooperation in a number of trade product areas, similar to the approach of the Montreal Protocol and controlling ozone-depleting substances.

Second, protecting a number of specific plant and animal species is needed, but the problems no doubt will require an integrated solution. Ideally, all species should have some measure of protection, but since one cannot protect all species, protecting habitats may be the best means for protecting endangered species. Such a focus on the habitat would be very complex, which would make it more difficult to construct multilateral legal regimes.

The third approach would focus on the use of the environment. Trade's greatest environmental impact may be in how it fosters or causes land-use changes. Land use changes are often the result of producing of particular commodities, such as sugar, and may require changing patterns of demand to solve these problems. In addition to land use changes, trade can lead to habitat impacts in the sea (over-fishing) and the air (pollution). These media too contain valuable biota.

3. *For dispute settlement to be successful in an environmental setting it needs to include the calculus or proportionality of economic and environmental measures.*

Proportionality suggests a relative basis from which to judge the environmental benefits and trade costs in a measure. This balancing is, at least, an important aspect of determining outcomes in World Trade Organization (WTO) cases insofar as "technical regulations shall not be more trade-restrictive than necessary to fulfil a legitimate objective."[32] Proportionality is important for creation of analytic systems to compare costs and benefits, only one of several reasons to investigate this issue from an environmental context.

Proportionality is also important because it establishes benchmarks for good public policy. Efficient use of economic resources follows the "theory of optimal intervention (which ranks various instruments according to the economic efficiency with which they attain policy goals), the optimal instrument is the one that attains the policy with the fewest undesired side-effects."[33]

The WTO Dispute Settlement Body (DSB) permits retaliation when a measure is inconsistent with WTO disciplines and a contracting member of the agreement fails to take adequate corrective measures. WTO DSB rules permit retaliation equivalent to the loss of trade incurred because of the measure. What is deemed or found to be equivalent depends on calculating trade losses and this can be complex, controversial, and highly technical in nature.

Involving the idea of proportionality is good public relations. It gives the public some sense of what choices decision-makers face in crafting a balance between competing economic and environmental instruments. The calculations can provide some tangible and understandable meaning to public policy choices on trade and environment issues.

Finally, cost proportionality and other analytic measures of trade-off can be important bridges between differing treaties and agreements that may apply to trade and environment issues. The recent WTO case on shrimp and turtles brought against the United States by several Asian countries also applies to an animal protected under the CITES agreement. This may be the first instance where a Multilateral Environment Agreement coincides with a WTO case. Proportionality can be instrumental in linking measurement systems in more than one agreement.

TABLE 4.2 Countries Attending the Ottawa Meeting

Armenia	Barbados	Croatia
Dominican Republic	Egypt	Greece
Iceland	Italy	Mexico
Senegal	South Africa	Sweden
Switzerland	Trinidad and Tobago	Tunisia
Ukraine	United Kingdom	Poland
Ivory Coast	Morocco	

Source: Government of Canada, "Overview of International Meeting on Cultural Policy" (Ottawa: Government of Canada, June 29–30, 1998).

NEW CULTURAL INITIATIVES

More countries are imposing additional barriers to cultural trade. In Mexico, proposed legislation would limit foreign broadcasts to a maximum of 30 percent of movies shown there. Already in Mexico there are limits to the amount of foreign commercials on television (three minutes per hour). Some Latin American countries attempt to impose indirect controls on culture through limitations on foreign ownership of movie theaters. India also imposes quotas on foreign film broadcasts, despite having the world's second-largest movie industry.

To address cultural issues in the next trade round, representatives from twenty countries met in Ottawa, Canada, in mid-1998 to discuss how to craft trade rules that would allow them to protect their cultures, and the industries tied to it, from outside trade threats (see Table 4.2 for a list of the attendees). The threats are presumably embodied in American culture and it was no surprise that a U.S. cultural minister was not invited (although the United States was given observer status). The purported reason for not inviting the United States was that it does not have a culture minister, but in fact, neither does Mexico who was invited (the United States does have a director for the National Endowment for the Arts). As some have proposed for environment, one purpose in the Canadian Initiative is to support a "differentiated" approach for cultural products. Sheila Copps, Minister of Canadian Heritage, believes culture is a critical issue for the trade negotiators to consider. "Now more than ever nations from every region of the world are discovering that globalization is not simply about trading commodities."[34]

One goal of the Canadian Initiative is to explicitly push for cultural diversity in trade disciplines. The avowed aim is to differentiate cultural from other trade products, no doubt to permit a wider range of restrictions.[35] As a first step they agreed to establish a permanent network among themselves for consultation. A second step, which Canada supports, is to include the issue in the next round of WTO negotiations. As a start, the group has built a Web site that links the culture ministries of several countries. A second meeting took place in Mexico in 1999 and a cultural summit is to convene in Greece in year 2000.

There are differing views among the attending countries on the implicit threat American culture holds. Mexico feels it is more protected from American culture because it is a Spanish-speaking country, which provides some degree of protective buffer. Some suggest the Canadian effort is a nationalistic push intending to deflect attention from its internal problems, the threat of Quebec's talk of succession, in large part due to cultural and language differences with its French-speaking province.

Canada did receive exemptions for cultural products under the NAFTA agreement, but not under WTO disciplines, where Canada has yet to win a culture case. Canada has long fought against American cultural intrusions, even since the early days of radio broadcasts. Canada's government believes that trade in books, magazines, film, art, and the like is strongly linked to a nation's identity.[36]

Some are quite critical of the Canadian Initiative in trying to impose trade barriers meant to protect culture, believing they are the consequence of bad policy.[37] Commentator Terry Teachout is unapologetic: "The Ottawa 19, however, appear to have in mind something altogether more ambitious, perhaps on the order of a *cordon sanitaire* designed to keep the deadly bacillus of American-made entertainment out of the international blood supply." The desire to promote one's culture through trade protection is not a new phenomenon: over half a century ago the British government subsidized English-language films.

Teachout believes that the reason for cultural protection is actually a reactionary impulse. Growing democracy tends to level out the elites in society, whose grip on culture in the past was undeniable. Teachout cites DeTocqueville's belief that where ever democracy goes, as evinced in the American model he saw, there tends to be a "middling ground" of knowledge and of the arts. American media is successful because it reaches out to the average person. Cultural protection, he argues, only acts to preserve elites.

The purpose of the Ottawa meeting was to "provide a forum for the ministers of 22 countries to discuss the importance of national cultures in an increasingly globalized world and ways to increase cooperation on common cultural objectives."[38] The sponsors gave three reasons for the initiative and focus on the issue, especially in terms of how countries will treat culture as one aspect of globalization.[39]

1. To build inter-cultural communications, information, and understanding.
2. To meet the challenges of globalization and technological change.
3. To promote the idea that cultural goods and services are unique from other goods and services.

The Canadian Initiative presents an important idea at an important time. The purpose, however, is sometimes not well served by the concepts. In the conference document, the term "culture" is used in a variety of contexts ranging from a tool of activist foreign policy, to the customs and rituals in people's everyday lives, to rather complicated academic theories on multidisciplinary phenomena. The problem with defining cultural policy is that defining culture, as noted at the onset of this book, is a difficult task and culture constitutes one of the most complicated words in the English language. No wonder the message is unclear, since the actual words are.

The Canadian Initiative offers an interesting link to traditional trade remedies. The conference document refers to issues of cultural "domestic content."[40] Thus, Canada is beginning the process of applying traditional trade measures (and the issues they relate to) to new issues and this is especially true in the case of culture. Domestic content once evoked images of automobile manufacturers, but now applies to country music television and other cultural products.

The next steps in the Canadian strategy is a four-part approach with 1) a search for new partners, 2) a series of ministerial policy forums, 3) collaborative projects, and 4) the establishment of research priorities on the issue. The order of this process seems completely the opposite of what it ought to be. First, there should be research into an issue, and then an addressing of policy questions.

The problem is that policymakers do not really understand, and more importantly cannot really control, the cultural impetus that globalization carries with it. The Canadian Initiative includes quite theoretical, and often quite complicated, claims of a near scientific nature about human behavior during extraordinary periods. For example, the document states "National cultural objectives are becoming increasingly linked to international development and global relations." Nowhere is this claim borne out or proven, much less defined.

The Canadian Initiative over-reaches the actual scientific understanding of—and consensus on—culture in the general developmental process because it is part of a latent policy agenda. As the document notes: "at the core of cooperative efforts is the concept of 'soft power' in which ideas are used to build influence and shared values."[41] Perhaps here is a challenge not to America's movie industry but its nuclear arsenal. Soft power suggests decentralized, popular approaches to global power sharing, in obvious distinction to the 'hard power' characteristic of the Cold War. This objective only makes the task of Canadian initiative that much more difficult. If the idea of the initiative is to somehow develop a respect for nascent cultural rights, why add to it a nebulous policy objective that uses a kind of cultural bully pulpit to achieve a separate policy objective?

A rush to create policy may compromise the need for understanding. Policymakers must assure that, in this effort to make cultural policies, science is not being left behind. Dissonance between policy needs and scientific understanding is not a new problem: the environmental policy implications and the science about environment did seem to arrive separately in time (hence issues of proof versus prevention as rationales for policy measures). This too may be the case with cultural policy. There are few hard indications as to how culture might be treated under proposed trade rules, but some general clues are given.

> Cultural industries and mass media are critical vehicles for promoting cultural development, diversity and freedom of expression. Books, magazines, performing and visual arts, sound recordings, film, radio and television broadcasting are all powerful expressions of new ideas and cultural points of view which can inform an entire society.[42]

Immediate questions on the implementation of special rules for cultural products arise. How strictly is culture defined by these industries? Do the industries and cases provide cogent examples of why this divergent attention is warranted? The evidence from cases that have attracted the greatest attention, most importantly Canada's defeat in the WTO case over the domestic content in Canadian versions of the magazine *Sports Illustrated*, is clearly a bad example for establishing persuasive precedent. American and

Canadian sports teams both participate in professional ice hockey, basketball, and baseball. Thus, it is hard to separate Canadian and American sports. Canada needs a better example of protecting culture in order to win a case in the WTO.

Canada lost the *Sports Illustrated* case (a magazine owned by Time Warner Inc., recently bought by America On-Line, an Internet company), where it placed an 80 percent tax on advertising in foreign magazines and required the publishing of a separate edition in Canada. The WTO panel found three different parts of the Canadian law inconsistent with WTO disciplines: 1) discrimination against imports of magazines with Canadian directed advertising, 2) a trade-distorting excise tax on split run magazines, and 3) differential postal rates for imported magazines. Canada's response was to argue that services are not part of international trade disciplines (as applied to national treatment provisions) and thus the case itself was illegitimate.[43] Canada did change its law on magazines but imposed limits on foreign-owned advertising. The United States counters that this violates the ruling of the dispute settlement panel.

Perhaps the observer can step back from the details of the case and think of the larger context of the culture at issue. *Sports Illustrated* is largely a man's magazine. By sales, its most popular issue focuses on women in abbreviated swimsuits. Would a certain percentage of the women in the issue need to be Canadian? Would there be restrictions on the types of swimsuits allowed? It is ironic that the same Canadian law on magazines also embraces the increased awareness of women's issues and their role in society. Perhaps the swimsuit issue would be illegal in Canada as part of the recognition of women's issues.

Another key culture case between the United States and Canada involves permission for the American company Borders Books to expand into Canada. The case lacks a compelling image of protecting culture. Rather, the issue is based primarily on profit. These two cases do not seem to link the broad cultural goals in documents such as the Canadian Initiative with the specific examples that represent legitimate aspects of national identity and development. Rather, they suggest base protectionist impulses for mostly materialistic purposes.

These cases aside, there is reason and need to protect one's culture. Bjorn Bjarnason, Iceland's Minister of Culture, Science and Education, noted in a speech at a meeting in Ottawa that "we do not want one kind of cultural influence to become so effective that it squeezes others aside." Later in his speech he is clearer on a perceived cultural threat and it is not the United States, but rather the European Union!

> It is the stated aim of the European Union to preserve the identities and cultural rights of each community and to guarantee the existence and flowering of their cultures but not to dilute them. This is a noble aim which I support, still one may question if it is reflected in the new framework programme. Coming from a small nation which is taking part in the programme though not a member of the European Union I am afraid that the emphasis on big projects to strengthen the cultural profile of the Union itself could make it difficult for small states to participate fully not to speak about initiating or leading any of the projects. At the same time as the cultural profile of the European Union is sharpened one should also focus on the cultural diversity of Europe.[44]

Minister Bjarnason gives a compelling example of culture that can have trade implications. Icelandic literary heritage springs from the Saga of the Icelanders, which was written about eight hundred years ago. These were monumental works. The novelist Milan Kundera believed the Sagas were the foundation for the modern European novel. For the first time, the epic has been almost completely translated into English in forty Sagas and forty-nine tales.

Would an Icelandic cultural tax on Saga book exports, in order to sustain a means to tell the world about Icelandic culture and history, be a legal WTO measure? It would certainly discriminate between domestic and foreign producers, but is this one way that small states can "level the playing field" in the Electronic Conjunction? What if there was an additional government requirement that the work be published on recycled paper? In this way, environmental and cultural policy might support one another.

Perhaps the focus of the Canadian Initiative should not be on excluding the United States, but rather, demonstrating how disputes that involve culture and trade can be resolved. For example, here are some unresolved cultural disputes between the very members of the Canadian Initiative, three areas where they might show policy leadership. Perhaps the effort should demonstrate how to connect the issues in the social context.

The first case they might resolve is the noted United Kingdom-Greece dispute on the Elgin Marbles and Greek demands for the return of these artifacts. For 150 years the marbles have resided in the British Museum. The U.K. government agrees that Lord Elgin took the marbles under unusual circumstances, but he also saved them from certain destruction by occupying Turkish forces. Moreover, some argue that if the marbles were in Athens all of this time they would have been subjected to the city's notorious air pollution. The case is simply the tip of the iceberg in terms of possible cases concerning stolen artifacts. "Countries that might be affected [by such a precedent] would include the following: Czech Republic (6,000 stolen artifacts), Russia (3,436 stolen artifacts), Germany (2,715 stolen artifacts), Cambodia (13 valuable antiques)"[45] and others.

The second dispute the Canadian Initiative could solve is the matter between the United Kingdom and Egypt over missing artifacts. Cleopatra's Needle sits along the Thames River in London, after having sat along the Nile for several millennia. It was actually built for Tuthmose III and later used to pay homage to Ramses. After that, perhaps the two countries can discuss the return of the Rosetta Stone, taken by the Napoleon in 1799 and later transferred to Great Britain under the Alexandria Agreement of 1801. Finally, Egyptians would like the return of some of the mummies and their bones that are in the British Museum and other places throughout the world.

The third dispute with cultural (and environmental) overtones is the noted dispute between Canada and the European Union regarding the import of furs and the use of leg traps. This long-lingering dispute could be a place to begin a case study in cultural and environmental dispute settlement, especially since it involves Canada (see Chapter 3).

Culture has always been a part of products, but its role will intensify in the Electronic Conjunction. One reason is the increasing commodification of culture as a product. Globalization will add to this trend because with so many more cultural alternatives to choose from in creating a product, more types of cultural products will occur. In the Industrial Conjunction the cultural aspects of products were mostly insular to the nation and its boundaries. In the Electronic Conjunction, the cultural-material mix will be much more global than ever before. Perhaps the Canadian Initiative, and other efforts, might anticipate and consider such trends.

SPILL-OVER PRINCIPLES IN TRADE, ENVIRONMENT, AND CULTURE

The Canadian Initiative intends to legitimize non-tariff measures in the WTO taken for cultural reasons. At the same time, the United States and France have committed themselves to the inclusion of environmental (and labor) issues in the WTO agenda. The inevitable conclusion is that the WTO will eventually need to directly address cultural and environmental measures and to treat them within its system of disciplines. These disciplines will need to rest on a general set of principles. These principles should be general enough that they can apply to a variety of non-tariff measures, including cultural and environment issues (and even labor).

Perhaps principles can spring from the twin goals of preventing extinction

FIGURE 4.3

The Five Principles of Cultural and Environmental Protection in International Trade

1. The Principle of the Right to Survive
Every culture and species has the right to survive and government can aid in that process using trade mechanisms.

2. The Principle of Diversity
All cultures and species not only have the right to survive, they also have the right to a diverse set of values and environments.

3. The Principle of Least Distortion
Governments can legitimately protect cultural and environmental rights but must do so in a manner that causes the least trade distortion.

4. The Principle of Sustainability
Cultures and environments should be sustainable, but they may need to change to meet changes in the world.

5. The Principle of Ownership
Individual cultures can own their own techniques of social ecology and economy.

and providing for diversity in both cultures and environments. Basic trade principles would still need to apply. One normative approach to crafting regimes and rules related to culture, especially in the context of protecting it, would be to use established environmental concepts and precepts. This approach would provide the added advantage of concentrating rule making. The disaggregating of culture and environment into specific WTO codes would fragment trade disciplines and make agreements more limited. Here are five basic principles that can apply to both culture and environment in the WTO (see Figure 4.3).

THE PRINCIPLE OF THE RIGHT TO SURVIVE Every culture and environment has the right to survive and thus a WTO contracting party may choose to enact survival measures that impact imports. The principle of preventing environmental extinction clearly conforms to the GATT Article

XX stipulation regarding the "conservation of natural resources" and can be certified through the CITES appendices based on the degree of endangerment. The principle of the Right to Survive would permit violations of Most Favored Nation (MFN) rights if a particular culture or species were at risk of extinction. If a type of beluga whale is threatened with extinction, or the Eskimo culture that prey on them, then the contracting party could request an exemption from WTO disciplines to assure survival of the species or culture.

Although there now exist some multilateral agreements with respect to environment, such as CITES, setting standards on culture may be much more difficult. Perhaps there is a need to develop a Convention on the International Trade in Endangered Cultures (CITEC), especially with reference to artifacts and intellectual property. Creating CITEC would need to begin with the difficult task of declaring the principles of cultural uniqueness and registering appropriate cultures.

Different from environmental cases, evidence of proof in culture cases would draw more from the social than the physical sciences. The obvious problem is that these standards would no doubt encounter a high degree of scientific uncertainty. It would expose the need to develop a vast group of new concepts and indicators to adequately judge issues and fairly settle disputes.

THE PRINCIPLE OF DIVERSITY All cultures not only have the right to survive, they also have a second related right; survival in the broadest possible sense as explained in the Principle of Diversity. Thus, the goal is to attain the highest level of "genetic" diversity, which means not only general species survival but also as many sub-species as possible (or as many subcultures as possible). Greater diversity also implies the most differences from the environmental or cultural norm.

The issue of survival may depend on diversity but it will be necessary to differentiate between general and specific examples. For environments, this means the difference between species and habitats. For cultures, diversity means the difference between customs and values. The narrower the issue, the species or the custom, the easier it will be to define rules. As this general policy promotes the most number of environments, so too does it promote the greatest number of cultures. The Principal of Diversity can lead to considerable controversy; it would permit some exceptions to trade rules where a cultural norm in one country applies to foreigners living in that country.

THE PRINCIPLE OF LEAST DISTORTION In trade disciplines, the general orientation is towards those measures that achieve their results with the least trade distortion in an economic sense. Many of the key GATT and WTO agreements mean to preserve this principle, especially in removing distortion between foreign and domestic operators in a country (existing transparency and non-discrimination trade principles). The Principle of Least Distortion would also apply to trade where culture and environment are at issue.

Because there are reasons to accept exemptions to trade disciplines on the basis of culture and environment, there also need to be standards for economic efficiency. Adopting inefficient policies to achieve cultural objectives serves little purpose. Adopting unfair programs to gain cultural advantage in third country markets should also be addressed by principles. Cultural or environmental goods could no more be dumped in third-country markets than televisions, steel, or computer chips. Thus, neither France nor the United States could subsidize their cultural exports to another country. An alternative approach would be to establish permissible and even minimum levels of subsidy in major projects, following the principles of the 1980s Gentlemen's Agreement on construction subsidies.[46]

THE PRINCIPLE OF SUSTAINABILITY The idea of environmental sustainability is somewhat well established, even if there is little agreement on the technical means for achieving it. Whether from the view of extracting a resource or depositing a pollutant, the goal should be to assure a long-term process of economic activity.

Cultures have the right to exist in diverse circumstances, but also may need to keep pace with current developments in perception and reality. Cultures are not static, nor are they without consequence. In some instances, a cultural custom may be found to harm an environmental species or even a labor practice. Somehow the priority of and timetable for change must be addressed and this may become enshrined in the dispute settlement process. The Principle of Sustainability recognizes that cultures and environments should survive but may need to change.

How much change would and can occur would differ by culture and time period. Some "Heritage Cultures," perhaps even linked to existing "Heritage Sites," may be exempt from trade rules. Through time designation, some cultures or habitats might be deemed "Traditional" or "Ancient" and therefore would be allowed to survive intact. For those cultures that are not "Ancient," but "Modern," they could receive some type of temporary protection. However, there would be an expectation of environmental, trade, and cultural self-sufficiency after a hiatus period of adjustment. This might follow an import surges model, like Section 201 of U.S. trade law, which provides temporary trade remedies based on significant, short-term increases in trade flows (the "escape clause").

THE PRINCIPLE OF OWNERSHIP Individual cultures and material representations of those cultures can be owned in the sense that they can belong to a specific country or environment. If flowers from Madagascar are part of a cure for cancer, then perhaps some percentage of the trade might include a tax to maintain and preserve the species in a general way, especially if the crops are wild. Here, the key word is wild, insofar as this is where the stocks of greatest chemical and cultural diversity are found. This approach might follow the arrangement of bio-diversity agreement between Costa Rica and the Merck Company.

Perhaps one solution would be the recognition of environmental and cultural ownership rights. By transferring the ownership principle to species or cultures, then perhaps they can acquire rights in a legal setting. Corporations in the United States have the legal standing of people. If something invented can have legal standing, it is not hard to believe that a species or a collective spirit of a people might seek equivalent standing, or at least representative standing.

Beyond adoption of such principles there is also a need to change technical procedures for dealing with non-economic cases that culture and environment embody. The evolution of trade disciplines promises to be a complex exercise in differentiating legitimate and proportional protective measures from those that mean to unfairly provide economic, cultural, or environmental advantages. Judging what is fair may pose the greatest barrier to progress.

Some trade experts believe adequate measures already exist in WTO disciplines to protect cultures and environments. If countries want to adopt standards that intend to protect environment and culture, they can choose to do so. They must however pay the cost. The cost is that the exporter countries, which promised reciprocal liberalization in exchange for further opening of their own markets, would lose concessions agreed to under multilateral trade negotiations such as the Uruguay Round. Therefore, the party denied potential exports, because of environmental or cultural protection, could withdraw concessions of a roughly equivalent amount. Thus, if Canada wants to protect its magazine industry it should permit the United States to remove concessions on other Canadian imports of an equal amount. The

U.S. government argues that Canada simply wants to erase agreed-upon concessions without providing the United States with equivalent concessions.

AFTER THE NEXT ROUND

This last section looks at four aspects of the Electronic Conjunction critical to the pace and direction of globalization in the twenty-first century. First, the role of culture may act as a limit to globalization. Second, new trade, environment, and culture cases will provide fuel for burning new disputes that may well challenge the WTO dispute settlement process. Third, the inclusion of culture and environment may be healthy to WTO disciplines by opening up a long-needed debate. Fourth, the Gene Conjunction will lead to new configurations and new meanings for trade, environment, and culture.

CULTURAL FEEDBACK AS A LIMIT TO GLOBALIZATION

There is a dynamic balance between a people's culture and their environment. The decline of local self-sufficiency that naturally comes with development and increased trade during a conjunction further disrupts this balance, or worsens the existing imbalance between culture and environment. As noted at the beginning of this book, trade severs the human-environment dynamic by removing the environment from the person's immediate consciousness and view. This distancing results in a type of ecological amnesia called a disconnect. In general, the greater the degree of globalization, the more it severs one's personal link to the environment and culture and hides the effect of economic activity on environments and cultures elsewhere in the world.

During a conjunction, the diffusion of new technologies occurs through trade. Globalization to some degree occurs in each historical conjunction, but over time the breadth and spread of each succeeding conjunction increases. Thus, the degree of separation and therefore disconnect today is greater than at any other point in history.

The disconnect in how people view trade, environment, and culture can itself be a barrier to the spread of globalization. Trade and environmental regimes can and will develop, and effective dispute settlement mechanisms evolve, but the idea of dispute settlement institutions that adjudicate on matters of cross-cultural differences may be simply too contentious of an issue to negotiate and institutionalize. Already, there are serious strains in the globalization movement and powerful objections to any attempts at further liberalizing trade. Voters in Europe and North America now express doubts about further commitments to greater trade liberalization in agreements such as the European Union and NAFTA.

The globalization of culture may simply be too difficult for people to accept at this point in time. Globalization can shift culture from a national to a regional level; this is possible because there is an existing basis for cultural relations mostly based on intimate geography. Common borders are often quite porous, especially with respect to culture. The further the geographic distance between countries, the less likely that these countries will agree on issues of trade and culture. This sense of distance suggests that regimes with the greatest potential for success may not be global but regional in nature. These regional systems are more likely to correspond to cultural and environmental systems in terms of actual geographic confines.

The objectivity of science may also limit globalization. It may well be that there can be some agreement on what are environmental principles and scientific understandings of the environment. The science of culture is a different matter. Scientific proof is qualitative in fields such as cultural anthropology and, therefore, the degree to which they possess truths and empirical proofs is often weak. The answer would seem to call for a major research effort into culture and specifically its relation to economics and institutions. This means returning to efforts begun by Margaret Meade and others earlier in the early twentieth century aimed at a widespread effort to better understand culture and anthropology. Perhaps including culture as a legitimate factor in the calculus of trade will force the greater study of it.

FUTURE CASES OF TRADE, ENVIRONMENT, AND CULTURE

The cases from the Electronic Conjunction are but the beginning of a closer mingling of products and ideas related to culture, trade, and environment. This closer mingling will invite dispute and disagreement that will need addressing. Consider the following hypothetical scenarios that may arise. The examples intend to sharpen the coincidence and confluence between the three factors in the social context and combine extrapolation of existing issues with newly emerging areas of discourse and debate.

JAPANESE SANCTIONS OF U.S. CHRISTMAS TREE EXPORTS Japan imposes an environmental tariff on U.S. Christmas Tree exports. The tariff is equal to the value of reasonable stumpage fees for the purpose of reforestation, a tactic used by the United States in prior lumber trade disputes with

Canada. Despite growing demand in Japan for Christmas trees, by Christians and Shintoists alike, the Japanese government believes that the constant re-cutting of young trees on Christmas tree farms is environmentally harmful and creates a monoculture. The Japanese government argues that the monocultures are deadly to several native species and inconsistent with the U.S. Endangered Species Act and agreements it has made under CITES to protect species that live in these forests. The government downplays the cultural importance of the tree, citing it as a pagan ritual that was attached to the celebrating of Christmas rites in the Middle Ages and thus not an integral part of the Christian religion.

CANADIAN IMPORT REGULATIONS ON BOOKS FOR CULTURAL AND ENVIRONMENTAL CONTENT In a continuing attempt to protect its heritage and culture, Canada announces new requirements on recycled paper used in books and magazines, in addition to new cultural content requirements. The United States objects to the new regulations because they favor Canadian wood and pulp manufacturers as well as Canadian publishers. The United States suggests that the measure is but another veiled attempt to protect Canada's cultural market from imports and is erecting new barriers in the aftermath of losing the WTO case on split-run magazine editions.

DUTCH SANCTIONS ON CHINA FOR BEAR FARM INHUMANITY Since the Dutch push for condemnation of Chinese human rights policy in the United Nations in 1997, there has been deterioration in relations between the two countries. The Netherlands, after a public campaign decrying practices at Chinese bear farms, imposes import sanctions on Chinese bear products. Not only do the Dutch ban bear imports from China, they also impose sanctions on China equal to the value of China's bear product exports to other countries. The Dutch argue that the Chinese system is inhumane and China should only be producing bear goods for domestic consumption, not for export. China is a leading exporter of bear bile and other bear products.

CHINESE PUSH FOR LIBERALIZATION OF RHINO HORN EXPORTS China sided with several South African countries to allow the export of elephant ivory at the CITES meeting in 1997 where Japan became the sole importer. Citing this case as precedent, China is pushing for limited liberalization in rhinoceros horn trade. Rhinoceros populations in some countries have not only recovered, but because of surpluses, must be culled on a regular basis. Some African countries ask CITES members to lift trade bans and allow exports, with China as the only buyer of horn. China argues that its need for keeping traditional medicines and the customs related to them should be considered along with maintaining sustainable rhinoceros populations.

ZAIRE'S RESTRICTIONS ON FRENCH PRINT EXPORTS Following the fall of Mobutu, the new Congo government under Kabila sought to reduce Francophone influence in the country and tilted towards the United States. There was also a mood of retaliation because of French support for Mobutu. To focus more on native languages in the country, the government imposes a 50 percent content rule on imported French-language broadcasts and French printed literature. The new government supported quota increases in English language print and television programs. Furthermore, print materials are given advantage if produced on paper originating from wood in the Congo.

THE RHEINHEITSGEBOT U.S. beer exporters bring a WTO case based on the German import law called the Rheinheitsgebot. The German law was enacted in 1516 and requires beer to be made from four products: water, hops, barley, and yeast. The U.S. government argues that the beer purity law has little to do with reality. The barley and hops used in German beer are often grown in polluted soil, the result of acid rain and high degrees of industrialization, using polluted water. Germany replies that beer is an esteemed part of German culture and the importance of local production carries a great cultural significance.[47]

OBSERVATIONS FROM THE HYPOTHETICAL CASES The six hypothetical cases illustrate how tomorrow's products will intertwine culture and environment along with the practical aspects of a product. In the process of this bundling, culture and environment can compliment one another, but in other cases they can come in conflict. Sometimes this intertwining betters both environment and culture and sometimes it harms both. These cases are only partially hypothetical. The premises in the cases stem from loose interpretations of law and some of them in fact reflect unsuccessful actions to impose regulations in these areas.

The internationalization of Christmas tree trade shows the varied ways that environment and culture might come into conflict. Most Christmas trees are not live trees that are later planted, but felled trees that are subsequently discarded and often mulched some weeks later. The period in which this product is actually used is only a few weeks; because of culture this durable product is treated as a non-durable one. The fir tree is a symbol of Christianity, but one added much later than the crucifixion of Jesus and probably after Christianity had spread into northern Europe where fir trees were more common. One question would be the appropriate trade category for classifying the tree. It can be argued that cross-border trade in such trees during late December is not merely a transaction involving a wood product, but in fact a type of religious artifact.

The case involving the French language and Democratic Republic of Congo concerning book trade is a purposeful entangling of culture and environment. The concordance in trade between culture (language) and environment (recycling) can become entangled as parts of policy decisions. This extends the cross-boundary dispute across disciplinary boundaries. For Canada, it is a natural balancing act: its environment provides a huge trade surplus but its culture is often in a huge deficit. A differing context would limit the measure of the Congo, a country that needs to export wood and import books.

China's hypothetical proposal to liberalize rhino trade shows how environment can abet culture. The rhinoceros population, rather than declining, has grown and populations have stabilized in some areas at historic levels. Thus, there is the need at times to cull certain animals. Logically, there is no reason to avoid income from the sale of these culled animals, especially if they were to die of natural causes and are properly registered and recorded. The use of the product for cultural reasons has little to do with the environment. But the environmental harm is directly the result of cultural demand. In some cases, the environmental product is part of the culture. Louisiana crawfish producers have brought an anti-dumping case against China over imports of the product. Besides economics and biological data, the case has also drawn considerable attention over the issue of its impact on Cajun culture and how embedded the crawfish is in it.

The German beer case brings a differing viewpoint on cultural ownership, where part of that ownership is based on its origination in a specific bio-geographic area. Liquor is one product where the source seems to matter a great deal, as the earlier case on pisco illustrates. The case does reveal an interesting conflict between environmental health now and before in a region. Can the environmental deterioration of a region act to undermine the intellectual property ownership claims of specific peoples to specific products in specific places? In the case of Germany, perhaps the answer is yes.

THE ENDLESS DEBATE

If culture and environment are in a constant state of change, then making rules about them, especially in the trade context, will also exist in constant flux. As evident in the development of legal regimes to protect the Eastern Pacific dolphin, this process can evolve in several stages. No doubt the regime for protecting the dolphin will continue to evolve in the future. The reasonable conclusion is that the uniting of trade, culture, and the environment within multilateral institutions will inevitably lead to an "endless debate." This debate will be a continuous process of negotiation and eternal discourse on the correct policies given a need to balance economic and social interests and national and multilateral forces.

Endless debate is probably an expected outcome from a conjunction that promises to cause more change faster than any other period in human history. Economic and trade patterns will change, environments will evolve through natural and anthropogenic means, and cultures will adapt to new economic and environmental realities. If there is reason to believe that the actual context for these three factors will quickly and constantly change, then it is also reasonable to assume the rules that govern them will also change.

The idea that people will need to constantly change the international rules and endlessly debate these issues is worrisome to many, especially those interests that are grounded in the stability of economic markets. The endless debate promises to be at times incoherent, rife with acrimony and dispute and a cause of friction among peoples. The debate will be endless because the issues at its core are timeless in the human experience.

The emergence of the endless debate will provide the impetus for a more general discussion that is generally needed in the post–Cold War era. The victory of free markets over communism did not clarify the relation between global economic forces and the future of local environments and cultures. The conclusion is that for local entities to survive there needs to be adequate checks and balances in the global system. Some countries may want to use such a system to their own advantage, a natural impulse in a world where the goal of international politics will still be the advancement of parochial interests. Undoubtedly, there will be cases where trade policy serves only to advance one country's own environmental or cultural interests at the expense of other countries. Hence, there must be some way of determining when such measures are appropriate or inappropriate. Further, this process must search for balance and harmony between competing trade, environmental, and cultural interests.

Perhaps the WTO might welcome (or at least accept) endless debate. Over the course of its first fifty years as the GATT, there were eight negotiating rounds and each one took longer to complete as the issues became more complex and the participants increased in number. The most recent

Uruguay Round took almost a decade to complete the negotiations and another decade for implementation. (The first few trade rounds were completed in less than a year.) It is now the norm that a new round begins even before the last one is completed. Even before fulfilling all commitments in the Uruguay Round, planning for the Millennium Round had already begun.

The WTO is, in many ways, a very different organization than was the GATT, if for no other reason than its greater complexity in jurisdiction and a strengthened system for dispute settlement. There have been as many disputes brought before the WTO in a few years as there were in the GATT's fifty years. The United States lost the first WTO case to Venezuela and Brazil over discriminatory aspects of the U.S. Clean Air Act. More recently, the United States lost a WTO case brought by four East Asian countries regarding shrimping requirements to protect sea turtles. As noted, the United States has also won a cultural case in a dispute with Canada in the WTO. The endless debate is beginning but the WTO continues to resist opening the dialog to the public and to issues other than trade.

This growing complexity to WTO rounds and disputes in it will only fuel the chaos of the endless debate. This "chaotic" quality of the endless debate may actually prove to be of great value. A free market of ideas and issues is the strength of democratic processes, especially those that intend to welcome broad-based participation. So far, this broad participation has not emerged in trade institutions. The more open the WTO process is to the public, the more the public's interests will be reflected in WTO trade disciplines and policy. It is clear that the public wants clarification on the role of culture and the environment in trade. The endless debate is not weakness, but strength in bringing together discourse and resolution among a number of differing points of view. The result will serve to strengthen support for free trade and work to reconnect the parts of the social context.

The Electronic Conjunction promises to provide a great leap forward in the human condition and in human development. At the same time, the conjunction may also increase threats to environments and cultures in different and stronger ways than those of forty thousand years ago, or in any subsequent conjunction. These new threats may arise much quicker and have more widespread consequences than in any earlier period. In turn, the disconnect will continue to grow unless efforts are undertaken to reverse it.

Trade rules relating to culture and environment will need to be flexible. Different cultures hold diametrically opposing beliefs about animals, plants, and habitats. Since each society ascribes different values to the materials around it based on its needs and wants, each value system differs in judgements of good and bad, acceptable and unacceptable, and normal and abnormal behaviors. If these cultures are different in part due to the different environments (both sociologically and physically) in which they live, then it seems illogical to assume that some normal or absolute state of cultural behavior exists.

The legitimization of culture in multilateral policy institutions might be ominous for some. Any overt institution charged with checking for global cultural correctness surely conjures images of Aldous Huxley and George Orwell. Culture is nonetheless evident in trade and environment issues and must be included as part of policy decisions. Without overtly attempting to favor one culture over another, some universal cultural norm vis-à-vis the environment needs to emerge, with the idea of sustainability of trade, environment, and culture serving as a key guideline.

Culture will not suffer by its inclusion in an endless debate because it is an enduring aspect of humanity. Culture is what makes us human. Culture has an enduring legacy and this is perhaps a good long-term basis for developing sustainable trade and environmental systems. As Fernand Braudel describes:

> The cultural and economic map cannot simply be super-imposed without anomaly, and this is after all only logical, if only because culture dates from even further back in time than the world-economy, impressive though the life span of the latter may be. Culture is the oldest character in human history: economies succeed each other, political institutions crumble, societies replace each other, but civilization continues along its way. Rome fell in the fifth century A.D., but the Church of Rome is still with us.[48]

Some scholars believe that the endless debate should begin with a new direction for human evolution. Paul Shepard, whose provocative ideas on historical imprints were presented earlier in the discussion about the Overkill Hypothesis, believes that the Electronic Conjunction is a potential mistake of enormous proportions precisely because it builds on earlier conjunctions. Shepard believes that the Agricultural Conjunction produced an unsustainable lifestyle because it led to the domestication of plants, animals and humans. For Shepard, the freedom promised by the Electronic Conjunction is simply a mirage.

> In the absence of some new synthesis that rejoins us to our natural heritage, the world of corporate organization pushes us towards the degenerating process of conformity, the frenzied outbreak of genetic engineering, and the pied piper's

technological tootle leading down the "information highway": toward "networked" insanity that confuses electronic regurgitation with wisdom.[49]

Shepard fears that the regularity of lifestyles in the Electronic Conjunction would level out the diversity of peoples and their ideas around the world. In this way, he would agree with the view expressed in the Bible with respect to the building of the Tower of Babel. Shepard also saw the emergence of a world of absolutes. He saw the "cultural excess" model winning out over the "cultural appropriateness" model. His solution was not to look forward to the Electronic Conjunction for solutions but backward to the Tool Conjunction where the macro or global world did not exist.

What we can do is single out those many things, large and small, that characterized the social and cultural life of our ancestors—the terms under which our genome itself was shaped—and incorporate them as best we can by creating a modern life around them. We take our cues from primal cultures, the best wisdom of the deep desires of the genome. We humans are instinctive culture makers, the culture will shape itself.[50]

Cultural adjustment, in looking back to the past and ahead to the future, may be the key to civil and institutional evolution. If Chinese demand shark fin soup then perhaps with education they will accept a chemical substance that tastes similar to shark fin. If Americans demand coral for their aquariums perhaps they will learn to accept fabricated stone that looks like coral. Unless there are alternatives and new thinking in the Electronic Conjunction it may become a disaster for many peoples and places, at the same time that real progress is being made for many peoples and places.

THE GENE CONJUNCTION AND BEYOND

The critical issue for this time in history is how to maintain the power and creativity nascent in new conjunctions while at the same time avoiding the disconnect that new technologies bring. This disconnect is an unintentional byproduct of progress and results in damage to social and ecological structures. The disconnect is a problem even in times of low technological change, but the rapid pace of change in the conjunction accelerates and elevates the problem. Should people or their governments try to slow down the pace of change during a conjunction?

The idea of controlling the pace of change is a proposition worthy of introspection but a subject often relegated to science fiction. Can human beings really manage history? Controlling change may effectively mean taking control of the new technology and its distribution. This control would of course leave ample room for imposing one's own values and views.

In the past, humans have let conjunctions happen and treated them like rain. By this logic, if it rains, one gets wet. In the process of getting wet however the grass and other things prosper. Thus, the cost of getting wet is well worth the overall benefits. Should people use some selective umbrellas to shield parts of cultures and environments from the influences of globalization? Should people see new technology as occasional nourishment for social growth, like watering the lawn to keep it green? In the end, there is probably more to fear from the concentration of the new technology or tool in the hands of a few rather than in letting natural processes take place in civil society. The image of Big Brother is simply too strong to allow ceding such control to governments.

It is nonetheless true that the occurrence of Conjunctions have become more frequent over time with shorter periods of duration between them. The Tool Conjunction began in 40,000 B.C. and may have taken thirty thousand years to develop and spread throughout most of the world. The Agricultural Conjunction, by contrast, began about 10,000 B.C. and spread within a few thousand years. The Industrial Conjunction was underway by about A.D. 1800 and spread worldwide within a century. The onset of the Electronic Conjunction was about A.D. 1970 and it has spread throughout the world in the matter of a few decades. It is obvious that from the standpoint of time, the conjunction is occurring more frequently and seemingly at an exponential pace.

Other types of technological breakthroughs will no doubt follow the Electronic Conjunction, beginning perhaps with the Gene Conjunction. Working in tandem with the advances in the Electronic Conjunction, this new period will focus on the manipulations and uses of genes in human and industrial practices. Computers will of course be required in order to understand and introduce the gene changes. The changes in gene structure, in essence creating new species, will first apply to flora and then to fauna, in a way mirroring the sequence of events in the Agriculture Conjunction. The Electronic Conjunction is driver of the Gene Conjunction, but it is also the result of the introduction of industrial processes originating in the Industrial Conjunction.

The early industries of the Industrial Revolution cotton textiles, iron, the railroadswere boom industries that created millionaires overnight, like Balzac's venture bankers and like Dickens's ironmaster, who in a few years grew from a lowly

> domestic servant into a "captain of industry." The industries that emerged after 1830 also created millionaires. But they took twenty years to do so, and it was twenty years of hard work, of struggle, of disappointments and failures, of thrift. This is likely to be true of the industries that will emerge from now on. It is already true of biotechnology.[51]

The Gene Conjunction will also change the natural world and peoples' cultures in a variety of ways. Trade may be dependent on ownership of gene sequences or unique genes, and this uniqueness may well be situated in specific environments (a product) and their use determined by specific cultures (a process). These issues will thus re-enforce a discussion on product and process begun in the Electronic Conjunction. The issues at the heart of the Gene Conjunction are more than simply eschewing tomatoes that have the gene from a shrimp that helps it withstand cold weather; they will also raise a multitude of new questions about the human relationship to culture and to the environment.

> But we have learned, from 10,000 years of history, that major reinventions of agriculture are not just little technological adjustments that take place down on the farm without having much effect on the rest of us. They are steps along the road of cultural and genetic evolution—large-scale systemic transformations that reshape societies, governments, economies, ecosystems. Most of them had uneven consequences—good for some, bad for others—and some have costly and destructive side-effects.[52]

The Gene Conjunction is already getting underway. Perhaps it is possible to understand the issues in Gene Conjunction through a series of three case studies.

First, one of the initial great achievements in the Gene Conjunction was the (ongoing) development of more productive plant strains as part of the "Green Revolution." This increase in productivity also relied on the use of pesticides to reduce insect damage to the crop. One place where the "Green Revolution" was important was India, where more resilient and productive strains of rice produced far greater agricultural outputs.[53]

The Bhopal pesticide facility, owned by the American chemical company Union Carbide, was a key part of India's Green Revolution. By the 1960s, India had become a large importer of such pesticides, but India's protectionist impulses, need for foreign exchange, and import substitution policies all played a part in forcing the company to set up a local operation in 1969 in Bhopal, capital city of Madhya Pradesh state and home to nearly a million people.

The Bhopal facility produced various pesticides, mainly carbaryl and aldicarb pesticides that use an intermediate chemical called Methyl Isocyanate or MIC, a highly volatile and lethal substance. Late at night on December 23, 1984, water somehow entered an MIC holding tank and led to a dangerous chemical reaction that caused a leak in the tank. By the time the leak was discovered, about forty tons of MIC escaped downwind, killing perhaps four thousand as they slept and injuring 400,000, the largest industrial accident in history. Deaths from the spill continued for many years.[54]

Second, the Basmati case is opening a new realm of intellectual property cases in the WTO that apply to environment and culture.[55] The word "basmati" translates as "the perfumed one" and refers to rice long grown in the Himalayan foothills. Basmati is the most expensive rice in the world and a leading product of India, especially in the Punjab, Haryana, and Uttar Pradesh regions. In 1997, the U.S. Patent Office granted RiceTec Inc. a license to call a U.S.-grown variant of the rice "Basmati" and to permit U.S. exports of the rice bearing that name. The company had previous marketed Indian-like rice grown in the United States under the brand name "Kasmati" and Thai-like Jasmine rice under the name "Jasmati."

India now exports forty-five thousand tons of basmati rice to the United States annually, 10 percent of its total rice exports of $250 million. The Indian government appealed the case to the WTO, objecting to the use of the name "basmati," where it awaits a decision. In an earlier case, the U.S. Patent Office allowed American scientists to patent the word "turmeric" in the sense of its use as a wound-healing agent. The decision was over-turned after India was able to show that the use of the spice as a healing agent had existed as common knowledge for millennia. This precedent may determine the outcome of ownership disputes over the names "champagne," "scotch," and "camembert."

Finally, the third case examines gene manipulation using meat hormones.[56] Beginning in the 1970s U.S. farmers used both natural and artificial hormones to increase the growth in livestock. One reason was to cut costs since the cattle could get to market much quicker, thus reducing feeding and housing costs. By the late 1980s, more than one-half of the U.S. beef farmers were using growth hormones. On January 1, 1989, the European Community banned meat from animals treated with growth inducing hormones and in particular, U.S. beef imports, which were running at nearly $150 million per year. In retaliation, the United States placed 100 percent tariffs on a variety of agricultural products including canned tomatoes, fruit juices, and ham (partly to spread the pain amongst EC member countries).

TABLE 4.3 **Past and Future Conjunctions**

No.	Name	Begin Time, Years Ago	End Time, Years Ago	Duration	Between Years
1*	Tool	50,000	10,000	40,000	500,000
2**	Agricultural	10,000	2,000	8,000	40,000
3	Industrial	300 (1700)	50 (1950)	250	11,700
4	Electronic	50 (1950)	+25 (2025)	75	250
5	Gene	+25 (2025)	+75 (2075)	50	75

* I assume a pre-conjunction period of inchoate development for the Tool Conjunction and it begins with the first evidence of tool use by human beings and their ancestors that began about 500,000 years ago.

** The basis for the "Years Ago" calculations assumes that "today" is the year 2000. Years in the future are indicated by a "+".

The EC further threatened retaliation against U.S. exports of nuts and fruits.

The United States took the case to the WTO and won (as did Canada which brought a separate but parallel case). The EU has not yet opened its market and the WTO has drawn up plans to allow the United States and Canada to seek and receive "compensation." This does not mean that the EU would "pay" the United States a certain amount (the value over several years was put at about $500 million). Rather, the decision would permit the United States to withdraw some concessions it had made to the EU in the last round of trade negotiations.

Even before the full onslaught of the Gene Conjunction there is growing evidence that gene enhancements will not only contribute to progress in the human social context but also to the current level of disconnect and discontent. Moves by differing countries to claim intellectual property ownership over cheeses, spirits, rice and other products foretell a legal battle over the ownership of life itself. Since these claims limit the ownership to a certain people living in a certain area, in many ways these issues epitomize the struggle of the local versus the cosmopolitan views of the world and the long-standing presence of the human as a local creature. Remembering history may provide some warning to the unintended consequences of technological advancement in this period.

This trickle of cases in the Gene Conjunction suggests an impending river of change that promises to be quicker, deeper, and broader than any conjunction before it. With the Gene Conjunction and another increase in the rate of social change, social anomie will also inevitably increase. Seattle showed that multilateral institutions are not yet capable of relieving such anxiety and the WTO no doubt the wrong place to seek solace. With this new conjunction, perhaps, it is time that human institutions take responsibility for producing a future that is welcoming to humans.

Table 4.3 provides a perspective on the current and future conjunctions. In this viewpoint, there continues a decline in the duration of a conjunction and its development period. Now the possibility and reality of the disconnect and its impact on the social context, what Toffler calls "future shock," becomes clearer. How short of a time can these periods of change become before they overwhelm the human imagination? It is clear that humans will see a higher rate of technological change in the future, but perhaps there is a "wall" to the extent that people can absorb such changes in lives and lifestyles. Perhaps this future shock will result in a feedback against more technological changes.

Will the pattern of shorter and quicker conjunctions continue? Will conjunctions come hurtling like hailstones and pummel people into madness or escapism? This disconnect can only further separate trade, environment, and culture into more discrete parts that may weaken the overall coherence of the social context. Thus, preservation of the natural world and natural society must be part of decision-making and investments for the future. The future will continue to stretch the limits of human capacity for change and shorten the period needed to prepare and accept those changes. People need to be ready for a cascade of new ideas and technologies in the wake of rapidly changing technological and environmental contexts. They also need to be part of developing responses to these changes.

Perhaps in time some people will live like the Batek from Malaysia, choosing to stay in a non-technological "forest" and not venturing out into the new world. With new technologies and new social contexts constantly arising, the feeling of being out of place and time will become more common. Those people who choose to come out of the forest will learn to cope with change and the new maladies it inspires. Among the maladies of today, one must surely include symptoms of the fast pace of change that produces the disconnect and perhaps it is possible to call this "global-phobia." Whether it will be possible to contain global-phobia to a limited outbreak or whether it will be an epidemic depends on the today's decisions. One thing is certain: the cure for global-phobia must include the search for authentic human experiences along the road to the endless debate.

NOTES

CHAPTER 1

1. Ulf Hannerz, "Cosmopolitans and Locals in World Culture," in *Global Culture: Nationalism, Globalization and Modernity*, ed. Michael Featherstone (London: Sage Publications, 1990), p. 237. See also Robert Merton, *Social Theory and Social Structure* (Glencoe, Ill.: Free Press, 1957).
2. Latin American Economic System (SELA) and United Nations Conference on Trade and Development (UNCTAD), *Trade and Environment: The International Debate* (1994).
3. Merwyn S. Garbarino, *Sociocultural Theory in Anthropology* (Prospect Heights, Ill.: Waveland Press, 1983), p. 49.
4. Bernard Campbell, *Human Ecology* (New York: Aldine Publishing Company, 1983), p. 8.
5. Raymond Williams, *Keywords: A Vocabulary of Culture and Society* (New York: Oxford University Press, 1976), pp. 76–77.
6. Immanuel Wallerstein, "Culture as the Ideological Battleground," in *Global Culture*, ed. Featherstone, p. 31.
7. Williams, *Keywords*, p. 77.
8. Williams, *Keywords*, p. 179.
9. Raymond Williams, *The Sociology of Culture* (Chicago: University of Chicago Press, 1981), pp. 10–11.
10. See Elvin Hatch, "Culture," in *The Social Science Encyclopedia*, ed. Adam Kuper and Jessica Kuper (London and Boston: Routledge and Kegan Paul, 1985) p. 179.
11. Hatch, "Culture," p. 179. Also, see Charles Singer, "The Concept of Culture," in *International Encyclopedia of the Social Sciences*, Volume 18, ed. David L. Sills (New York: Free Press, 1968), p. 528.
12. Garbarino, *Sociocultural Theory in Anthropology*, p. 49.
13. Garbarino, *Sociocultural Theory in Anthropology*, p. 49.
14. John T. Zadrozny, *Dictionary of Social Science* (Washington, D.C.: Public Affairs Press, 1959), pp. 78–79.

15. Lawrence E. Harrison, *Who Prospers? How Cultural Values Shape Economic and Political Success* (New York: Basic Books, 1992), p. 9.
16. Williams, *The Sociology of Culture*, p. 11.
17. Harrison, *Who Prospers*, p. 9.
18. Walter Truett Anderson, *Evolution Isn't What It Used to Be: The Augmented Animal and the Whole Wired World* (New York: W.H. Freeman and Company, 1996), p. 185.
19. Stephen Mennell, "The Globalization of Human Society as a Very Long-term Social Process: Elias' Theory," in *Global Culture*, ed. Featherstone, p. 359.
20. Herbert Simon, *Sciences of the Artificial* (Cambridge: M.I.T. Press, 1969).
21. Charles L. Redman, "The Impact of Food Production: Short-Term Strategies and Long-Term Consequences," in *Pleistocene Extinctions*, ed. P. S. Martin and H. S. Wright (New Haven, Conn., and London: Yale University Press, 1967), p. 123.
22. Stephen D. Cohen, Joel R. Paul and Robert A. Blecker, *Fundamentals of U.S. Foreign Trade Policy: Economics, Politics, Laws, and Issues* (Boulder, Colo.: Westview Press, 1996).
23. Stephen K. Sanderson, *Social Evolution* (Cambridge, Mass.: Basil Blackwell, 1990), p. 170.
24. A. L. Kroeber, *Cultural and Natural Areas of Native North America* (Berkeley: University of California Press, 1947), p. 251.
25. William J. Hamilton III, "Omnivorous Primate Diets and Human Overconsumption of Meat," in *Food and Evolution: Toward a Theory of Human Food Habitats*, ed. Marvin Harris and Eric B. Ross (Philadelphia, Pa.: Temple University Press, 1987), pp. 117–32.
26. In the interior of Europe, the high price of meat forced farmers to turn to dairy products focusing on cheese and milk (the poor man's "meat"). Domesticated animals were ordinarily only eaten if they died of natural causes, usually old age.
27. See William H. Durham, *Coevolution: Genes, Culture, and Human Diversity* (Stanford, Calif.: Stanford University Press, 1991). See also June Helm, "The Ecological Approach in Anthropology," in *Perspectives in Cultural Anthropology*, ed. Herbert Applebaum (Albany: State University of New York Press, 1987).
28. Julian Steward, *Theory of Cultural Change* (Urbana, Ill.: University of Illinois Press, 1957), p. 37.
29. Steward, in *Theory of Cultural Change*, p. 37.
30. Clifford Geertz, *Agricultural Innovation* (Berkeley: University of California Press, 1963).
31. Marvin Harris, *Cannibals and Kings: The Origins of Cultures* (New York: Random House, 1977), pp. 9–17.
32. See Marvin Harris, *Cows, Pigs, Wars, and Witches* (New York: Vintage Books, 1974) and *Good to Eat: Riddles of Food and Culture* (New York: Simon and Schuster, 1985).
33. Harris, *Cows, Pigs, Wars, and Witches*, p. 28 and Harris, *Good to Eat*, p. 130.

34. Harris, *Good to Eat*, p. 109.
35. Robert Lowie, "The Determinants of Culture," in *Perspectives on Cultural Anthropology*, ed. Herbert Applebaum (Albany: State University of New York Press, 1987), p. 92.
36. Harris, *Cows, Pigs, Wars, and Witches*, pp. 30-31.
37. Paul Shepard, *Coming Home to the Pleistocene* (Washington, D.C.: Island Press, 1998), p. 1.
38. Campbell, *Human Ecology*, pp. 16–17. Roy Ellen, *Environment, Subsistence, and System* (Cambridge: Cambridge University Press, 1982), Chapter 2.
39. Alvin Toffler, *Future Shock* (New York: Random House, 1970), p. 27.
40. Maurice Daumas, ed., *A History of Technology and Invention: Progress through the Ages*, Volume I, "The Origins of Technological Civilization" [translated by Eileen B. Hennessy] (New York: Crown Publishers, 1969). See also V. Gordon Childe, "Early Forms of Society," in *A History of Technology*, Volume I, "From Early Time to Fall of Ancient Empires," ed. Charles Singer, E. J. Holmyard, and A. R. Hall (New York and London: Oxford University Press, 1954), p. 40.
41. Daumas, ed., *A History of Technology and Invention*, p. 3.
42. Daumas, ed., *A History of Technology and Invention*, p. 2. See also V. Gordon Childe, "Early Forms of Society," p. 40.
43. Daumas, ed., *A History of Technology and Invention*, p. 6.
44. Daumas, ed., *A History of Technology and Invention*, p. 7.
45. See Richard Klein, "The Impact of Early People on the Environment: The Case of Large Mammal Extinctions," in *Human Impact on the Environment: Ancient Roots, Current Challenges*, ed. Judith E. Jacobson and John Furor (Boulder, Colo.: Westview Press, 1992), p. 21.
46. Shepard, *Coming Home to the Pleistocene*, p. 69.
47. Redman, "The Impact of Food Production," p. 35.
48. Ester Boserup, *Evolution agraire et pression demographique* [The Condition of Agricultural Growth: The Economics of Agrarian Change under Population Pressure] (New York: Aldine Publishing Co., 1965).
49. Karl Marx, *Capital: A Critique of Political Economy*, Vol. 1 (New York: Vintage Books, 1977), p. 878.
50. Michael Albert and Robin Hahnel, *Marxism and Socialist Theory* (Boston: South End Press, 1981).
51. Marx, *Capital: A Critique of Political Economy*, p. 876.
52. Arnold J. Toynbee, "Preface to the Beacon Paperback Edition," in Arnold Toynbee, *The Industrial Revolution* (Boston: Beacon Press, 1884), p. ix.
53. Toynbee, *The Industrial Revolution*, p. 7.
54. Toynbee, *The Industrial Revolution*, p. 12, "It is known that 334,974 acres were enclosed between 1710 and 1760, while nearly 7,000,000 were enclosed between 1760 and 1843."
55. Toynbee, *The Industrial Revolution*, p. 13.
56. Toynbee, *The Industrial Revolution*, p. 19.

57. Simon Kuznets, *Modern Economic Growth: Rate, Structure, and Spread*, Fourth Printing (New Haven, Conn.: Yale University Press, 1969), p. 2. For Kuznets, several elements comprise a conjunction:

    "First, the distinction and definition of epochs in the long stretch of human life on this planet is partly a matter of judgment, based on the scholar's interest. He may wish to distinguish the 500,000 years of food-gathering, hunting, and fishing from the following five to seven thousand years of food production and concentrate on the slow but significant changes in the techniques of making stone implements."
58. Kuznets, *Modern Economic Growth*, pp. 5–6.
59. Kuznets, *Modern Economic Growth*, p. 5.
60. Kuznets, *Modern Economic Growth*, p. 4.
61. Alvin Toffler, *The Third Wave* (New York: William Morrow, Inc., 1980), p. 20.
62. Barraclough argues that the Industrial Conjunction centers about the year 1870 as opposed to Toynbee, who saw the beginnings of this period driven by water and steam power. Barraclough sees combustion engines burning fossil fuels as the driver of these trends. The FrancoPrussian War occurred in 1870, but there were few events around then associated with creating such a largescale impact. A greater impact than this brief war may have been the publishing of Charles Darwin's *Ascent of Man* a year later. See Geoffrey Barraclough, reprint ed., *An Introduction to Contemporary History* (Harmondworth, Middlesex, England: Penguin Books, 1984).
63. Unless otherwise noted, time dates refer to anno domini (A.D.) time, before present (B.P.), before Christ (B.C.) and before the common era (B.C.E.).
64. Toffler, *The Third Wave*, pp. 30, 33.
65. George Thomson, *The Foreseeable Future* (New York: Viking, 1960), p. 1.
66. Herbert Read, "New Realms of Art," in *The Semi-Artificial Man*, ed. M. B. Schnapper (Washington, D.C.: Public Affairs Press, 1957), p. 77.
67. Kenneth Boulding, *The Meaning of the Twentieth Century* (New York: Harper and Row, 1964), p. 7. Alvin Toffler, *The Third Wave* and *Future Shock* (New York: Random House, 1970), pp. 12–13.
68. Julius Huxley, *On Living in a Revolution* (New York: Harper and Row, 1942), pp. viii–ix. Also see Julius Huxley, *Man in the Modern World* (New York: New American Library, 1959).
69. Toffler, *The Third Wave*, p. 132.
70. Toffler, *The Third Wave*, p. 33.
71. Toffler, *The Third Wave*, p. 307.
72. Toffler, *The Third Wave*, p. 136.
73. Toffler, *The Third Wave*, p. 167.
74. Alvin Toffler, *Future Shock* (New York: Random House, 1970), p. 326. William Ogburn, (Toffler, *Future Shock*, p. 3), developed the idea of a cultural lag, where uneven rates of change between societal entities can cause stress.
75. Fernand Braudel, *The Structures of Everyday Life: Civilization and*

Capitalism, Fifteenth–Eighteenth Century (Paris: Librarie Armund Colin, 1979) Volume I, p. 431.

76. Barraclough, *An Introduction to Contemporary History*, p. 93
77. Barraclough, *An Introduction to Contemporary History*, p. 44. On this distinction, see also Thomas Kuhn, *The Structure of Scientific Revolutions* (Chicago: University of Chicago Press, 1962).
78. Barraclough, *An Introduction to Contemporary History*, pp. 1920.
79. Roland Robertson, "Mapping the Global Condition: Globalization as the Central Concept" in *Global Culture*, ed. Featherstone, p. 21.
80. Peter Drucker, "Beyond the Information Revolution," *The Atlantic Monthly* (October 1999), <www.theatlantic.com/issues/99oct/9910drucker.htm>.

CHAPTER 2

1. Judith E. Jacobsen, and John Firor, eds., *Human Impact on the Environment: Ancient Roots, Current Challenges* (Boulder, Colo.: Westview Press, 1992), pp. 25–26.
2. P. Mellars and C. Stringer, eds., *The Human Revolution: Behavioral and Biological Perspectives on the Origins of Human Beings* (Edinburgh: Edinburgh University Press, 1989). Some scholars have even suggested that a gene mutation occurring around the same time was responsible for the sudden human changes.
3. In fact, we separate the modern from the older human lines by the appearance of culture and signs of identity on the part of these people. One of the first signs of humanity was the practice of burying one's dead.
4. Jensen, *The Prehistory of Denmark* (London: Methennard Co., 1982), p. 53.
5. Robert Lowie, "The Determinants of Culture," in *Perspectives in Cultural Anthropology*, ed. Herbert Applebaum (Albany: State University of New York Press, 1987), p. 89.
6. Maurice Daumas, ed., *A History of Technology and Invention: Progress through the Ages*, Volume I, "The Origins of Technological Civilization," tr. Eileen B. Hennessey (New York: Crown Publishers, 1969), p. 59.
7. Walter Truett Anderson, *Evolution Isn't What It Used to Be: The Augmented Animal and the Whole Wired World* (New York: W.H. Freeman and Company, 1996), pp. 52–53.
8. Further, "the effects of culture on humans themselves in the hunter-gatherer phase included impacts on techniques of food-gathering, and especially of hunting." Stephen Boyden, *BioHistory: The Interplay between Human Society and the Biosphere*, Man and the Biosphere Series, Volume 8 (Paris: UNESCO, 1992), p. 95. Additionally, the use of fire resulted not only in the introduction of cooked foods into the diet, but also burns as a new form of injury.
9. J. Lawrence Angel, "Paleoecology, Paleodemography and Health," in *Perspectives in Cultural Anthropology*, ed. Herbert Applebaum (Albany: State University of New York Press, 1987), p. 168.

10. V. Gordon Childe, "Early Forms of Society," in *A History of Technology*, Volume I, "From Early Time to Fall of Ancient Empires," ed. Charles Singer, E. J. Holmyard and A. R. Hall (New York and London: Oxford University Press, 1954), p. 43.
11. Paul Shepard, *Coming Home to the Pleistocene* (Washington, D.C.: Island Press, 1998), p. 82.
12. Daumas, *A History of Technology and Invention*, p. 12.
13. Daumas, *A History of Technology and Invention*, p. 13.
14. Daumas, *A History of Technology and Invention*, p. 30.
15. Childe, "Early Forms of Society," p. 44.
16. Daumas, *A History of Technology and Invention*, p. 4.
17. Daumas, *A History of Technology and Invention*, p. 13.
18. Daumas, *A History of Technology and Invention*, p. 13. This trend parallels the diminishing size of computers today.
19. Marvin Harris, *Culture, People, Nature: An Introduction to General Anthropology* (New York: Harper Row, 1980), p. 138.
20. Harris, *Culture, People, Nature*, p. 143.
21. Colin Tudge, *The Day before Yesterday: Five Million Years of Human History* (London: Pimlico, 1995), p. 2.
22. Harris, *Culture, People, Nature*, p. 122.
23. Harris, *Culture, People, Nature*, p. 128.
24. This is not to imply that older humans, or even Neanderthals, lacked creative abilities to use technology or create art.
25. Robert Hughes, "Behold This Stone Age," *Time*, Volume 145, Number 6 (February 13, 1995), pp. 52–63.
26. Richard Klein, "The Impact of Early People on the Environment: The Case of Large Mammal Extinctions," in *Human Impact on the Environment: Ancient Roots, Current Challenges*, ed. Judith E. Jacobsen and John Firor (Boulder, Colo.: Westview Press, 1992), p. 21.
27. However, in places where humans had entered into the Agricultural Conjunction and the woolly mammoth survived, this may not have been the case. Recent finds in Ukraine suggest humans and mammoths lived side by side for a long period.
28. Harris, *Culture, People, Nature*, p. 130. One way that early peoples conducted commerce was through "silent trade." One group would leave a product in an open space; another would come along, see it, and leave a product of equal value. If the first group returned and saw that an equal product existed, that was the consummation of the deal. "In this fashion the Mbuti of the Ituri forest trade meat for bananas with the Bantu agriculturalists, and the Vedda of Sri Lanka trade honey for iron tools with the Sinhalese," p. 229.
29. Klein, "The Impact of Early People," pp. 25–26.
30. Tudge, *The Day before Yesterday*, p. 262.
31. Shepard Krech III, *The Ecological Indian: Myth and History* (New York: W.W. Norton and Company, 1999), pp. 36–37.

32. Tudge, *The Day before Yesterday*, p. 315.
33. Tudge, *The Day before Yesterday*, p. 321.
34. Klein, "The Impact of Early People," pp. 25–26.
35. Marvin Harris, *Cannibals and Kings* (New York: Vintage Books Edition, 1991, first edition, Random House, 1977), p. 31. Harris points to the fact that New World megafauna extinctions exceeded those in the Old World. In the New World, thirty-one large mammals became extinct. Harris, *Culture, People, Nature*, p. 167, suggests it was a matter of opportunity: "because of the more extensive range of extinctions affecting the New World Pleistocene fauna, opportunities for animal domestication were limited by a lack of suitable wild species."
36. Klein, "The Impact of Early People," pp. 13–34.
37. Klein, "The Impact of Early People," p. 27.
38. Popular renditions of these ancient cultures include Jean Auel, *The Mammoth Hunters* (New York: Bantam Books, 1986).
39. Anderson, *Evolution Isn't What It Used to Be*, p. 83.
40. Russian scientists have recently found a type of woolly mammoth on Wrangel Island that sits between Russia and the U.S. state of Alaska in the Bering Sea that survived much later. Carbon dating of ivory tusks suggests the mammoths survived there until about two thousand years ago and there is no evidence of humans living there at the time. Because of the limited space on the island, the mammoths evolved into a pygmy size. On Catalina Island, off California, there are similar pygmy mammoth finds and again with no evidence of human presence around this time.
41. Harris, *Culture, People, and Nature*, p. 136.
42. Harris, *Culture, People, and Nature*, p. 136.
43. Matt Creson, "Mammoth Tusks Tell Ancient Tales of Life and Murder," *Denver Post* (November 6, 1996), p. 32a.
44. R. Dale Guthrie, "Late Pleistocene Faunal Revolution—A New Perspective on the Extinction Debate," in *Megafauna and Man: Discovery of America's Heartland*, ed. Larry D. Agenbrod, Jim I. Mead and Lisa W. Nelson (Hot Springs, S.Dak.: The Mammoth Site of Hot Springs, South Dakota, Inc., Scientific Papers, Volume 1, 1990), p. 42.
45. Krech III, *The Ecological Indian*, p. 40.
46. Guthrie, "Late Pleistocene Faunal Revolution," p. 45.
47. Guthrie, "Late Pleistocene Faunal Revolution," p. 45.
48. Guthrie, "Late Pleistocene Faunal Revolution," p. 48.
49. Shepard, *Coming Home to the Pleistocene*, pp. 31–32.
50. Shepard, *Coming Home to the Pleistocene*, p. 32.
51. Shepard, *Coming Home to the Pleistocene*, p. 33.
52. Shepard, *Coming Home to the Pleistocene*, pp. 82–83.
53. Shepard, *Coming Home to the Pleistocene*, p. 20.
54. Shepard, *Coming Home to the Pleistocene*, p. 37.
55. Shepard, *Coming Home to the Pleistocene*, pp. 92–93.

"In hoe or subsistence agriculture, we usually find a greater diversity of plants, a polycultural system with small-scale mixed planting, and fewer specialized crops than with advanced agriculture. According to David Harris, the transition to the specialized systems from more generalized systems required not only genetic engineering but stratified societies." Shepard, *Coming Home to the Pleistocene*, p. 87. Also see David R. Harris, "Agricultural Systems, Ecosystems, and the Origin of Agriculture," *The Domestication and Exploitation of Plants and Animals* (Chicago: Aldine Press, 1969), p. 4.

56. Benjamin Burack, *Ivory and Its Uses* (Rutland, Vt.: Charles E. Tuttle Company, 1984), p. 15.
57. Mammoth ivory finds show up in places where mammoths did not live and researchers surmise that trade must have spread the products.
58. Ivory has come largely from elephants, but ivory can also be obtained from the mammoth, mastodon, walrus, hippo, narwhal, boar, and wart hog. Sperm whale teeth are also a form of ivory. Ivory was one of the products to return with European adventurers from their first trips to Africa in the fifteenth century. Sometime between 10,000 and 3000 B.C., the mammoths disappeared and the focus of ivory demand turned to the elephant. At this time, elephants lived as far north as Libya and Mauritania in Africa and herds stretched all the way to Syria. Their extinction was mainly the result of ivory demand. *Ivory: An International Survey* (New York: Harry N. Abrams, Inc., Publishers, 1987), p. 35. Evidence of ivory carving in Asia has a long history and samples date back four thousand years. See James R. Lee, "Ancient Mammoth Ivory Trade," *TED Case Studies* #465, (January 1998), <www.american.edu/TED/mammoth.htm>.
59. Adrian Lister and Paul Bahn, *Mammoths* (New York: Macmillan, 1994), p. 93.
60. Lister and Bahn, *Mammoths*, p. 93.
61. Paul G. Bain and Jean Vertot, *Images of the Ice Age* (New York: Facts on File Books, 1988), p. 74.
62. *Ivory: An International Survey*, p. 34.
63. Lister and Bahn, *Mammoths*, p. 114.
64. George C. Frison, "Clovis, Goshen, and Folsom: Lifeways and Cultural Relationships," p. 101, in *Megafauna and Man*, ed. Agenbrod, Mead and Nelson. Clovis peoples were less developed than Old World upper Paleolithic peoples were.
65. Frison, "Clovis, Goshen, and Folsom," p. 138.
66. L. Adrien Hannus, "The Lange-Ferguson Site: A Case of Mammoth Bone-Butchering Tools," p. 86, in *Megafauna and Man: Discovery of America's Heartland*, ed. Agenbrod, Mead, and Nelson.
67. Hannus, "The Lange-Ferguson Site," p. 90.
68. Frison, "Clovis, Goshen, and Folsum," p. 138.
69. Daumas, *A History of Technology and Invention*, p. 30.
70. Frison, "Clovis, Goshen, and Folsum," p. 139.
71. Frison, "Clovis, Goshen, and Folsom," p. 106.

72. Krech III, *The Ecological Indian*, p. 129.
73. Frison, "Clovis, Goshen, and Folsom," p. 139.
74. Alfred W. Crosby, *Ecological Imperialism: The Biological Expansion of Europe, 900–1900* (Cambridge: Cambridge University Press, 1986), p. 182.
75. Krech III, *The Ecological Indian*, p. 131.
76. Marvin Harris, *Cannibals and Kings* (New York: Vintage Books edition, 1991, first edition, Random House, 1977), p. 29. One famous spot for this was located in Alberta, Canada, at a place called "Head Smashed in Buffalo Jump."
77. Harris, *Culture, People, Nature*, p. 177.
78. Krech III, *The Ecological Indian*, p. 138.
79. Richard A. Barrett, *Culture and Conduct* (Belmont, Calif.: Wadsworth Publishing Co., 1991), p. 88.
80. Krech III, *The Ecological Indian*, p. 136.
81. Lewis Mumford, "The First Megamachine," *Diogenes* (Fall 1966), pp. 1–5.
82. Anderson, *Evolution Isn't What It Used to Be*, p. 114.
83. Tudge, *The Day before Yesterday*.
84. Harris, *Cannibals and Kings*, p. 31.
85. Anderson, *Evolution Isn't What It Used to Be*, p. 113.
86. Jane Jacobs, *The Economy of Cities* (New York: Random House), 1963.
87. Tudge, *The Day before Yesterday*, p. 277.
88. Shepard, *Coming Home to the Pleistocene*, p. 81.
89. Harris, *Culture, People, Nature*, pp. 142–43.
90. Harris, *Culture, People, Nature*, p. 147.
91. Harris, *Culture, People, Nature*, p. 148.
92. Bernard Campbell, *Human Ecology* (New York: Aldine Publishing Company, 1983), pp. 171–72.
93. Campbell, *Human Ecology*, p. 172.
94. Fekri A. Hassan, "Determination of the Size, Density, and Growth Rate of Hunting-Gathering Populations," in *Population, Ecology, and Social Evolution*, ed. Steven Polgar (The Hague and Paris: Mouton Publishers, 1975), p. 34.
95. Charles L. Redman, "The Impact of Food Production: Short-Term Strategies and Long-Term Consequences," in *Pleistocene Extinctions*, ed. P. S. Martin and H. S. Wright (New Haven, Conn., and London: Yale University Press, 1967), p. 124.
96. White, *Medieval Technology and Social Change* (Oxford: Clarendon Press, 1962), p. 41.
97. White, *Medieval Technology and Social Change*, p. 60–61.
98. White, *Medieval Technology and Social Change*, p. 44.
99. White, *Medieval Technology and Social Change*, p. 1.
100. White, *Medieval Technology and Social Change*, p. 2.
101. White, *Medieval Technology and Social Change*, p. 57.
102. Inventions need not only be a new type of product but also a new type of

process. White, *Medieval Technology and Social Change*, p. 69, asserts "the three-field system of crop rotation has been called 'the greatest agricultural novelty of the Middle Ages in Western Europe.'"

103. The critical role of the horseshoe was made clear by Benjamin Franklin, who said in *Poor Richard's Almanac* (1738) that "A little neglect may breed mischief . . . for want of a nail the shoe was lost; for want of a shoe the horse was lost; and for want of a horse the rider was lost."
104. Shepard, *Coming Home to the Pleistocene*, p. 115.
105. See Doug Jacobsen, "Amber Trade: Old and New," *TED Case Studies* #451 (January 1998), <www.american.edu/TED/amber.htm>.
106. Arnolds Spekke, *The Ancient Amber Routes and the Geographical Discovery of the Eastern Baltic* (Stockholm: M. Goppers, 1957), p. 16.
107. Jensen, *The Prehistory of Denmark*, p. 103.
108. Lowie, "The Determinants of Culture," p. 86.
109. Spekke, *The Ancient Amber Routes*, p. 48.
110. Spekke, *The Ancient Amber Routes*, p. 72.
111. Spekke, *The Ancient Amber Routes*, p. 3. See also J. M. de Navarro, "Prehistoric Routes between Northern Europe and Italy Defined by Amber Trade," *The Geographical Journal*, Volume LXVI (1925).
112. Spekke, *The Ancient Amber Routes*, p. 47.
113. David A. Grimaldi, *Amber: Window to the Past* (New York: Henry N. Abrahms, 1996), p. 160.
114. Grimaldi, *Amber: Window to the Past*, p. 167.
115. Grimaldi, *Amber: Window to the Past*, pp. 47–53.
116. Doug Jacobsen, "Amber Trade."
117. John Gardner and John Maier, *Gilgamesh: Translated from the Sin-leqi-unnunni version* (New York: Alfred A. Knopf, 1984), p. 16.
118. Gardner and Maier, *Gilgamesh*, p. 146. This is quoted in Marvin W. Mikesell, "The Deforestation of Mount Lebanon," *The Geographical Review*, Volume LIX, Number 1 (January 1969), p. 13.
120. The Bible, Isaiah 14:7–8.
121. The section draws from Benjamin T. Kasoff, "Cedars of Lebanon," *TED Case Studies* #187 (May 1995), <www.american.edu/TED/cedars.htm>.
122. Ellen Churchill Semple, *Geography of the Mediterranean Region* (New York: Henry Holt and Co., 1931), pp. 267–68.
123. Russell Meiggs, *Trees and Timber in the Ancient Mediterranean and the World* (Oxford: Clarendon Press, 1982), p. 59.
124. Dmitri Baramki, *Phoenicia and the Phoenicians* (Khayats: Lebanon, 1961), p. 18.
125. Meiggs, *Trees and Timber*, p. 55.
126. Semple, *Geography of the Mediterranean Region*, p. 267, also noted that Sidon sent logs for the building of the Temple.
127. The Bible notes a figure of thirty thousand men but Meiggs, *Trees and Timber* and others dispute this total as being far too high (p. 70).

128. Donald Harden, *The Phoenicians* (New York: Frederick A. Praeger, Inc., 1963), p. 41, and p. 91 and Mikesell, "The Deforestation of Mount Lebanon," p. 18.
129. Meiggs, *Trees and Timber*, pp. 71–72.
130. Semple, *Geography of the Mediterranean Region*, p. 283.
131. Semple, *Geography of the Mediterranean Region*, p. 282.
132. Leften Stavrianos, *Global Rift: The Third World Comes of Age* (New York: Morrow, 1981), p. 256.
133. Karl Polyani, *The Great Transformation: The Political and Economic Origins of Our Time* (Boston: Beacon Press, 1944), p. 7.
134. White, *Medieval Technology and Social Change*, p. 89. "Our purpose is not to demonstrate this astonishing rise in productivity, but rather to examine the new exploratory attitude towards the forces of nature which enabled medieval Europe to discover and to try to harness other sources of power which have been culturally effective in modern times."
135. Martin J. Wiener, *English Culture and the Decline of the Industrial Spirit, 1850–1980* (Cambridge: Cambridge University Press, 1981), p. 4.
136. Ralf Dahrendof, quoted in Wiener, *English Culture and the Decline of the Industrial Spirit*, p. 4.
137. Peter Drucker, "Beyond the Information Revolution," *The Atlantic Monthly* (October 1999), <www.theatlantic.com/issues/99oct/9910drucker.htm>.
138. E. J. Hobsbawm, *Industry and Empire*, p. 13.
139. M. Fores, "The Myth of the British Industrial Revolution," *History* (1981), p. 66.
140. Peter Mathias, "The Industrial Revolution: Concept and Reality," in *The First Industrial Revolutions*, ed. Peter Mathias and John A. Davis (Oxford: Basil Blackwell, 1989), p. 1.
141. Mathias, "The Industrial Revolution," pp. 1–2.
142. Mathias, "The Industrial Revolution," p. 2, also notes that it is in fact an "initial phase in long-term industrialization that is marked by higher rates of growth and consequent structural change."
143. John W. Osborne, *The Silent Revolution: The Industrial Revolution in England as a Source of Social Change* (New York: Charles Scribner's Sons, 1970), p. 21.
144. John W. Osborne, *The Silent Revolution*, p. 23.
145. Drucker, "Beyond the Information Revolution."
146. Arnold Toynbee, *The Industrial Revolution* (Boston: Beacon Press, 1884), p. 63.
147. Arnold Toynbee, *Lectures on the Industrial Revolution in England: Popular Addresses, Notes and Other Fragments Together with a Short Memoir to B. Jowett* (London: 1884).
148. Toynbee, *The Industrial Revolution*, pp. 27–32.
149. Al Gore, *Earth in the Balance: Ecology and the Human Spirit* (Boston: Houghton Mifflin Company, 1992), p. 22.
150. J. Tyndall, "On the Absorption and Radiation of Heat by Gasses and Vapors,

and on the Physical Connection of Radiation, Absorption, and Conduction," *Philosophy Magazine*, Serial Volume 4, Number 22 (1861), pp. 169–94 and 237–76.

151. "The best were harvested by the Ehattesehat and Quatsino people, on the west coast of Vancouver Island," *National Geographic*, Volume 183, Number 1 (January 1993), p. 110.
152. *National Geographic* (January 1993), p. 110. Also see Chad P. Cummins, "Hudson Bay Fur Trade in 1800s," *TED Case Studies* #113 (January 1994), <www.american.edu/TED/hudson.htm>.
153. The trade to Asia also helped a balance of payments problem that was taking place in Europe at this time. Europe had been running large trade deficits with China because of silk imports. This problem actually persisted for a century; one reason Western countries forced China to open its borders for trade. The export of British-owned opium from India to China was in part to alleviate this still persistent trade gap. Britain forced China to open up for opium (and other) trade in the Opium Wars.
154. This part uses information found in Theresa Purcell's "Irish Potato Famine," *TED Case Studies* #274 (June 1996), <www.american.edu/TED/potato.htm>.
155. Joseph Judge, "The Travail of Ireland," *National Geographic*, Volume 159, Number 4 (April 1981), p. 440.
156. Hugh A. Mulligan, "Irish Potato Famine Painfully Remembered," *Hickory Daily Record* (September 10, 1995), p. C8. Potatoes contain nutrients such as proteins, carbohydrates, and vitamin C, which are necessary for a healthy diet, but they lack vitamin A and calcium. Combined with milk, potatoes supply almost all food elements required for a healthy diet. To fulfill the daily nutritive requirement in the mid-1800s, one person had to eat three kilograms (six and a half pounds) of potatoes. According to historical accounts, a "burley farmer could down 15 potatoes" at one meal.
157. Liam Kennedy, "The Great Exodus: The Nineteenth Century," *Ireland of the Welcomes*, Volume 41, Number 4 (July–August 1992), pp. 10–15.
158. Judge, "The Travail of Ireland," p. 440.
159. Mulligan, "Irish Potato Famine Painfully Remembered," p. C8.
160. Kennedy, *Ireland of the Welcomes*, pp. 11–13.
161. Mulligan, "Irish Potato Famine Painfully Remembered," p. C8.
162. Mulligan, "Irish Potato Famine Painfully Remembered," p. C8.
163. Judge, *The Travails of Ireland*, p. 440.
164. Shepard, *Coming Home to the Pleistocene*, pp. 93–94.
165. This part uses information found in George Arvantides, "The Elgin Marbles," *TED Case Studies* #445 (January 1998), <www.american.edu/TED/monument.htm>.
166. "The Restitution," Hellenic Ministry of Culture, 1997.
167. "Marbles Requested and Refused," Newsletter of the British Committee for the Restitution of the Parthenon Marbles (July 1984). UNESCO determines the legality of claims based on the 1970 Convention on the Means of Prohibiting and Preventing the Illicit Import, Export and Transfer of Ownership of

Cultural Property.

168. Jules Dassin, "The Parthenon Marbles" (Athens: Melina Mercouri Foundation, 1994).

169. John Henry Merryman, "Who Owns the Elgin Marbles?" *ARTNEWS*, Volume 85, Number 7 (September 1986), p. 106.

CHAPTER 3

1. Eric Hobsbawm, *The Age of Extremes: A History of the World, 1914–1991* (New York: Pantheon Books, 1994).
2. G. Harry Stine, *The Untold Story of the Computer Revolution: Bits, Bytes, Bauds, and Brains* (New York: Arbor House, 1985), p. 14.
3. Zbigniew Brzezinski, *Between Two Ages: America's Role in the Technotronic Era* (New York: Viking Press, 1970).
4. Daniel Bell, *The Coming of Post-Industrial Society* (New York: Basic Books, 1973), p. 53.
5. Walter Truett Anderson, *Evolution Isn't What It Used to Be: The Augmented Animal and the Whole Wired World*, (New York: W.H. Freeman and Company, 1996), p. 57.
6. Bell, *The Coming of Post-Industrial Society*, p. 37.
7. Amitai Etzioni, *The Active Society* (New York: Free Press, 1968), p. vii.
8. Peter Drucker, "Beyond the Information Revolution," *The Atlantic Monthly* (October 1999), <www.theatlantic.com/issues/99oct/9910drucker.htm>.
9. Stine, *The Untold Story of the Computer Revolution*, p. 18.
10. Stine, *The Untold Story of the Computer Revolution*, p. 14.
11. Robert Slater, *Portraits in Silicon* (Cambridge: M.I.T. Press, 1987), p. 10.
12. Stine, *The Untold Story of the Computer Revolution*, p. 30.
13. Stine, *The Untold Story of the Computer Revolution*, p. 36.
14. Stine, *The Untold Story of the Computer Revolution*, p. 94.
15. Stine, *The Untold Story of the Computer Revolution*, p. 100.
16. P. D. Hall, "Computer Systems," in *Technological Forecasting and Corporate Strategy*, ed. Gordon Wills, David Ashton and Bernard Taylor (New York: American Elsevier Publishing Company, Inc., 1969), p. 190.
17. Drucker, "Beyond the Information Revolution."
18. Daniel Bell, *The Coming of Post-Industrial Society*. Bell believes that social context is comprised of three parts: "the social structure, the polity, and the culture" (p. 19).
19. This section draws from Jennifer Fedor and Janet Herrlinger, "The EC Fur Ban," *TED Case Studies* #22 (June 1992), <www.american.edu/TED/ecfurban.htm>.
20. Following are the thirteen species expressly encompassed by the Council regulation and amendment: Beaver (*Castor canadensis*), Otter (*Kutra canadensis*), Coyote (*Canis latrans*), Wolf (*Canis lupus*), Lynx (*Lynx canadensis*), Bobcat (*Felis rufus*), Sable (*Martes zibellina*), Raccoon (*Procyon lotor*), Muskrat

(*Ondatra zibethicus*), Fisher (*Martes pennanti*), Badger (*Taxidea taxus*), Marten (*Martes americana*) and Ermine (*Mustela erminea*). See *Amendment to the Proposal for a Council Regulation (EEC) on the Importation of Certain Furs*, as contained in the *Official Journal of the European Communities* 34 (April 13, 1991).

21. Trade data provided by the Office of the United States Trade Representative.
22. Trade data provided by the Office of the United States Trade Representative.
23. The Harmonized Tariff System (HTS) only provides a choice between apparel/clothing accessories made of mink and those of all "other" furs. Similar complications arise with Subheading 4302.30.00, which groups together all assembled tanned or dressed fur skins.
24. Kathryn Knight, "Canadian Indians Protest at Ban on Fur Imports," *The Times*, London (April 12, 1997), p. 7.
25. Knight, "Canadian Indians Protest," p. 7.
26. Knight, "Canadian Indians Protest," p. 7.
27. Chief Mercredi of the Cree nation quoted in Kathryn Knight, "Canadian Indians Protest," p. 7.
28. "Pride in Fur Is Promoted by Alaskans," *The New York Times* (March 20, 1990), p. A20.
29. "Thus, in Canada, though beaver was already exploited before the arrival of the Europeans, increasing involvement by Indians such as the Cree in the fur trade seems to have increased the role of the beaver as a food source." Eric B. Ross, "An Overview of Trends in Dietary Variation from Hunter-Gatherer to Modern Capitalist Societies," pp. 7–55, in Marvin Harris and Eric B. Ross, *Food and Evolution: Toward a Theory of Human Food Habits* (Philadelphia, Pa.: Temple University Press, 1987).
30. This part uses information in Tung-Lin Wu and David Diluciano, "Bears and Trade," *TED Case Studies* #5 (January 1992), <www.american.edu/TED/bear.htm>.
31. CITES Appendix I bans commercial trade by participating nations. Appendix II regulates commercial trade. Appendix III listings are self-imposed restrictions instituted by individual countries, which may or may not choose to grant export and import permits for listed species. Appendices I and II require joint approval by CITES member nations, while Appendix III does not.
32. H.R. 4427, 102nd Congress, second session, "Export of Black Bear Viscera" (March 11, 1992), required the establishment of "a computer information system in Fish and Wildlife Service to record data on [bear] exports and imports."
33. Kathy Griffin, "Fake Bear Gall Bladder Scam," *South China Morning Post* (January 27, 1994), p. 2.
34. "Asian Gourmets and Canada's Bears," *Economist*, Volume 339, Number 7963 (April 27, 1996), p. 50.
35. Media Release, "Fines for Bear Part Trafficking Still too Lenient," *Bear Watch*, Vancouver (January 12, 1996).
36. Lawrence Carter-Long, Associated Press, Vancouver (April 10, 1996).

37. Kathy Griffin. "Bid to Stop Suffering of China's Black Bears," *South China Morning Post* (June 29, 1993), p. 9.
38. See James R. Lee, "Trade Policy, Worker Rights, and the Environment," *The Ritsumeikan Journal of International Relations and Area Studies*, Volume 8 (August 1995).
39. This part draws from Karen Sack, "Elephant Ivory Trade Ban," *TED Case Studies* #26 (January 1992), <www.american.edu/TED/elephant.htm>.
40. TRAFFIC USA, *Elephant Ivory Trade* (August 1990).
41. David Western, "The Ecological Value of Elephants: A Keystone Role in African Ecosystems," *The Ivory Trade and the Future of the African Elephant* (Geneva: CITES Secretariat, 1989).
42. Ivory Trade Review Group, "The Ivory Trade and the Future of the African Elephant: Interim Report," Gaborone, Botswana (1989).
43. "South Africa's Terrorists Butcher Elephants," *New Scientist* (January 5, 1984), p. 8.
44. Sarah Fitzgerald, *International Wildlife Trade: Whose Business Is It?*" (Washington, D.C.: World Wildlife Fund, 1989), pp. 62–65.
45. TRAFFIC USA, *Elephant Ivory Trade* (August 1990).
46. ITRG, "The Ivory Trade," p. 17.
47. Fitzgerald, *Whose Business*, p. 66.
48. Fitzgerald, *Whose Business*, p. 73.
49. *New Scientist* (March 14, 1992), p. 11.
50. Arthur MacGregor, *Bone, Antler, Ivory, and Horn* (Totowa, N.J.: Barnes and Noble Books, 1985), p. 17.
51. *Ivory: An International Survey and Illustrated History* (New York: Harry N. Abrams, Inc., Publishers, 1987), p. 12.
52. MacGregor, *Bone, Antler, Ivory, and Horn*, p. 40. Chariots in Rome had decorations made with ivory pieces, along with amber. Ivory found in Saxon graves in the fifth and sixth century in England may have been mammoth ivory manufactured for sale at a relatively cheap price.
53. Lister and Bahn, *Mammoths*, p. 115.
54. Lister and Bahn, *Mammoths*, p. 115.
55. This part draws from Jenny Jones, "Hawksbill Turtle," *TED Case Studies*, #32 (January 1992), <www.american.edu/TED/hawksbil.htm>.
56. Keith Bradsher, "Sea Turtles Put New Friction in U.S.-Japan Trade Quarrels," *The New York Times* (May 17, 1991), p. D4.
57. See Jenny Jones, "Shrimp and Sea Turtle," *TED Case Studies* #62 (January 1993), <www.american.edu/TED/shrimp.htm>.
58. David E. Sanger, "Japan, Backing Down, Plans Ban on Rare Turtle Import," *The New York Times* (June 20, 1991), p. D6.
59. John Lancaster, "Endangered Sea Turtle Seen Jeopardized by Japan," *The Washington Post* (January 19, 1991), p. A3.
60. See also Keith Schneider, "US Moves to Punish Japan," *The New York Times* (March 21, 1991), p. A12.

61. Douglas Harbrecht, “How an Obscure Law Is Saving Turtles,” *National Wildlife*, Volume 30 (April/May 1992), p. 22.
62. Makiko Shinohara, “Japan and US at Loggerheads Over Endangered Sea Turtles,” *Christian Science Monitor* (May 10, 1991), p. 7.
63. T. R. Reid, “Japan to End Imports of Endangered Turtle,” *The Washington Post* (May 18, 1991), p. A17.
64. James Sterngold, “Japan Agrees to Gradual Ban on Imports of Turtle Shells,” *The New York Times* (May 18, 1991), p. A35.
65. This part uses information in Jeanine Mackay, “Shark Protection,” *TED Case Studies* #62 (January 1993), <www.american.edu/TED/shark.htm>.
66. Philip E. Ross, “Man Bites Shark,” *Scientific American*, Volume 262 (June 1990).
67. Richard Conniff, “From Jaws to Laws—Now the Big, Bad Shark Needs Protection from US,” *Smithsonian*, Volume 24 (June 1990).
68. Keith Highley, “Shark Attack,” *One Earth* (Hong Kong: Friends of the Earth Spring, 1993).
69. This part uses information in Andrew Hamm, “Guam Bat Imports,” *TED Case Studies* #111 (January 1994), <www.american.edu/TED/guambat.htm>.
70. Lucy Young, “Bat-Eating an Endangered Custom,” *Gannett News Service* (March 24, 1990).
71. Jan Zeigler, “The Necessary Bat,” *United Press International* (April 2, 1986).
72. David Briscoe, “Humans with Taste for Fruit Bats Endanger Species,” *Dallas Morning News* (September 26, 1993), p. 9A.
73. Sheeline, “Cultural Significance,” p. 9.
74. Diane Dumanoski, “Flying Foxes Join List of Species at Risk,” in Environmental Notebook, *The Boston Globe* (January 6, 1990), p. 3.
75. Hilts, “Big Snakes Wiping Out Native Guam Animals,” p. A9.
76. Ken Miller, “U.S. Backs Guam Habitats, Could Alter Military Plans,” *Gannett News Service* (June 17, 1991).
77. Sheeline, “Cultural Significance,” p. 17.
78. The section drew from Mary-Ellen Foley and Andrew Hamm, “James Bay Project,” *TED Case Studies* #91 (January 1993), <www.american.edu/TED/james.htm>.
79. Sean McCutcheon, *Electric Rivers: The Story of the James Bay Project* (Montreal and New York: Black Rose Books, 1991), p. 33.
80. Peter O’Neil, “Warning from MP Jim Fulton Ignites Firestorm in Quebec,” *The Vancouver Sun* (February 19, 1993), p. A4.
81. Christian Jaekl, “James Bay: Prometheus vs. the Environment,” *Swiss Review of World Affairs* (April 1993).
82. Stephen Dale, “Canada: Cree Indians Accept Reward but Want Hydro Plants Halted,” Inter Press Service (January 21, 1993).
83. Graeme Hamilton, Philip Authier and Jeff Heinrich, “Cree Beat Hydro in Top Court: But Dam Project Gets Go-Ahead,” *The Gazette* (February 25, 1994), p. A1.

84. Frank Rutter, "Cuomo Electrocutes Quebec Separatism by Bailing New York Out of Hydro Deal," *Vancouver Sun* (March 31, 1992), p. A8.
85. Deborah Charles, "Canada: Hydro-Quebec Faces More Environmental, Demand Pressure," *Reuter Textline* (March 3, 1994).
86. *Euromoney Trade Finance and Banker International*, "USA: Hydro Quebec Left in the Dark," Reuter Textline in Lexis Nexis (April 1, 1994).
87. Patti Singer, "The Damming of Rivers Threatens Hunting Grounds of the Cree," *Gannett News Service* (October 6, 1993).
88. Barry Came, "Fighting for the Land," *Maclean's* (February 27, 1995).
89. Penny Park, "Canadian Cree Take Quebec's Hydro Scheme to Tribunal," *New Scientist*, Volume 133, Number 1806 (February 1, 1992).
90. Barry Brown, "Aboriginal Rights Seen Touching off 'Civil War' if Quebec Secedes," *The Buffalo News* (May 22, 1994).
91. This section draws from Jeanine MacKay, "Swift Protection," *TED Case Studies* #66 (1993), <www.american.edu/TED/swift.htm>.
92. Bruce Campbell and Elizabeth Lack, *A Dictionary of Birds* (London: Buteo Books, 1985).
93. Diane Summers, "Dark World of Gourmet Soup," *International Wildlife*, Volume 22 (January/February 1992).
94. Roy Andries de Groot, "On the Trail of Bird's Nest Soup: Caves, Climbs and High Stakes," *Smithsonian*, Volume 14 (September 1993).
95. This is included on the packaging of a bottle of bird's nest soup.
96. Jeanine MacKay correspondence from Clement Ngai (Hong Kong: World Wide Fund for Nature, October 19, 1993).
97. This section draws from Yuri Honda, "Sugar and Philippines," *TED Case Studies* #250 (January 1996), <www.american.edu/TED/philsug.htm>.
98. Belinda Coote, *The Hunger Crop—Poverty and the Sugar Industry* (Oxford: Oxfam, 1987), p. 4.
99. Richard W. Franke, "The Effects of Colonialism and Neocolonialism on the Gastronomic Patterns of the Third World," in *Perspectives in Cultural Anthropology*, ed. Herbert Applebaum (Albany: State University of New York Press, 1987), p. 460. See also Sidney Wilfred Mintz, *Sweetness and Power: The Place of Sugar in Modern History* (New York: Viking, 1985).
100. "Environment Chief Warns Ormoc Deluge Could Be Repeated," Japan Economic Newswire (November 11, 1991).
101. The section draws from Pamela Oakes, "Pisco Liquer and Chile," *TED Case Studies* #145 (June 1994), <www.american.edu/TED/pisco.htm>.
102. Henk Milne, "Dancing with the Demon; Peruvian Liquor," *Latin Finance* (1995), p. 103.
103. Milne, "Dancing with the Demon," p. 103.
104. Flora Metzer and Derek Fetzer, "Peru: Pollution Control Equipment," *National Trade Data Bank* (March 21, 1995), p. 68.
105. Roger Atwood, "Sweet Liquor Sparks Bitter Trade Dispute," *Reuter Business Report* (March 29, 1991), p. 1.

106. Atwood, "Sweet Liquor," p. 1.
107. Atwood, "Sweet Liquor," p. 1.
108. Betty Fussell, "The Face of the Country: Chicha, Peru's Favorite Drink," *New York Times* (February 15, 1995), p. 6.
109. This section draws from Nicole Lewis, "CITES Watch on Coral," *TED Case Studies* #18 (January 1992), <www.american.edu/TED/coral.htm>.
110. Peter K. Weber, "Saving the Coral Reefs," *The Futurist*, Volume 27, Number 4 (July 1993), p. 28.
111. Weber, "Saving," p. 28.
112. Worldwatch Institute, *State of the World, 1993* (New York: W.W. Norton and Company, 1993), p. 43.
113. Worldwatch, *State of the World, 1993*, p. 43.
114. Doug Tsuruoka, "Vanishing Coral Reefs," *Far Eastern Economic Review*, Volume 156, Number 1 (January 7, 1993), p. 25.
115. Weber, "Saving," p. 28.
116. Mark Derr, "Raiders of the Reef," *Audubon* (March/April 1992), p. 54.
117. Weber, "Saving," p. 28.
118. This section draws from Deborah Meisegeier, "Great Barrier Reef," *TED Case Studies* #179 (January 1995), <www.american.edu/TED/barrier.htm>.
119. "Sanctuarial Movement Growing in U.S. Waters," *Offshore* (September 1991), p. 42.
120. Derr, "Raiders," p. 50.
121. Mary T. Schmich, "Coral Reef War Pits Nature vs. Tourists," *Chicago Tribune* (July 22, 1990), p. C15.
122. Derr, "Raiders," p. 52.
123. Derr, "Saving," p. 48.
124. A. L. Kroeber, "The Nature of Culture," in *Perspectives in Cultural Anthropology*, ed. Herbet Applebaum (Albany: State University of New York Press, 1987), pp. 83–84.
125. Jean Michel Cousteau, "Cousteau Watch: Paradise Reef Tests Traders' Ecological Scruples," *Planet ENN*, September 2, 1996, <www.enn.com/planetenn/090296/fe.htm>. See also Christopher Clawery, "Mexico and Tourism," *TED Case Studies* #86 (June 1993), <www.american.edu/TED/cancun.htm>.
126. This section is based on Antonio Santiago and Jay Allen Schmidt, "Costa Rica Beef Exports," *TED Case Studies* #82 (June 1993), <www.american.edu/TED/costbeef.htm> and see Dina Lehman, "Buffalo and Native Americans," *ICE Case Studies* (January 1998), <www.american.edu/TED/ice/buffalo.htm>.
127. George Armelagos, "Biocultural Aspects of Food Choice," in *Food and Evolution: Toward a Theory of Human Food Habits*, ed. Marvin Harris and Eric B. Ross (Philadelphia, Pa.: Temple University Press, 1987), pp. 581–82.
128. Eric B. Ross, "An Overview of Trends in Dietary Variation from Hunter-Gatherer to Modern Capitalist Societies," in *Food and Evolution: Toward a Theory of Human Food Habits*, ed. Marvin Harris and Eric B. Ross (Philadelphia, Pa.: Temple University Press, 1987), pp. 7–55.

129. Ross, "Patterns of Diet and Forces of Production," pp. 181–82.
130. J. Hermardinquer, "The Family Pig of the Ancien Regime: Myth or Fact?" in *Food and Drink in History*, ed. R. Forster and O. Ranum (Baltimore, Md.: Johns Hopkins University Press, 1979), pp. 50–72. Also, see H. C. Darby, "The Clearing of the Woodland in Europe," in *Man's Role in Changing the Face of the Earth*, ed. W. L. Thomas (Chicago: University of Chicago Press, 1956), pp. 183–216.
131. Fernand Braudel, *Capitalism and Material Life, 1400–1800* (New York: Harper and Row, 1967).
132. Drucker, "Beyond the Information Revolution." "By World War I, 40 percent of British beef was imported and, by 1938, beef imports rose to account for 80 percent of total beef sold, at least in the London area." R. Perren, "The North American Beef and Cattle Trade with Great Britain, 1870–1914," *The Economic History Review*, 2nd Ser., Volume 24, Number 3, pp. 430–44 and G. Harrison, *Borthwicks: A Century in the Meat Trade, 1863–1963* (London: Borthwicks, 1963).
133. Alfred W. Crosby, *Ecological Imperialism: The Biological Expansion of Europe, 900–1900* (Cambridge: Cambridge University Press, 1986), p. 176. Also see Jeremy Rifkin, *Beyond Beef: The Rise and Fall of the Cattle Culture* (New York: Dutton, 1992) who looks at the historical role of beef in society, relating it to environmental degradation, market forces, gender, culture, and a host of other factors.
134. S. Vestal, *Queen of Cowtowns, Dodge City* (New York: Harper and Row, 1952), pp. 41–44.
135. Vestal, *Queen of Cowtowns*, pp. 41–44.
136. V. Clark, *History of Manufactures in the United States, 1860–1914* (Washington, D.C.: Carnegie Institution, 1928), p. 35.
137. "U.S. Is World's Largest Exporter of Cattle Hides," *News* (Washington, D.C.: U.S. International Trade Commission, March 4, 1997).
138. Crosby, *Ecological Imperialism*, pp. 177–78.

CHAPTER 4

1. Judy Mills, "Milking the Bear Trade," *International Wildlife*, Volume 22, Number 3 (May 1992), pp. 38–45. Also see Michael Tennesen, "Poaching, Ancient Traditions, and the Law," *Audubon*, Volume 93 (July/August 1991), p. 92.
2. Peter Drucker, "Beyond the Information Revolution," *The Atlantic Monthly* (October 1999), <www.theatlantic.com/issues/99oct/9910drucker.htm>.
3. There may even be cases where differing countries treat the same product differently. This could produce a situation where pork sausage trade, say to or from countries such as Germany, Israel, Saudi Arabia, or India, may have completely different sets of regulatory requirements that have a cultural basis.
4. Vincent Cable, "The New Trade Agenda: Universal Rules Amid Cultural Diversity," in *International Affairs*, Volume 72, Number 2 (April 1996), pp.

234–35.

5. Cable, "The New Trade Agenda," p. 241.
6. Cable, "The New Trade Agenda," p. 242.
7. Amilcar Cabral, *Liberation National y Cultural* (San Pablo: Medellin Corporacion Educativa, 1977).
8. Ismail Serageldin, "The Challenge of a Holistic Vision: Culture, Empowerment, and the Development Paradigm," in *Culture and Development in Africa*, ed. Ismail Serageldin and June Taboroff (Washingon, D.C.: World Bank, 1994), p. 21.
9. Serageldin, "The Challenge of a Holistic Vision," p. 31.
10. Ismail Serageldin, *Culture and Development at the Millennium: The Challenge and the Response* (Washington, D.C.: World Bank, 1998), pp. 1–9. Speech distributed in pamphlet form.
11. Serageldin, *Culture and Development*, p. 8.
12. Robert Klitgaard, "Taking Culture into Account: From 'Let's' to 'How'," in *Culture and Development in Africa*, ed. Serageldin and Taboroff, p. 76.
13. Serageldin, *Culture and Development*, p. 11.
14. Ali Mazrui, *Cultural Forces in World Politics* (London: James Currey, 1990), pp. 1, 4.
15. Aaron Wildavsky, "How Cultural Theory Can Contribute to Understanding and Promoting Democracy, Science, and Development," in Serageldin and Taboroff, p. 160.
16. Daniel Etounga Manguelle, "Culture and Development: African Responses," paper presented at the International Conference on Culture and Development in Africa (Washington, D.C.: World Bank, April 2–3, 1992).
17. Klitgaard, "Taking Culture into Account," p. 87.
18. Alan Thein Durning, "Guardians of the Land: Indigenous Peoples and the Health of the Earth," Worldwatch Paper 112 (Washington, D.C.: Worldwatch Institute, 1995).
19. See Karen Rinaman, "Sports Magazine in Canada," *TED Case Studies* #352 (January 1997), <www.american.edu/TED/sportsil.htm> and Nina Joshi, "US Canada Softwood Lumber Dispute," *TED Case Studies* #75 (January 1993), <www.american.edu/TED/uscanada.htm>.
20. *Rockefeller Brothers Fund* (New York: Rockefeller Foundation, Annual Report, 1995).
21. Walter Truett Anderson, *Evolution Isn't What It Used to Be: The Augmented Animal and the Whole Wired World* (New York: W.H. Freeman and Company, 1996), p. 172. "Ecologist Aldo Leopold started perhaps the first restoration project on a prairie in Wisconsin in 1934. But restoration ecology becomes very subjective at some point, especially in choosing which habitat to restore over the course of a bioregion's life."
22. Stan Stevens, ed., *Conservation through Cultural Survival: Indigenous Peoples and Protected Areas* (Washington, D.C.: Island Press, 1997), p. 9.
23. Stevens, "The Legacy of Yellowstone," p. 19.
24. Stevens, "The Legacy of Yellowstone," p. 20.

25. Karen Siune and Wolfgang Truetzshler, *Dynamics of Media Politics* (London: Sage Publications, 1992), p. 47.
26. Durning, "Guardians of the Land."
27. John Jackson, in "World Trade Rules and Environmental Policies: Congruence or Conflict?" *Washington and Lee Law Review*, Volume 49, Number 4 (Fall 1992), p. 1228, adds one other interesting dimension:

    "To some extent, the conflicts between the trade liberalization proponents and the environmental protection proponents derive from a certain 'difference in cultures' between the trade policy experts and the environmental policy experts. Oddly enough, even when operating within the framework of the same society, these different 'policy cultures' have developed different attitudes and perceptions of the political and policy processes, and these different outlooks create misunderstandings and conflict between the groups."

    Also see Robert W. Jerome, "Traders and Environmentalists," *Journal of Communications* (December, 27, 1991), p. 4a.
28. Jackson, "World Trade Rules and Environmental Policies: Congruence or Conflict?" p. 1241.
29. "WTO Committee on Trade and the Environment Invites MEA Secretariats to Information Session, and Discusses Items Related to the Linkages between the Multilateral and Trade Agendas," *Trade and Environment Bulletin* (Geneva: World Trade Organization, August 13, 1998, Press/TE 025).
30. *WTO Bulletin*, p. 6.
31. See James R. Lee, "Process and Product: Making the Link between Trade and the Environment," in *International Environmental Affairs: A Journal for Research and Policy*, Volume 6, Number 4 (Fall 1994), pp. 320–47.
32. Article 2.2 of the TBT Agreement noted in Jeffrey L. Gertler, "WTO Dispute Settlement: The Environmental Dimension," pp. 118–39, in *Trade and Environment: Conflict or Compatibility*, ed. Duncan Brack (London: Earthscan Publications and the Royal Institute of International Affairs, 1998).
33. Gertler, 1998, p. 120.
34. "Ministers From Twenty-two Countries Expected at Ottawa Meeting on Culture" (Ottawa: Office of the Minister of Canadian Culture, June 1998).
35. "Culture Ministers Say They Will Meet Again, Probably Without U.S." *Wall Street Journal* (July 1, 1998).
36. Anthony DePalma, "Nineteen Nations See U.S. as Threat to Cultures," *New York Times* (July 1, 1998).
37. Terry Teachout, "Cultural Protectionism: The World's Culture Czars Move to Repel the Hollywood Invasion," *The Wall Street Journal* (July 10, 1998).
38. "Overview of International Meeting on Cultural Policy" (Ottawa: Government of Canada, June 29–30).
39. "Ottawa Group Forms International Alliance on Culture Ministers" (Ottawa: Government of Canada, June 30, 1998).
40. "Overview of International Meeting," p. 11.
41. "Ottawa Group Forms International Alliance," p. 2.
42. "Ottawa Group Forms International Alliance," p. 6.

43. "USTR Criticizes Proposed Canadian Action to Continue Restrictions on Market Access for Magazines," *Office of U.S. Trade Representative* (October 9, 1998).
44. Bjorn Bjarnason, "The Role of Culture in Global Relations," Conference on *Putting Culture on the World Stage* (Ottawa: June 30, 1998).
45. John Henry Merryman, "Who Owns the Elgin Marbles," *ARTNEWS*, Volume 85, Number 7 (September 1986), p. 104.
46. See James R. Lee and David Walters, *International Trade in Construction, Design and Engineering Services* (Boston: Ballinger Publishing Company, 1989).
47. See Mary-Ann Kocian, "German Beer Laws," *TED Case Studies* #219 (June 1995), <www.american.edu/TED/germbeer.htm>.
48. Fernand Braudel, *The Perspective on the World*,Volume 3, "Civilization and Capitalism, Fifteenth–Eighteenth Century" (New York: Harper and Row, 1984), p. 65.
49. Paul Shepard, *Coming Home to the Pleistocene* (Washington, D.C.: Island Press/Shearwater Books, 1998), p. 5.
50. Shepard, *Coming Home to the Pleistocene*, "Some Cultures Are More Socially and Culturally Attuned Than Others," p. 173.
51. Drucker, "Beyond the Information Revolution."
52. Anderson, *Evolution Isn't What It Used to Be*, p. 115.
53. See Trupti Patel, "Bhopal Disaster," *TED Case Studies* #233 (January 1996), <www.american.edu/TED/bhopal.htm>.
54. See David Weir, *The Bhopal Syndrome: Pesticides, Environment, and Health* (San Francisco: Sierra Club Books, 1987).
55. See Yemi Adewumi, "The Basmati Case," *TED Case Studies* #493 (Summer 1998), <www.american.edu/TED/basmati.htm>.
56. See Richard Weir, "EU BST Import Ban," *TED Case Studies* #160 (June 1994), <www.american.edu/TED/bst.htm>.

KEY TO TERMS

A.D.	Anno Domini
ASEAN	Association of Southeast Asian Nations
B.P.	Before Present
B.C.	Before Christ
BCE	Before the Common Era
BSJCEAP	Baltic Sea Joint Comprehensive Environmental Action Program
CITEC	Convention on the International Trade in Endangered Cultures
CITES	Convention on International Trade in Endangered Species
DSB	Dispute Settlement Body
EC	European Community
EEZ	Exclusive Economic Zone
EU	European Union
ISA	International Sugar Agreements
ITRG	Ivory Trade Review Group
MEA	Multilateral Environmental Agreement
NAFTA	North American Free Trade Agreement
NMFS	U.S. National Marine Fisheries Service
OECD	Organization for Economic Cooperation and Development
PRC	People's Republic of China
TED	Trade Environment Database
U.K.	United Kingdom
UNESCO	United Nations Educational, Scientific, and Cultural Organization
U.S.	United States
WTO	World Trade Organization

BIBLIOGRAPHY

CHAPTER 1

Albert, Michael and Robin Hahnel. *Marxism and Socialist Theory*. Boston: South End Press, 1981.

Anderson, Walter Truett. *Evolution Isn't What It Used to Be: The Augmented Animal and the Whole Wired World*. New York: W.H. Freeman and Company, 1996.

Applebaum, Herbert, ed. *Perspectives in Cultural Anthropology*. Albany: State University of New York Press, 1987.

Barraclough, Geoffrey. *An Introduction to Contemporary History*. Harmondworth, Middlesex, England: Penguin Books, 1984, reprint edition.

Boserup, Ester. *Evolution agraire et pression demographique* [The Condition of Agricultural Growth: The Economics of Agrarian Change under Population Pressure]. New York: Aldine Publishing Co., 1965.

Boulding, Kenneth. *The Meaning of the Twentieth Century*. New York: Harper & Row, 1964.

Braudel, Fernand. *The Structures of Everyday Life: Civilization and Capitalism, Fifteenth–Eighteenth Century*. Paris: Librarie Armund Colin, 1979, Volume I.

Campbell, Bernard. *Human Ecology*. New York: Aldine Publishing Company, 1983.

Childe, V. Gordon. "Early Forms of Society." In *A History of Technology*. Charles Singer, E. J. Holmyard and A. R. Hall, eds. Volume I, "From Early Time to Fall of Ancient Empires. New York and London: Oxford University Press, 1954.

Daumas, Maurice, ed. *A History of Technology and Invention: Progress through the Ages*, Volume I, "The Origins of Technological Civilization." Eileen B. Hennessy, tr. New York: Crown Publishers, 1969.

Drucker, Peter. "Beyond the Information Revolution." *The Atlantic Monthly* (October 1999), <www.theatlantic.com/issues/99oct/9910drucker.htm>.

Durham, William H. *Coevolution: Genes, Culture, and Human Diversity*. Stanford, Calif.: Stanford University Press, 1991.

Ellen, Roy F. *Environment, Subsistence, and System*. Cambridge: Cambridge University Press, 1982.

———. "Trade, Environment, and the Reproduction of Local Systems in the Moluccas." In *The Ecosystem Concept in Anthropology*. Emilio F. Moran, ed.

Boulder, Colo.: Westview Press, 1984.

Garbarino, Merwyn S. *Sociocultural Theory in Anthropology*. Prospect Heights, Ill.: Waveland Press, 1983.

Geertz, Clifford. *Agricultural Involution*. Berkeley: University of California Press, 1963.

Hannerz, Ulf. "Cosmopolitans and Locals in World Culture." In *Global Culture: Nationalism, Globalization and Modernity*. Michael Featherstone, ed. London: Sage Publications, 1990.

Hamilton III, William J. "Omnivorous Primate Diets and Human Overconsumption of Meat." In *Food and Evolution: Toward a Theory of Human Food Habits*. Marvin Harris and Eric B. Ross, eds. Philadelphia, Pa.: Temple University Press, 1987.

Harris, Marvin. *Cannibals and Kings: The Origins of Cultures*. New York: Random House, 1977.

———. *Cultural Materialism: The Struggle for the Science of Culture*. New York: Random House, 1979.

———. *Culture, People, Nature: An Introduction to General Anthropology*. New York: Harper and Row, 1980.

———. *Cows, Pigs, Wars, and Witches*. New York: Vintage Books, 1974.

———. *History, Man, and Nature*. New York: Crowell, 1971.

——— and Eric B. Ross. *Food and Evolution: Toward a Theory of Human Food Habits*. Philadelphia, Pa.: Temple University Press, 1987.

Harrison, Lawrence E. *Who Prospers? How Cultural Values Shape Economic and Political Success*. New York: Basic Books, 1992.

Hatch, Elvin. "Culture." In *The Social Science Encyclopedia*. Adam Kuper and Jessica Kuper, eds. London and Boston: Routledge and Kegan Paul, 1985.

Helm, June. "The Ecological Approach in Anthropology." In *Perspectives in Cultural Anthropology*. Herbert Applebaum, ed. Albany: State University of New York Press, 1987.

Huxley, Julius. *On Living in a Revolution*. New York: Harper and Row, 1942.

———. *Man in the Modern World*. New York: New American Library, 1959.

Jacobsen, Judith E., and John Firor, eds. *Human Impact on the Environment: Ancient Roots, Current Challenges*. Boulder, Colo.: Westview Press, 1992.

Kroeber, A. L. *Cultural and Natural Areas of Native North America*. Berkeley: University of California Press, 1947.

Kuhn, Thomas. *The Structure of Scientific Revolutions*. Chicago: University of Chicago Press, 1962.

Kuznets, Simon. *Modern Economic Growth: Rate, Structure, and Spread*. New Haven, Conn., and London: Yale University Press, New Haven and London, Fourth Printing, 1969.

Latin American Economic System (SELA) and United Nations Conference on Trade and Development (UNCTAD). *Trade and Environment: The International Debate*, 1994.

Lowie, Robert. "The Determinants of Culture." In *Perspectives in Cultural Anthropology*. Herbert Applebaum, ed. Albany: State University of New York Press, 1987.

Marx, Karl. *Capital: A Critique of Political Economy*, Volume 1. New York: Vintage Books, 1977.

Mennel, Stephen. "The Globalization of Human Society as a Very Long-term Social Process: Elias' Theory." In *Global Culture: Nationalism, Globalization and Modernity*. Michael Featherstone, ed. London: Sage Publications, 1990.

Merton, Robert. *Social Theory and Social Structure*. Glencoe, Ill.: Free Press, 1957.

Read, Herbert. "New Realms of Art." In *The Semi-Artificial Man*. M. B. Schnapper, ed. Washington, D.C.: Public Affairs Press, 1957.

Redman, Charles L. "The Impact of Food Production: Short-Term Strategies and Long-Term Consequences." In *Pleistocene Extinctions*. P. S. Martin and H. S. Wright, eds. New Haven, Conn., and London: Yale University Press, 1967.

Robertson, Roland. "Mapping the Global Condition: Globalization as the Central Concept." In *Global Culture: Nationalism, Globalization and Modernity*. Michael Featherstone, ed. London: Sage Publications, 1990.

Sanderson, Stephen K. *Social Evolution*. Cambridge: Basil Blackwell, 1990.

Shepard, Paul. *Coming Home to the Pleistocene*. Washington, D.C.: Island Press, 1998.

Simon, Herbert. *Sciences of the Artificial*. Cambridge: M.I.T. Press, 1969.

Singer, Charles. "The Concept of Culture." In *International Encyclopedia of the Social Sciences*, Volume 18. David L. Sills, ed. New York: Free Press, 1968.

Steward, Julian. *Theory of Cultural Change*. Urbana: University of Illinois Press, 1957.

Toffler, Alvin. *Future Shock*. New York: Random House, 1970.

———. *The Third Wave*. New York: William Morrow Inc., 1980.

Thomson, George. *The Foreseeable Future*. New York: Viking, 1960.

Toynbee, Arnold J. "Preface to the Beacon Paperback Edition." In Arnold Toynbee, *The Industrial Revolution*. Boston: Beacon Press, 1884.

Wallerstein, Immanuel. "Culture as the Ideological Battleground." In *Global Culture: Nationalism, Globalization and Modernity*. Michael Featherstone, ed. London: Sage Publications, 1990.

Williams, Raymond. *Keywords: A Vocabulary of Culture and Society*. New York: Oxford University Press, 1976.

———. *The Sociology of Culture*. Chicago: University of Chicago Press, 1981.

Zadrozny, John, T. *Dictionary of Social Science*. Washington, D.C.: Public Affairs Press, 1959.

CHAPTER 2

Anderson, Walter Truett. *Evolution Isn't What It Used to Be: The Augmented Animal and the Whole Wired World*. New York: W.H. Freeman and Company, 1996.

Angel, J. Lawrence. "Paleoecology, Paleodemography and Health." In *Perspectives in Cultural Anthropology*. Herbert Applebaum, ed. Albany: State University of New York Press, 1987.

Auel, Jean. *The Mammoth Hunters*. New York: Bantam Books, 1986.

Bain, Paul G. and Jean Veertot. *Images of the Ice Age*. New York: Facts on File Books, 1988.

Baramki, Dimitri. *Phoenicia and the Phoenicians*. Lebanon: Khayats, 1961.

Barrett, Richard A. *Culture and Conduct*. Belmont, Calif.: Wadsworth Publishing Co., 1991.

Boyden, Stephen. *BioHistory: The Interplay between Human Society and the Biosphere*. Man and the Biosphere Series, Volume 8. Paris: UNESCO, 1992.

Burack, Benjamin. *Ivory and Its Uses*. Rutland, Vt.: Charles E. Tuttle Company, 1984.

Childe, V. Gordon. "Early Forms of Society." In *A History of Technology*, Volume I, "From Early Time to Fall of Ancient Empires." Charles Singer, E. J. Holmyard and A. R. Hall, eds. New York and London: Oxford University Press, 1954.

Connery, Clare. "Food before the Famine." *Ireland of the Welcomes*, Volume 44, Number 3 (May/June 1995).

Creson, Matt. "Mammoth Tusks Tell Ancient Tales of Life and Murder." *Denver Post* (November 6, 1996).

Crosby, Alfred W. *Ecological Imperialism: The Biological Expansion of Europe, 900–1900*. Cambridge: Cambridge University Press, 1986.

Dassin, Jules. "The Parthenon Marbles." Athens: Melina Mercouri Foundation, 1994.

Daumas, Maurice, ed. *A History of Technology and Invention: Progress through the Ages*, Volume I, "The Origins of Technological Civilization." Eileen B. Hennessey, tr. New York: Crown Publishers, 1969.

de Navarro, J. M. "Prehistoric Routes between Northern Europe and Italy Defined by Amber Trade." *The Geographical Journal*, Volume LXVI (1925).

Drucker, Peter. "Beyond the Information Revolution." *The Atlantic Monthly* (October 1999), <www.theatlantic.com/issues/99oct/9910drucker.htm>.

Fores, M. "The Myth of the British Industrial Revolution." *History* (1981).

Frison, George C. "Clovis, Goshen, and Folsom: Lifeways and Cultural Relationships." In *Megafauna and Man: Discovery of America's Heartland*. Larry D. Agenbrod, Jim I. Mead and Lisa W. Nelson, eds. Hot Springs, S.Dak.: Mammoth Site of Hot Springs, South Dakota, Inc., Scientific Papers Volume 1, 1990.

Gardner, John and John Maier. *Gilgamesh: Translated from the Sin-leqi-unnunni version*. New York: Alfred A. Knopf, 1984.

Gore, Al. *Earth in the Balance: Ecology and the Human Spirit*. Boston: Houghton Mifflin Company, 1992.

Grimaldi, David A. *Amber: Window to the Past*. New York: Henry N. Abrams, 1996.

Guthrie, R. D. "Mosaics, Allelochemicals, and Nutrients: An Ecological Theory of Late Pleistocene Megafaunal Extinctions." In *Quaternary Extinctions*. P. S. Martin and R. G. Klein, eds., pp. 259–98. Tucson: University of Arizona Press, 1984.

Hannus, L. Adrien. "The Lange-Ferguson Site: A Case of Mammoth Bone-Butchering Tools." In *Megafauna and Man: Discovery of America's Heartland*. Larry D. Agenbrod, Jim I. Mead and Lisa W. Nelson, eds. Hot Springs, S.Dak.: The Mammoth Site of Hot Springs, South Dakota, Inc., Scientific Papers Volume 1, 1990.

Harden, Donald. *The Phoenicians*. New York: Frederick A. Praeger, Inc., 1963.

Harris, David R. "Agricultural Systems, Ecosystems, and the Origin of Agriculture." In *The Domestication and Exploitation of Plants and Animals*. David R. Harris, ed. Chicago: Aldine Press, 1969.

Harris, Marvin. *Cannibals and Kings: The Origins of Cultures*. New York: Random House, 1977.

———. *Culture, People, Nature: An Introduction to General Anthropology*. New York: Harper Row, 1980.

Hassan, Fekri A. "Determination of the Size, Density, and Growth Rate of Hunting-Gathering Populations." In *Population, Ecology, and Social Evolution*. Steven Polgar, ed. The Hague and Paris: Mouton Publishers, 1975.

Hobsbawm, A. J. *Industry and Empire*. Harmondsworth, Middlesex, England: Penguin Books, 1969.

Hughes, Robert. "Behold This Stone Age." *Time*, Volume 145, Number 6 (February 13, 1995), pp. 52–63.

Ivory: An International Survey and Illustrated History. New York: Harry N. Abrams, Inc., Publishers, 1987.

Jacobs, Jane. *The Economy of Cities*. New York: Random House, 1963.

Jacobsen, Judith E., and John Firor, eds. *Human Impact on the Environment: Ancient Roots, Current Challenges*. Boulder, Colo.: Westview Press, 1992.

Jensen, Jorgen. *The Prehistory of Denmark*. London: Methenn and Co., 1982.

Judge, Joseph. "The Travail of Ireland." *National Geographic*, Volume 159, Number 4 (April 1981).

Kennedy, Liam. "The Great Exodus: The Nineteenth Century." *Ireland of the Welcomes*, Volume 41, Number 4 (July–August 1992).

Klein, Richard. "The Impact of Early People on the Environment: The Case of Large Mammal Extinctions." In *Human Impact on the Environment: Ancient Roots, Current Challenges*. Judith E. Jacobsen and John Firor, eds. Boulder, Colo.: Westview Press, 1992.

Krech III, Shepard. *The Ecological Indian: Myth and History*. New York: W.W. Norton and Company, 1999.

Lister, Adrian and Paul Bahn. *Mammoths*. New York: Macmillan, 1994.

Lowie, Robert. "The Determinants of Culture." In *Perspectives in Cultural Anthropology*. Herbert Applebaum, ed. Albany: State University of New York Press, 1987.

"Marbles Requested and Refused." Newsletter of the British Committee for the Restitution of the Parthenon Marbles. July 1984.

Mathias, Peter. "The Industrial Revolution: Concept and Reality." In *The First Industrial Revolutions*. Peter Mathias and John A. Davis, eds. Oxford: Basil Blackwell, 1989.

——— and John A. Davis. *The First Industrial Revolutions*. Oxford: Basil Blackwell, 1989.

Meiggs, Russell. *Trees and Timber in the Ancient Mediterranean and the World*. Oxford: Clarendon Press, 1982.

Mellars, P. and C. Stringer, eds. *The Human Revolution: Behavioral and Biological Perspectives on the Origins of Human Beings*. Edinburgh: Edinburgh University Press, 1989.

Merryman, John Henry. "Who Owns the Elgin Marbles?" *ARTNEWS*, Volume 85, Number 7 (September 1986).

Mikesell, Marvin W. "The Deforestation of Mount Lebanon." *The Geographical Review*, Volume LIX, Number 1 (January 1969).

Mulligan, Hugh A. "Irish Potato Famine Painfully Remembered." *Hickory Daily Record* (September 10, 1995).

Mumford, Lewis. "The First Megamachine." *Diogenes* (Fall 1966).

National Geographic, Volume 183, Number 1 (January 1993).

Osborne, John W. *The Silent Revolution: The Industrial Revolution in England as a Source of Social Change*. New York: Charles Scribner's Sons, 1970.

Polyani, Karl. *The Great Transformation: The Political and Economic Origins of Our Time*. Boston: Beacon Press, 1944.

Redman, Charles L. "The Impact of Food Production: Short-Term Strategies and Long-Term Consequences" in *Pleistocene Extinctions*. P. S. Martin and H. S. Wright, eds. New Haven, Conn., and London: Yale University Press, 1967.

Sahlins, M. *Stone Age Economics*. New York: Aldine, 1972.

Sanger, David E. "Japan, Backing Down, Plans Ban on Rare Turtle Import." *The New York Times* (June 20, 1991).

Semple, Ellen Churchill. *Geography of the Mediterranean Region*. New York: Henry Holt and Co., 1931.

Shepard, Paul. *Coming Home to the Pleistocene*. Washington, D.C.: Island Press, 1998.

Singer, Charles, E. J. Holmyard and A. R. Hall, eds. *A History of Technology*, Volume I, "From Early Time to Fall of Ancient Empires." New York and London: Oxford University Press, 1954.

Spekke, Arnold. *The Ancient Amber Routes and the Geographical Discovery of the Eastern Baltic*. Stockholm: M. Goppers, 1957.

Stavrianos, Leften. *Global Rift: The Third World Comes of Age*. New York: Morrow, 1981.

"The Restitution of the Pantheon Marbles." Athens: Hellenic Ministry of Culture, Government of Greece, 1997.

Toynbee, Arnold. *The Industrial Revolution*. Boston: Beacon Press, 1884.

———. *Lectures on the Industrial Revolution in England: Popular Addresses, Notes and Other Fragments Together with a Short Memoir to B. Jowett*. London: 1884.

Tudge, Colin. *The Day before Yesterday: Five Million Years of Human History*. London: Pimlico, 1995.

Tyndall, J. "On the Absorption and Radiation of Heat by Gasses and Vapors, and on the Physical Connection of Radiation, Absorption, and Conduction." *Philosophy Magazine*, Volume 4, Number 22 (1861).

Weiner, Martin J. *English Culture and the Decline of the Industrial Spirit, 1850–1980*. Cambridge: Cambridge University Press, 1981.

White, *Medieval Technology and Social Change*. Oxford: Clarendon Press, 1962.

CHAPTER 3

Anderson, Walter Truett. *Evolution Isn't What It Used to Be: The Augmented Animal and the Whole Wired World*. New York: W.H. Freeman and Company, 1996.

Bell, Daniel. *The Coming of Post-Industrial Society: A Venture in Social Forecasting*. New York: Basic Books, 1973.

Brzezinski, Zbigniew. *Between Two Ages: America's Role in the Technotronic Era*. New York: Viking Press, 1970.

Drucker, Peter. "Beyond the Information Revolution." *The Atlantic Monthly* (October 1999), <www.theatlantic.com/issues/99oct/9910drucker.htm>.

Etzioni, Amitai. *The Active Society*. New York: Free Press, 1968.

Hall, P. D. "Computer Systems." In *Technological Forecasting and Corporate Strategy*. Gordon Wills, David Ashton and Bernard Taylor, eds. New York: American Elsevier Publishing Company, Inc., 1969.

Hobsbawm, Eric. *The Age of Extremes: A History of the World, 1914–1991*. New York: Pantheon Books, 1994.

Slater, Robert. *Portraits in Silicon*. Cambridge: The M.I.T. Press, 1987.

Stine, G. Harry. *The Untold Story of the Computer Revolution: Bits, Bytes, Bauds, and Brains*. New York: Arbor House, 1985.

CASE 1: EU FUR BAN

Amendment to the Proposal for a Council Regulation (EEC) on the Importation of Certain Furs. Official Journal of the European Communities, Volume 34 (April 13, 1991).

Knight, Kathryn. "Canadian Indians Protest at Ban on Fur Imports." *The Times*, London (April 12, 1997), p. 7.

"Pride in Fur Is Promoted by Alaskans." *The New York Times* (March 20, 1990), p. A20.

Ross, Eric B. "An Overview of Trends in Dietary Variation from Hunter-Gatherer to Modern Capitalist Societies." In *Food and Evolution: Toward a Theory of Human Food Habits*. Marvin Harris and Eric B. Ross, eds., pp. 7–55. Philadelphia, Pa.: Temple University Press, 1987.

CASE 2: BEAR WINE

"Asian Gourmets and Canada's Bears." *Economist*, Volume 339, Number 7963 (April 27, 1996), p. 50.

Carter-Long, Lawrence. Associated Press, Vancouver (April 10, 1996).

"Fines for Bear Part Trafficking Still too Lenient," *Bear Watch*, Vancouver (January 12, 1996).

Griffin, Kathy. "Bid to Stop Suffering of China's Black Bears." *South China Morning Post* (June 29, 1993), pp. 7–9.

———. "Fake Bear Gall Bladder Scam." *South China Morning Post* (January 27, 1994), p. 2.

H.R. 4427. *Congressional Record* E582-585 (March 9, 1992).

CASE 3: IVORY WARS

Fitzgerald, Sarah. *International Wildlife Trade: Whose Business Is It?* Washington, D.C.: World Wildlife Fund, 1989.

Frison, George C. "Clovis, Goshen, and Folsom." In *Megafauna and Man: Discovery of America's Heartland*. Larry D. Agenbrod, Jim I. Mead and Lisa W. Nelson, eds. Hot Springs, S.Dak.: Mammoth Site of Hot Springs, South Dakota, Inc., Scientific Papers Volume 1, 1990.

Ivory: An International Survey and Illustrated History. New York: Harry N. Abrams, Inc., Publishers, 1987.

Lister, Adrian and Paul Bahn. *Mammoths*. New York: Macmillan, 1994.

MacGregor, Arthur. *Bone, Antler, Ivory, and Horn*. Totowa, N.J.: Barnes and Noble Books, 1985.

New Scientist, March 14, 1992, p. 11.

"South Africa's Terrorists Butcher Elephants." *New Scientist* (January 5, 1984), p. 8.

"The Ivory Trade and the Future of the African Elephant: Interim Report." Gaborone, Botswana: Ivory Trade Review Group, 1989.

TRAFFIC (USA). *CITES*. Washington, D.C.: World Wildlife Fund, 1992.

TRAFFIC (USA). *Elephant Ivory Trade*. Washington, D.C.: World Wildlife Fund, August 1990.

Western, David. "The Ecological Value of Elephants: A Keystone Role in African Ecosystems." *The Ivory Trade and the Future of the African Elephant*. Geneva: CITES Secretariat, 1989.

CASE 4: HAWSKBILL TURTLE

Bradsher, Keith. "Sea Turtles Put New Friction in U.S.-Japan Trade Quarrels." *The New York Times* (May 17, 1991).

Charnovitz, Steve. "GATT and the Environment: Examining the Issues." *International Environmental Affairs*, Volume 26, Number 4 (Summer 1992).

Harbrecht, Douglas. "How an Obscure Law Is Saving Turtles." *National Wildlife*, Volume 30 (April/May 1992).

"Japan Bans by '93 Imports of Endangered Sea Turtles." *The Wall Street Journal* (June 20, 1991), p. A10.

Lancaster, John. "Endangered Sea Turtle Seen Jeopardized by Japan." *The Washington Post* (January 19, 1991), p. A3.

Reid, T. R. "Japan to End Imports of Endangered Turtle." *The Washington Post* (May 18, 1991), p. A17.

Sanger, David E. "Japan, Backing Down, Plans Ban on Rare Turtle Import." *The New York Times* (June 20, 1991), p. D6.

Schneider, Keith. "US Moves to Punish Japan for Trade in Turtles." *The New York Times* (March 21, 1991), p. A12.

Shinohara, Makiko. "Japan and US at Loggerheads Over Endangered Sea Turtles." *Christian Science Monitor* (May 10, 1991), p. 7.

Sterngold, James. "Japan Agrees to Gradual Ban on Imports of Turtle Shells." *The New York Times* (May 18, 1991).

CASE 5: SHARKFIN SOUP

Deborah Cramer. "Troubled Waters." *The Atlantic Monthly*, Volume 275, Number 6 (June 1995).

Conniff, Richard. "From Jaws to Laws — Now the Big, Bad Shark Needs Protection from Us." *Smithsonian*, Volume 24 (June 1990).

Highley, Keith. "Shark Attack." *One Earth*. Hong Kong: Friends of the Earth (Spring 1993).

Ross, Philip E. "Man Bites Shark." *Scientific American*, Volume 262 (June 1990).

CASE 6: GUAM FRUIT BATS

Briscoe, David. "Humans with Taste for Fruit Bats Endanger Species." *Dallas Morning News* (September 26, 1993), p. 9A.

Dumanoski, Diane. "Flying Foxes Join List of Species at Risk." In Environmental Notebook, *The Boston Globe* (January 6, 1990), p. 3.

Hilts, Philip J. "Big Snakes Wiping out Native Guam Animals." In *Science Notebook*, *The Washington Post* (January 30, 1989), p. A2.

Miller, Ken. "U.S. Backs Guam Habitats, Could Alter Military Plans." *Gannett News Service* (June 17, 1991).

Sheeline, Leonora. *Cultural Significance of Pacific Fruit Bats (Pteropus) to the Chamorro People of Guam: Conservation Implications*. Report to World Wildlife Fund/Traffic USA, 1993.

Young, Lucy. "Bat-Eating an Endangered Custom." In *Gannett News Service* (March 24, 1990).

Zeigler, Jan. "The Necessary Bat." *United Press International* (April 2, 1986).

CASE 7: CREE AND ELECTRICITY

Brown, Barry. "Aboriginal Rights Seen Touching off 'Civil War' if Quebec Secedes." *The Buffalo News* (May 22, 1994).

Came, Barry. "Fighting for the Land." *Maclean's* (February 27, 1995).

Charles, Deborah. "Canada: Hydro-Quebec Faces More Environmental, Demand Pressure." *Reuter Textline* (March 3, 1994).

Dale, Stephen. "Canada: Native Indians Fight Against Hydro-Electric Project." Inter Press Service (April 22, 1993).

Euromoney Trade Finance and Banker International. "USA: Hydro Quebec Left in the Dark." Reuter Textline in Lexis Nexis (April 1, 1994).

Hamilton, Graeme, Philip Authier and Jeff Heinrich. "Cree Beat Hydro in Top Court: But Dam Project Gets Go-Ahead." *The Gazette* (February 25, 1994), p. A1.

Heinrich, Jeff. "Hydro under the Microscope." *The Gazette*, March 14, 1994, p. F8.

Jaekl, Christian. "James Bay: Prometheus vs. the Environment." *Swiss Review of World Affairs* (April 1993).

Johnson, William. "Blow to Quebec: Ottawa Wins in Court Ruling over James Bay."

The Gazette (February 25, 1994), p. B3.

McCutcheon, Sean. *Electric Rivers: The Story of the James Bay Project*. Montreal and New York: Black Rose Books, 1991.

O'Neil, Peter. "Warning from MP Jim Fulton Ignites Firestorm in Quebec." *The Vancouver Sun* (February 19, 1993), p. A4.

Park, Penny. "Canadian Cree Take Quebec's Hydro Scheme to Tribunal." *New Scientist*, Volume 133, Number 1806 (February 1, 1992).

Rutter, Frank. "Cuomo Electrocutes Quebec Separatism by Bailing New York Out of Hydro Deal." *Vancouver Sun* (March 31, 1992), p. A8.

Singer, Patti. "The Damming of Rivers Threatens Hunting Grounds of the Cree." *Gannett News Service* (October 6, 1993).

CASE 8: SWIFTS

Campbell, Bruce and Elizabeth Lack. *A Dictionary of Birds*. London: Buteo Books, 1985.

de Groot, Roy Andries. "On the Trail of Bird's Nest Soup: Caves, Climbs and High Stakes." *Smithsonian*, Volume 14 (September 1993).

MacKay, Jeanine. Correspondence from David S. Melville, Executive Director, World Wildlife Fund-Hong Kong (November 11, 1993).

Summers, Diane. "Dark World of Gourmet Soup." *International Wildlife*, Volume 22 (January/February 1992).

CASE 9: SUGAR

"Aquino Promises to Bring Illegal Loggers to Justice." *Agence France Presse* (November 11, 1991).

Coote, Belinda. *The Hunger Crop—Poverty and the Sugar Industry*. Oxford: Oxfam, 1987.

"Environment Chief Warns Ormoc Deluge Could Be Repeated." Japan Economic Newswire (November 11, 1991).

Franke, Richard W. "The Effects of Colonialism and Neocolonialism on the Gastronomic Patterns of the Third World." In *Perspectives in Cultural Anthropology*. Herbert Applebaum, ed. Albany: State University of New York Press, 1987.

Mintz, Sidney Wilfred. *Sweetness and Power: The Place of Sugar in Modern History*. New York: Viking Press, 1985.

CASE 10: PISCO

Atwood, Roger. "Sweet Liquor Sparks Bitter Trade Dispute." *The Reuter Business Report* (March 29, 1991).

Bowen, Sally. "Survey of Peru." *Financial Times* (September 29, 1993).

Fussell, Betty. "Fare of the Country; Chicha, Peru's Favorite Drink." *The New York Times* (February 15, 1995).

Metzer, Flora and Derek Fetzer. "Peru: Pollution Control Equipment." *National Trade Data Bank* (March 21, 1995).

Milne, Henk. "Dancing with the Demon; Peruvian Liquor." *Latin Finance* (January 1995).

Nyrop, Richard, ed. *Peru: A Country Study*. Washington, D.C.: United States Government, 1981.

CASE 11: CORAL

"China Moves to Protect Coral Reefs in South China Sea." *Agence France Presse* (August 20, 1992).

Cousteau, Jean Michael. "Cousteau Watch: Paradise Reef Tests Traders' Ecological Scruples." *Planet ENN* (September 2, 1996), <www.enn.com/planetenn/090296/fe.htm>.

Derr, Mark. "Raiders of the Reef." *Audubon* (March/April 1992).

Kroeber, A. L. "The Nature of Culture." In *Perspectives in Cultural Anthropology*. Herbert Applebaum, ed. Albany: State University of New York Press, 1987.

"Sanctuarial Movement Growing in U.S. Waters." *Offshore* (September 1991), p. 42.

Schmich, Mary T. "Coral Reef War Pits Nature vs. Tourists." *Chicago Tribune* (July 22, 1990).

Tsuruoka, Doug. "Vanishing Coral Reefs." *Far Eastern Economic Review*, Volume 156, Number 1 (January 7, 1993).

Weber, Peter K. "Saving the Coral Reefs." *The Futurist*, Volume 27, Number 4 (July 1993).

Worldwatch Institute. *State of the World, 1993*. New York: W.W. Norton & Company, Inc., 1993.

CASE 12: HAMBURGER

Armelagos, George. "Biocultural Aspects of Food Choice." In *Food and Evolution: Toward a Theory of Human Food Habits*. Marvin Harris and Eric B. Ross, eds. Philadelphia, Pa.: Temple University Press, 1987.

Braudel, Fernand. *Capitalism and Material Life, 1400–1800*. New York: Harper and Row, 1967.

Clark, V. *History of Manufactures in the United States, 1860–1914*. Washington, D.C.: Carnegie Institution, 1928.

Crosby, Alfred W. *Ecological Imperialism: The Biological Expansion of Europe, 900–1900*. Cambridge: Cambridge University Press, 1986.

Darby, H. C. "The Clearing of the Woodland in Europe." In *Man's Role in Changing the Face of the Earth*. W. L. Thomas, ed. Chicago: University of Chicago Press, 1956.

Drucker, Peter. "Beyond the Information Revolution," *The Atlantic Monthly* (October 1999), <www.theatlantic.com/issues/99oct/9910drucker.htm>.

Harrison, G. *Borthwicks: A Century in the Meat Trade, 1863–1963*. London: 1963.

Hermardinquer, J. "The Family Pig of the Ancien Regime: Myth or Fact?" In *Food and Drink in History*. R. Forster and O. Ranum, eds. Baltimore, Md.: Johns Hopkins University Press, 1979.

Perren, R. "The North American Beef and Cattle Trade with Great Britain, 1870–1914." *The Economic History Review*, 2nd Serial, Volume 24, Number 3, pp. 430–44.

Rifkin, Jeremy. *Beyond Beef: The Rise and Fall of the Cattle Culture*. New York: Dutton, 1992.

Ross, Eric B. "An Overview of Trends in Dietary Variation from Hunter-Gatherer to Modern Capitalist Societies." In *Food and Evolution: Toward a Theory of Human Food Habits*. Marvin Harris and Eric B. Ross, eds., pp. 7–55. Philadelphia, Pa.: Temple University Press, 1987.

Vestal, S. *Queen of Cowtowns, Dodge City*. New York: Harper and Row, 1952.

"U.S. Is World's Largest Exporter of Cattle Hides." *News* (Washington, D.C.: U.S. International Trade Commission, March 4, 1997).

CHAPTER 4

Anderson, Walter Truett. *Evolution Isn't What It Used to Be: The Augmented Animal and the Whole Wired World*. New York: W.H. Freeman and Company, 1996.

Bjorn Bjarnason. "The Role of Culture in Global Relations." Ottawa: Conference on "Putting Culture on the World Stage," June 30, 1998.

Braudel, Fernand. *The Perspective on the World*, Volume 3, "Civilization and Capitalism, Fifteenth–Eighteenth Century." New York: Harper and Row, 1984.

Cable, Vincent. "The New Trade Agenda: Universal Rules Amid Cultural Diversity." *International Affairs*, Volume 72, Number 2 (April 1996).

Cabral, Amilcar. "Liberation National y Cultural." San Pablo: Medellin Corporacion Educativa, 1977.

"Culture Ministers Say They Will Meet Again, Probably Without U.S." *Wall Street Journal* (July 1, 1998).

DePalma, Anthony. "Nineteen Nations See U.S. as Threat to Cultures." *The New York Times* (July 1, 1998).

Drucker, Peter. "Beyond the Information Revolution." *The Atlantic Monthly* (October 1999), <www.theatlantic.com/issues/99oct/9910drucker.htm>.

Durning, Alan Thein. "Guardians of the Land: Indigenous Peoples and the Health of the Earth." Washington, D.C.: Worldwatch Institute, Worldwatch Paper #112, 1995.

Gertler, Jeffrey L. "WTO Dispute Settlement: The Environmental Dimension." In *Trade and Environment: Conflict or Compatibility*. Duncan Brack, ed., pp. 118–39. London: Earthscan Publications and the Royal Institute of International Affairs, 1998.

Government of Canada. "Overview of International Meeting on Cultural Policy." Ottawa: Government of Canada, June 29–30, 1998.

Jackson, John. "World Trade Rules and Environmental Policies: Congruence or Conflict?" *Washington and Lee Law Review*, Volume 49, Number 4 (Fall 1992).

Jerome, Robert W. "Traders and Environmentalists." *Journal of Communications* (December 27, 1991).

Klitgaard, Robert. "Taking Culture into Account, From 'Let's' to 'How'." In *Culture and Development in Africa*. Ismail Serageldin and June Taboroff, eds. Washington, D.C.: World Bank, 1994.

Lee, James R. "Process and Product: Making the Link between Trade and the Environment." *International Environmental Affairs: A Journal for Research and Policy*, Volume 6, Number 4 (Fall 1994).

——— and David Walters. *International Trade in Construction, Design and Engineering Services*. Boston: Ballinger Publishing Company, 1989.

Manguelle, Daniel Etounga. "Culture and Development: African Responses." *Culture and Development in Africa*. Ismail Serageldin and June Taboroff, eds. Washington, D.C.: World Bank, 1994.

Mazrui, Ali. *Cultural Forces in World Politics*. London: James Currey, 1990.

Merryman. John Henry. "Who Owns the Elgin Marbles." *ARTNEWS*, Volume 85, Number (September 1986).

Mills, Judy. "Milking the Bear Trade." *International Wildlife*, Volume 22, Number 3 (May 1992), pp. 38–45.

"Ministers From Twenty-two Countries Expected at Ottawa Meeting on Culture." Ottawa: Office of the Minister of Canadian Culture, June 1998.

Rockefeller Brothers Fund Annual Report—1995. New York: Rockefeller Brothers Fund, 1995.

Serageldin, Ismail. "The Challenge of a Holistic Vision: Culture, Empowerment, and the Development Paradigm." In Ismail Serageldin and June Taboroff, eds. *Culture and Development in Africa*. Washington, D.C.: World Bank, 1994.

———. *Culture and Development at the Millennium: The Challenge and the Response*. Washington, D.C.: World Bank, 1998. Speech distributed in pamphlet form.

Shepard, Paul. *Coming Home to the Pleistocene*. Washington, D.C.: Island Press/Shearwater Books, 1998.

Siune, Karen and Wolfgang Truetzshler. *Dynamics of Media Politics*. London: Sage Publications, 1992.

Stavrianos, Leften. *Global Rift: The Third World Comes of Age*. New York: Morrow, 1981.

Stevens, Stan, ed. *Conservation through Cultural Survival: Indigenous Peoples and Protected Areas*. Washington, D.C.: Island Press, 1997.

Teachout, Terry. "Cultural Protectionism: The World's Culture Czars Move to Repel the Hollywood Invasion." *The Wall Street Journal* (July 10, 1998).

Tennesen, Michael. "Poaching, Ancient Traditions, and the Law." *Audubon*, Volume 93 (July–August 1991).

"USTR Criticizes Proposed Canadian Action to Continue Restrictions on Market Access for Magazines." Washington, D.C.: Office of U.S. Trade Representative,

October 9, 1998. Press Release.

Weir, David. *The Bhopal Syndrome: Pesticides, Environment, and Health*. San Francisco: Sierra Club Books, 1987.

Wildavsky, Aaron. "How Cultural Theory Can Contribute to Understanding and Promoting Democracy, Science, and Development." In *Culture and Development in Africa*. Ismail Serageldin and June Taboroff, eds. Washington, D.C.: World Bank, 1994.

Williams, Francis and Guy Jounquieres. "US Appeal on Shrimp Import Ban Rejected." *Financial Times* (October 13, 1998).

"WTO Committee on Trade and the Environment Invites MEA Secretariats to Information Session, and Discusses Items Related to the Linkages between the Multilateral and Trade Agendas." *Trade and Environment Bulletin*. Geneva: World Trade Organization, Press/TE 025, August 13, 1998.

BIBLIOGRAPHY OF RELEVANT TED CASE STUDIES

Adewumi, Yemi. "The Basmati Case." *TED Case Studies* #493 (Summer 1998), <www.american.edu/TED/basmati.htm>.

Arvantides, George. "The Elgin Marbles." *TED Case Studies* #445 (January 1998), <www.american.edu/TED/monument.htm>.

Clawery, Christopher. "Mexico and Tourism." *TED Case Studies* #86 (June 1993), <www.american.edu/TED/cancun.htm>.

Cummins, Chad P. "Hudson Bay Fur Trade in 1800s." *TED Case Studies* #113 (January 1994), <www.american.edu/TED/hudson.htm>.

Fedor, Jennifer and Janet Herrlinger. "The EC Fur Ban." *TED Case Studies* #22 (June 1992), <www.american.edu/TED/ecfurban.htm>.

Foley, Mary-Ellen and Andrew Hamm. "James Bay Project." *TED Case Studies* #91 (January 1993), <www.american.edu/TED/james.htm>.

Hamm, Andrew. "Guam Bat Imports." *TED Case Studies* #111 (January 1994), <www.american.edu/TED/guambat.htm>.

Hond, Yuri. "Sugar and Philippines." *TED Case Studies* #250 (January 1996), <www.american.edu/TED/philsug.htm>.

Jacobsen, Doug. "Amber Trade Old and New." *TED Case Studies* #451 (June 1997), <www.american.edu/TED/amber.htm>.

Jones, Jenny. "Shrimp and Sea Turtle." *TED Case Studies* #62 (January 1993), <www.american.edu/TED/shrimp.htm>.

———. "Hawksbill Turtle." *TED Case Studies* #32 (January 1992), <www.american.edu/TED/hawksbil.htm>.

Joshi, Nina. "US Canada Softwood Lumber Dispute." *TED Case Studies* #75 (January 1993), <www.american.edu/TED/uscanada.htm>.

Kasoff, Benjamin T. "Cedars of Lebanon." *TED Case Studies* #187 (June 1995), <www.american.edu/TED/cedars.htm>.

Kocian, Mary-Ann. "German Beer Laws." *TED Case Studies* #219 (June 1995), <www.american.edu/TED/germbeer.htm>.

Lee, James R. "Ancient Mammoth Ivory Trade." *TED Case Studies* #468 (June 1996), <www.american.edu/TED/mammoth.htm>.

Lewis, Nicole. "CITES Watch on Coral." *TED Case Studies* #18 (January 1992), <www.american.edu/TED/coral.htm>.

MacKay, Jeanine. "Swift Protection." *TED Case Studies* #66 (January 1993), <www.american.edu/TED/swift.htm>.

———. "Shark Protection." *TED Case Studies* #62 (January 1993), <www.american.edu/TED/shark.htm>.

Meisegeier, Deborah. "Great Barrier Reef." *TED Case Studies* #179 (January 1995), <www.american.edu/TED/barrier.htm>.

Oakes, Pamela. "Pisco Liquer and Chile." *TED Case Studies* #145 (June 1994), <www.american.edu/TED/pisco.htm>.

Patel, Trupti. "Bhopal Disaster." *TED Case Studies* #233 (January 1996), <www.american.edu/TED/bhopal.htm>.

Purcell, Theresa. "Irish Potato Famine." *TED Case Studies* #274 (June 1996), <www.american.edu/TED/potato.htm>.

Rinaman, Karen. "Sports Magazine in Canada." *TED Case Studies* #352 (January 1997), <www.american.edu/TED/sportsil.htm>.

Sack, Karen. "Elephant Ivory Trade Ban." *TED Case Studies* #26 (January 1992), <www.american.edu/TED/elephant.htm>.

Santiago, Antonio and Jay Allen Schmidt. "Costa Rica Beef Exports." *TED Case Studies* #82 (June 1993), <www.american.edu/TED/costbeef.htm>

Weir, Richard. "EU BST Import Ban." *TED Case Studies* #160 (June 1994), <www.american.edu/TED/bst.htm>.

INDEX

CHRIS ZIMMER

ABOUT THE AUTHOR

JAMES R. LEE is a professor at American University, in the School of International Service in Washington, D.C. He directs the Mandala Projects, a set of interrelated efforts that examine key issues in trade, environment, culture, and rights. These Projects are all Web-based efforts that intend to add to and encourage further research in these areas. He has worked in academia, the private sector, and as a policymaker in the Office of the U.S. Trade Representative and the U.S. Environmental Protection Agency. His last book was *The Chinese House Game: A Computer Simulation for Students of International Relations*, and he is co-author of *International Trade in Construction, Design and Engineering Services*.

Books of related interest from Kumarian Press

Beyond Globalization: Shaping a Sustainable Global Economy

Hazel Henderson
for the New Economics Foundation

Hazel Henderson sets out a panoramic vision of the changes required to reshape the global economy toward social justice and sustainability at every level from the global to the local and personal.

US $ 10.95 / Paper: 1-56549-107-6

Inequity in the Global Village: Recycled Rhetoric and Disposable People

Jan Knippers Black

As globalization rapidly replaces the cold war paradigm, disturbing aspects of this transition are often glossed over. The narrow distribution of benefits from globalization has created a yawning gap in wealth and power both among and within states. Jan Black incisively describes increased nationalism, growing refugee populations, and the politics of exclusion in her impassioned style.

US $24.95 / Paper: 1-56549-099-1
US $55.00 / Cloth: 1-56549-100-9

How Context Matters: Linking Environmental Policy to People and Place

George Honadle

This book presents a unique method of looking at environmental policy and contextual implementation. Drawing upon a range of disciplines, the author identifies specific elements of the natural resource condition and the social and political settings that present opportunities, create implementation hurdles, and affect policy performance.

US $24.95 / Paper: 1-56549-104-1
US $59.00 / Cloth: 1-56549-105-X

Mediating Sustainability: Growing Policy from the Grassroots

Jutta Blauert, Simon Zadek, editors

This book explores how mediation between grassroots and policy formation processes can and does work in practice by focusing on experiences in Latin America. Contributions are drawn from the work of researchers, activists, farmers and policymakers.

US $25.95 / Paper: 1-56549-081-9
US $55.00 / Cloth: 1-56549-082-7

Kumarian Press is dedicated to publishing and distributing books and other media that will have a positive social and economic impact on the lives of peoples living in "Third World" conditions no matter where they live.

Kumarian Press publishes books about Global Issues and International Development, such as Peace and Conflict Resolution, Environmental Sustainability, Globalization, Nongovernmental Organizations, and Women and Gender.

To receive a complimentary catalog or to request writer's guidelines call or write:

Kumarian Press, Inc.
14 Oakwood Avenue
West Hartford, CT 06119-2127
U.S.A.

Inquiries: (860) 233-5895
Fax: (860) 233-6072
Order toll free: (800) 289-2664

e-mail: kpbooks@aol.com
Internet: www.kpbooks.com